10,001 WAYS TO DECLUTTER YOUR HOME ON A SMALL  BUDGET

10,001 WAYS TO DECLUTTER YOUR HOME ON A SMALL BUDGET

ED MORROW, SHEREE BYKOFSKY, AND RITA ROSENKRANZ

Skyhorse Publishing

Skyhorse Publishing books may be purchased in bulk at special discounts for sales promotion, corporate gifts, fund-raising, or educational purposes. Special editions can also be created to specifications. For details, contact the Special Sales Department, Skyhorse Publishing, 555 Eighth Avenue, Suite 903, New York, NY 10018 or info@skyhorsepublishing.com.

www.skyhorsepublishing.com

10 9 8 7 6 5 4 3 2 1

Library of Congress Cataloging-in-Publication Data

Morrow, Ed.
    10,001 ways to declutter your home on a small budget / Ed Morrow,
Shree Bykofsky, and Rita Rosenkranz.
        p. cm.
    Includes index.
    ISBN 978-1-60239-952-5 (pbk. : alk. paper)
    1. House cleaning. 2. Orderliness. 3. Storage in the home. I. Bykofsky,
Sheree. II. Rosenkranz, Rita. III. Title. IV. Title: Ten thousand and one ways
to declutter your home on a small budget.
    TX324.M66 2010
    648'.5--dc22

                                            2009048766

Printed in China

Contents

Introduction

A Cluttered House Is Like an Overweight Body

Is your house fat? Can it barely squeeze itself into that new coat of aluminum siding you purchased last summer? Is it more likely to be featured in a Richard Simmons video than a Bob Vila video? Houses can get overweight. We overfeed them with clutter. Each day, we go out to work to earn money to buy stuff that we bring home and cram into every cupboard, drawer, and closet till one day, when we leave, we can't shut the door behind us.

The house-cramming process is much like what happens to our bodies if we overindulge in food while under-indulging in exercise. They become a burden and a source of unhappiness. Health-minded people turn to dieting and exercise to regain control of their bodies, and in the same way you can put your home on a diet.

Home "dieting" consists of buying less and getting rid of things you don't need. Home "exercise" involves organizing those possessions you do need so that they don't interfere with your life. *10,001 Ways to Declutter Your Home on a Small Budget* offers practical, room-by-room advice on how to combine both into an anticlutter diet and exercise plan.

There is a need for this book because, in America the Bountiful, we can acquire so much stuff. Indeed, there's a whole industry—advertising—devoted to convincing us that we need as much of that stuff as we can possibly afford, plus a little more. Ads appear on everything from park benches to barn roofs. It has been estimated that the average American reaching the age of 80 will have watched 2.5 million television commercials. From home shopping networks to online sites, we can shop 24 hours a day—and we do! Sometimes we buy because we legitimately need the item, but all too often we buy to satisfy a psychological need.

As is true for overeating, we tend to use shopping as self-reward, as recreation, as a diversion to relieve boredom, or to fill vague longings hidden in a remote corner of our souls. How often have you purchased something, brought it home, and wondered, "What was I thinking?" Probably about as often as you've eaten something when you weren't hungry.

Clutter is more than an inconvenience that can trip you as you go from room to room. A house with too much stuff is physically, emotionally, and spiritually draining. Every extraneous object becomes a psychological hurdle that you have to jump over to accomplish anything.

Like being overweight, clutter isn't just a matter of appearances. Once you bring possessions home, your work has only begun. You have to maintain them. You have to clean them. You have to pay rent or a mortgage to put a roof over them. You have to protect them. You have to organize them. Eventually, you may have to pole vault over them.

It doesn't have to be this way. You can fight against the rising tide of clutter that threatens to engulf your home, disrupt your life, and deplete your energy. *10,001 Ways to Declutter Your Home on a Small Budget* can help you establish a balance of beauty, comfort, practicality, and well-being for your home. You'll find tips on what to save, what to forsake, and what to do to reclaim the harmony in your household—and your life. From regifting to online auctions to innovative charitable outlets, this book will show you many clever guilt- and regret-free ways to rid your home of excess pounds of ugly clutter. While you're streamlining, set a goal of losing 7 to 10 items an hour and you'll be well on your way. Remember: Inside every jam-packed home is a svelte *House Beautiful* centerfold just waiting to get out!

OUR FAT HOUSES

A typical Southern California home is now approaching 3,000 square feet in size, with two-car garages standard and three-car garages common. By contrast, a typical home from the 1950s and 1960s was about 1,000 square feet, with a one-car garage. According to the National Association of Home Builders, this trend can be seen across the country. Our bloated homes aren't explained by growing families. The average household fell from about 3 people in the 1960s to just 2.59 in 2000, and it is still shrinking. Homebuilders attribute the increase in home size to a greater demand for both living area and storage space for our stuff.

As you uncover your slimmed-down new home, you'll enjoy a sense of freedom, spiritual vigor, and pride. You'll feel and act lighter. If this is hard to imagine, picture yourself with the energetic step of a newly thin person carrying bags full of old "fat clothes" to the Salvation Army. Once you've done the equivalent with your home clutter, you'll free up both room and time for new inspirations, more meaningful and more carefully chosen belongings, and maybe even new relationships. When you relieve yourself of burdens, the whole world becomes a lighter, if not enlightened, place to live.

CLUTTA
THE ANCIENT ROMAN GODDESS OF EXCESSIVE ACCUMULATION

ONE

Are You a Pack Rat?

You can't have everything. Where would you put it?"

—Steven Wright

You know when it's time to diet. You can't fit into your favorite jeans. You get winded on the second flight of stairs. You actually eat that fruitcake Aunt May sent for Christmas. Your belt screams.

There also are indicators when your home has a weight problem because of accumulated clutter. Try the quiz on the following pages to find your clutter quotitent.

7 WAYS TO MEASURE YOUR CLUTTER QUOTIENT

In each of the categories below, find the statement that best describes your situation. Add up your score, then see how you measure up compared to fictional TV icons of neatness and slovenliness.

1. Your General Housekeeping Principles

- There is a place for everything, everything is in its place, and everything is dusted. (**4 points**)
- There is a place for most things, and most things are in their place. Most are dusted. (**3 points**)
- There is a place for most things but hardly anything is in its place, and many more things are in something else's place. All places and all things are dusty. (**2 points**)
- There isn't a place for anything, but you've never noticed because everything is hidden under an inch of dust. (**1 point**)

2. Your Toothpaste Habits

- You always put the cap back on the toothpaste and put the tube back in the medicine cabinet. You never squeeze from the middle. (**4 points**)
- You put the cap back and leave the tube on the bathroom counter. You sometimes squeeze from the middle but immediately regret it and contritely squeeze the tube back into shape. (**3 points**)
- You often squeeze from the middle, forget the cap, and leave the tube on your bedroom dresser. Toothpaste gets on your socks. You wear them anyway. (**2 points**)
- You always squeeze from the middle, lost the cap a month ago, and left the tube on the kitchen counter beside the toaster, where the toaster's heat melted

it, gluing the tube to the counter. Rather than pry it up, you now brush your teeth in the kitchen. **(1 point)**

3. Your Laundry

- Your hamper is clean and nearly empty. Thanks to a sachet of dried apples and spices hanging inside it, it smells like Mom's warm apple pie. **(4 points)**
- Your hamper is nearly clean and nearly full and smells of apple pie–scented disinfectant spray. **(3 points)**
- Your hamper is full and smells like spoiled apple pie. **(2 points)**
- Your hamper is full and you've piled more dirty laundry on top of it. The thing smells like Johnny Appleseed's feet after a 20-mile stretch of his frontier wanderings. **(1 point)**

4. Your Refrigerator

- There is plenty of room in your refrigerator, its shelves are clean, and nothing in it is spoiled. You have a fresh box

of baking soda on each shelf. **(4 points)**
- Your refrigerator is full, and a few items need to be tossed out. You have leftovers from last night. There's one box of baking soda. **(3 points)**
- Your refrigerator is full, the shelves are crusty, and there are items inside that are spoiled. You have three-day-old leftovers. The baking soda has turned green. **(2 points)**
- Your refrigerator is crammed full, things are cemented to the shelves by sticky goo, and there is a pool of brown glop at the bottom. Many items are soft with decay or blue-green with

mold. There are leftovers from meals you can't remember. (**1 point**)

5. Your Work Space

- There are no loose papers on your desk. Your pens are functioning, the pencils are sharpened, and they all are neatly collected in a china penholder. (**4 points**)
- There are a few papers scattered on your desk. Some of your pens are dry, and one or two pencils are dull. Your penholder is a souvenir mug. (**3 points**)
- There is a mix of papers, books, and junk mail on your desk. Your penholder is an old, chipped coffee mug. It contains many pens and pencils, but only one pen works and only one pencil has a point. (**2 points**)
- You can't see your desktop for the papers, books, and candy wrappers piled on top of it. There are broken pens, a fistful of pointless (and, hence, pointless to possess) pencils,

and a spatula in the unwashed beer mug that serves as your penholder. A torn sneaker rests on top of your computer. (**1 point**)

6. Your Acquiring Habits

- You buy things only when necessary, and then only after waiting a day or two to be sure you need them. (**4 points**)
- You buy things when they're needed but also pick up items when they're on sale or you have a coupon. (**3 points**)
- You buy things on impulse and save things because they may be useful someday. If you have a coupon, you buy two. (**2 points**)
- You see something shiny. You buy it. Then you buy another for a spare, in case the first shiny thing gets dull. You cram both into your home, where you have hundreds of other once-shiny things, all of which are now dull, but you promise yourself to polish them one day. You buy polish. (**1 point**)

7. Your Disposal Habits

- You dispose of possessions as soon as you no longer need them. You also generously dispose of other people's possessions when you think they no longer need them. You get lots of healthful aerobic exercise running away from these people when they learn you've disposed of their possessions. (**4 points**)
- You dispose of unneeded possessions regularly, keeping your home tidy. (**3 points**)
- You dispose of possessions when they fall from the piles in which you've stacked them, and they hit you on the head. (**2 points**)
- You dispose of things when they're pulled from your cold, dead fingers. (**1 point**)

Add up your points and check the chart below.

If you score a June Cleaver or better, you may not need this book. But you undoubtedly have lots of relatives and friends who don't match your level of tidiness, so send them all copies. If you score a Roseanne, you're like most people today. You struggle to balance work and family life, with little time to tidy. You barely keep ahead of the clutter, and all it would take to plunge into Sanford-hood is a weekend binge of buying at garage sales. A Sanford score means you'll need lots of hard

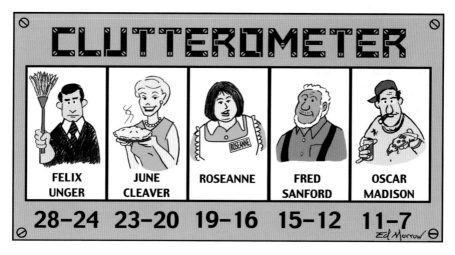

CLUTTEROMETER

FELIX UNGER	JUNE CLEAVER	ROSEANNE	FRED SANFORD	OSCAR MADISON
28–24	23–20	19–16	15–12	11–7

Ed Morrow

work to improve. If you score an Oscar Madison, you not only need this book but also should have it tattooed on your person for easy reference.

On the positive side, if you're the average Roseanne, a weekend of cleaning and the adoption of an anticlutter strategy can edge you up to a Cleaver. Of course, you can become *too* tidy and wind up in the neurotic domain of Ungerville. While you may want a Felix for a cleaning service worker, Neil Simon demonstrated in *The Odd Couple* that an obsessive level of orderliness can turn an easygoing slob of a roommate into a spaghetti-throwing menace.

Whatever your score on this quiz, you probably know if you're a pack rat living in a home choked with clutter. All it takes is an honest look around the place to answer the question: Does your home need to diet?

YOUR HOME'S DIET

"Always use one of the new—and far more reliable—elastic measuring tapes to check on your waistline."

—Miss Piggy

Some people choose to be overweight, accepting the health risks and stigmas that ensue, because they enjoy food so much or just feel that being thin isn't important. Some people embrace clutter, enjoying collecting objects that others might cast out. It's important to note that those who make these choices aren't bad people. The greatest soul on Earth may be wrapped in the 600-pound body of a sumo wrestler, while as many an exhausted exerciser might suspect, the most twisted soul may reside in the perfectly toned body of a perky aerobics instructor. Similarly, you aren't evil if your home isn't absolutely clutter-free; and banishing

every item of clutter from your home won't elevate you into sainthood.

But losing weight and cutting clutter can improve your life. Fairly or unfairly, people respond more favorably to thin people than to "non-thin" people. A thinner you is likely to be a healthier, more energetic you, capable of accomplishing more. People also value neatness and order. A home that is efficiently organized will impress visitors and suggest its owner is efficient. A home containing less clutter is likely to be more pleasant as well. It's a place where your life isn't hindered by physical and psychological obstacles created by clutter. So there are both exterior and interior reasons for dieting to reduce weight and to eliminate clutter.

But weight or clutter dieting is difficult. To lose weight, you must eat less and exercise more. As many a plump person will tell you, this is all but impossible. You slip and eat just one cookie, which becomes two, then an entire box. You skip a session at the gym because it's raining, then because it might rain, then because you've missed so many sessions that you're embarrassed to appear in your now-too-tight exercise wear.

For a pack rat, putting your household on a diet can be just as hard. To trim household clutter, it's necessary to buy less, throw out more, and organize what you keep. As with dieting, it's hard to avoid impulsive acquisition. There's a great sale on sweaters, so you get one in red and one in blue, then decide you need pants in a complementary tone—and don't forget shoes.

There's also a parallel between failing to exercise and failing to dispose of clutter. You may find it difficult to throw out unneeded possessions. It would make sense to get rid of a couple of old sweaters to make room for the new ones, but everything in your closet seems potentially useful, even the shabby old sweatshirt from your high school band camp. You could organize your closet to better accommodate your new possessions, but it's easier to keep its door shut and avoid confronting the mess. The result: Your home gets fatter and fatter.

4 WAYS TO RESIST THE URGE TO ACCUMULATE

"I can resist everything except temptation."

—Oscar Wilde

Overeaters are overcome by the impulse to indulge. The smell of fresh-baked cookies wafting from a bakery may be impossible to resist. In the same way, the pack rat can be tempted to accumulate on a whim. The best way to defeat impulsive acquisition is through self-discipline. You have to force yourself to think twice, and even thrice if that's what it takes to resist. Here are a few suggestions on ways to bolster your self-discipline.

1. Delay the purchase. If you're in the mall and see a sale for thingamajigs at 50 percent off, you can reduce the urge to buy by telling yourself you'll pick up the item after visiting another store. Then pick a store that has goods you enjoy browsing through but can't afford to buy—perhaps an art gallery displaying expensive paintings. By the time you've finished looking through the big-ticket stuff, the urge to pick up a bargain may have faded.

   Some shoppers become more easily tempted after seeing costly merchandise they can't have. If this describes you, find some other activity to use to help you delay making purchases. Perhaps pausing for a nice, crisp salad in the mall's food court will give you time for your burning desire to cool down to a more platonic admiration that doesn't require possession.

2. Try adopting a bargain-hunter's attitude. If you're eager to buy a nonessential item, spend some time searching for the best price in town or on the

Internet. This will give you a chance to calm down and reconsider.

3. Ask yourself where in the world you're going to stash the new item. Will you have to shove something else aside? Will the purchase interfere with your everyday life? That driftwood hat rack may look nice, but if it snags your shoulder every time you squeeze down your over-crowded hallway, it'll become a pest. Do you even wear enough hats to make the thing earn its share of your living space?

4. Try to anticipate the buying impulse. Avoid going to shops that you know will make you itch to spend. Just as dieters learn to stay away from bakeries and ice cream parlors, clutter addicts should steer clear of stores with merchandise that they find particularly tempting. Instead of visiting a den of cluttery iniquity, go someplace you enjoys that doesn't have price tags, where you can't buy more clutter. Do you like dino-saur bones? Go to a museum. Enjoy tennis? Grab a friend and go play. Treat yourself to a good time–without bringing anything home.

6 THINGS TO DO INSTEAD OF SHOPPING

"Depression is just lazy anger."
—**Anonymous**

After getting kicked in the can by life, the overeater often seeks comfort from food. Similarly, the pack rat may use acquisition to soothe his or her frayed soul. Shop-ping can make you feel catered to and special. The rest of the world may hate you, but the folks at the mall smile and say "thank you" when you hand them your credit card. Owning things can also calm anxiety if you see them as

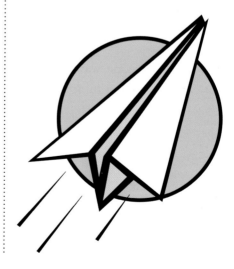

solutions to anticipated problems. Is winter on its way? Four new coats will defeat its chills.

When you're feeling forlorn or anxious, going on a buying spree is especially seductive. A better solution is to find comfort elsewhere.

1. Go to the gym or just take a walk when you're tempted to resort to shopping to improve your mood. Doctors recommend it as a way to beat the blues.
2. Feed the ducks in the park.
3. Visit the library.
4. Noodle on your trombone.
5. Organize your vacation photos.
6. Call that relative you've neglected.

OVERCOMING PREMATURE VICTORIES AND DEPRESSING DEFEATS

"Nothing recedes like success."
—Walter Winchell

Perversely, overeaters sometimes react badly when they start having success with their slimming efforts. The scale greets them with the report of 10 pounds gone missing, and they take this as

---

QUICK FIX

PAMPER YOURSELF

If you enjoy being catered to, take the money that might go to acquiring more stuff and hire a cleaning service to take on household jobs you loathe. Your home will doubly benefit. It will be tidier both from the shopping trip you didn't take and from the professional cleaning.

---

an opportunity to ease up on their diet. All too soon, they have erased months of discipline and healthful habits.

If you're a pack rat, you may stumble in a similar way. After clearing out the garage or making a couple of shelves available in a bedroom closet, you declare a premature victory and return to your old habits. Before long, the hard-won space is taken up by new clutter.

While success can cause you to relax your resolve, failure can trigger a depression that leads you to abandon your efforts. After all, if a regimen isn't working, why continue the struggle? You may seek out the comfort of food—or clutter—to counter your misfortune.

The solution to handling either success or a lack of it is to realize that dieting, both to reduce weight and to reduce clutter, is a lifelong, ongoing struggle. It doesn't end with a victorious day of ticker tape parades and sailors kissing nurses in Times Square. It's more like the war on organized crime. A hit man may be thwarted, a shipment of drugs may be confiscated, and a sinister godfather may be dispatched to Sing Sing, but the struggle goes on. We may never completely dispose of our clutter, just as we may never extinguish the Mob, but we can minimize the harm it does.

Once you've had some success in trimming down your possessions, avoid overestimating your success. Mentally divide the space you think you have freed *by half.* Then avoid allowing yourself to acquire more than this halved space will hold. For tactics to deal with failure, try the suggestions given below for managing poor self-image, misdirected anger, and self-protection.

WHEN SELF-DEPRIVATION DOESN'T DO IT

"The unfortunate thing about this world is that good habits are so much easier to give up than bad ones."

—W. Somerset Maugham

Overeaters not only eat too much, but also tend to make poor choices when deciding what and

when to eat. They may skip meals, become overly hungry, then over-indulge. They may plan meals that are too large or too small, alternately overeating or failing to satisfy their hunger which then can lead to eating an extra meal. Another pitfall is failing to prepare an appetizing variety of meals, and then finding it difficult to stick to a boring diet.

Similarly, well-intentioned pack rats may virtuously postpone buying a needed item for so long that, when they finally allow themselves to shop, they do so too quickly for sound decision-making. They tend to overestimate or underestimate their needs, causing unnecessary clutter or creating more opportunities to be tempted to acquire. And just as a strict diet can turn dieting into drudgery, an overly tight grip on your wallet can make your lifestyle feel cramped, increasing the desire to indulge.

To handle poor acquisitive habits, you need to develop an attitude that balances necessary purchases with the disposal of clutter. In other words, cultivate the habit of asking yourself what's needed and what's not. For example, you may fall prey to an overwhelming desire to collect beer cans, which then requires you to adjust some other aspect of your life. Perhaps you could give away your collection of baseball caps to make room for the cans.

At times, adjusting to compensate for acquisitions can be difficult and your possessions may overwhelm you, but you can recover and purge yourself of excess clutter. Don't think of these misadventures as failures. They are evolutionary steps toward building a happy life—a life that, in this case, includes a massive beer can collection.

6 SUGGESTIONS FOR MAKING ORGANIZATION MORE EXCITING

"I get my exercise being a pall-bearer for those of my friends who believe in regular running and calisthenics."

—Winston Churchill

Reducing food intake isn't enough to produce healthful weight loss. It must be accompanied by exercise. While good exercise habits

can be hard to develop and maintain, there are tactics to win the battle. This is also true of *organizing* and *tidying*, the decluttering equivalents of exercise.

Boredom is particularly difficult to overcome when building good exercise habits. It can be hard, for example, to generate the inner fire to run an extra mile on your home treadmill when every mile is identical to the last. Boredom is similarly hard to avoid when building good organizational habits. Putting things in their proper place is repetitive and monotonous. If your decluttering plan has become tedious, try changing its order. Begin with a particularly easy task for a sense of accomplishment that will carry you through more tiresome tasks. Or conversely, deliberately choose the most onerous task first, plug your way through it, then enjoy the greater sense of accomplishment it yields and the knowledge that the rest of your tasks will be easier by comparison.

Another tactic that you can use to fight boredom while decluttering, organizing, and tidying is to try to introduce novelty into the process.

1. In *Star Speak*, Doug McClelland quotes the Dutch film star Nina Foch as saying, "When I'm cleaning the house I wear an apron, but nothing else." Try it.

2. Try some new cleaning products or alter your methods.

3. Incorporate diversions to make the time pass more quickly,

such as using a portable phone with a headset to chat with friends and family while you work.

4. Put some music on. Dancing while you dust may seem silly, but if it gets you through the task, why not? And you can always pull the drapes so the neighbors won't think you're nuts.

5. If you can't dance, try listening to talk radio or books on tape. A little political controversy or good literature can divert you during dull chores.

6. Or make your own music—singing has been a traditional way of lightening the work-load for folks as varied as Irish women pulling yarn, sailors hauling on ropes, and soldiers marching off to battle.

5 WAYS TO REWARD A JOB WELL DONE

You can reinforce neat habits by rewarding yourself. After setting a room straight:
1. Enjoy a bubble bath.
2. Get your hair done.
3. Play a round of golf.

4. Have a special meal at your favorite restaurant.

5. Better yet, find rewards that are directly related to the task itself. As an example, allow yourself to take the time to enjoy a newly uncluttered area of your home. Sit back in an easy chair in your well-ordered living room and listen to some well-ordered Bach. Or invite friends over for a party. Your newly cleaned home will be on display, and you can show off a little of the singing and dancing you practiced while tidying.

Extra Hands Make the Work Go Fast

Have you ever tried doing household tasks with a friend? Chatting while you work can make the dullest job pass more quickly. Take turns working at each other's home a few hours each week.

TIDYING TAKES TIME

"An occasional trip to a fast-food restaurant is not the worst of all possible sins."

—Hillary Rodham Clinton

For people on the run, fast food and slapped-together meals seem like necessities. Unfortunately, eating fast usually means eating fat. For the pack rat, this is equivalent to skipping clutter-controlling measures—or taking shortcuts because you don't have time to do a better job.

To handle the pressure of limited time, you need to be as efficient as possible. If your household maintenance tasks can be accomplished with reasonable ease, you're more likely to do them even when in a hurry. Give some thought to better planning jobs that otherwise tend to create clutter because you're rushed. Each night, for example, you might plan how to fix your breakfast the next morning in a way that generates less of a mess to straighten up later. Or you could organize your cosmetics so that putting on your morning face will be simple and fast, and not leave your bathroom counter a mess of makeup bottles and applicators.

A subtle source of clutter is the secondary mess that may result from performing a decluttering task. For example, consider what might happen after you spend a day diligently cleaning out your closet. You've made many hard decisions about your possessions, tossing out box after box of clutter. Finally, you close the door on a tidy closet. But look at the room itself. There are hangers piled up on the floor; you neglected to carry out the trash you generated; and you didn't get around to packing up things meant for charity. Too often, the declutterer, tired of decluttering, postpones taking care of this mess, convincing himself that he's been virtuous enough for one day.

Actually, his good work has been tainted by creating more clutter.

Put off any reward until you've handled the entire job. A good motivational device is to increase your reward when you do both the work and the final cleanup. If you were going to indulge yourself by curling up with a mystery novel for organizing that closet, give yourself that treat plus a cup of your favorite tea for tidying up as well.

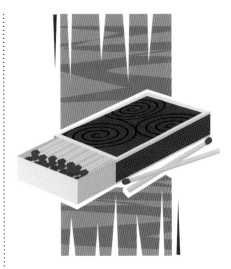

ARE YOU IN DENIAL?

Denial is a psychological mechanism that allows us to persist in negative behaviors by lying to ourselves. For the pack rat, denial can be evident in the belief that if clutter is out of sight, it doesn't exist. If you can jam one more box under the bed or into the closet, then you really don't have a clutter problem.

The best way to counter denial is to routinely take a mental step back and evaluate your condition dispassionately. Imagine you're visiting someone else's home as you look at your own. Would you be impressed if, while in search of an aspirin, you opened a medicine cabinet and fell victim to an avalanche of ancient prescription bottles, twisted tubes of ointment, and fluttering Band-Aids? Would heaps of old magazines behind a sofa suggest your host was a well-organized person? Would you feel comfortable eating a meal with cutlery you pulled from a silverware drawer jammed with matchboxes, keys, and flashlight batteries?

GET PSYCHED!

Overweight people sometimes see themselves as unworthy of being thin. For them, being heavy and unattractive is just punishment for their lack of discipline. Failed attempts to diet only serve to increase self-loathing and confirm this unworthy feeling. For pack rats, the equivalent would be thinking you don't deserve a well-kept, junk-free home because you've been chronically lax in the past. This is a vicious little logical loop that produces only negative consequences.

Two possible remedies to a poor self-image are visualization and self-love. Psychologists have found that athletes who visualize themselves playing adroitly will perform better. This makes intuitive sense. Consider what could have happened if those athletes had concentrated on all the mistakes they might make and the possibility of losing. In sports, allowing negative thoughts to spoil a perfor-mance is called "choking," and it's second only to physical injury as a dread misfortune because it's very hard to overcome. Don't choke when it's time to declutter.

Imagine putting everything away neatly in clean, well-ordered rooms. Imagine how pleased this will make you feel. Imagine a future of such contentment.

Self-love can help combat self-doubts, too. Have you stayed in a fine hotel room with crisp linens, beautiful furniture, and a spotless bath? Have you stayed in a cheap motel with sticky carpets, ciga-rette-burned furniture, and stained sinks? Didn't you feel better about yourself in the nicer place? Don't

If You Can't Find It, You Don't Have It

If you can't find a thing when you want it, you can't use it. In effect, you don't "have" the thing. This can lead you to buy a duplicate, which means you're spending twice as much money and devoting twice as much space in your home for the object's purpose. Organizing your home to make it easy to find things when you need them can help you avoid this.

you deserve to feel that way in your own home? Summon up your self-regard, and make your home an orderly oasis worthy of housing you. You deserve it.

HARNESS YOUR ANGER

Some overweight people are comfortable being plump and consequently they feel little reason to change. If challenged, they may explain that they're happier because they have less stress in their lives than calorie-counters who starve themselves and spend hours straining away in a gym. Some pack rats take the same approach to rationalizing the mess they live in. They may label those who are neater as obsessive and neurotic. While the chronically overweight and clutter prone should be treated with respect and have a right to live as they please, we needn't agree with their choices.

If you're reading this book, you probably believe clutter is a bad thing. Even so, you may feel some anger because others seem to have less trouble handling the clutter in their lives. This anger can turn to bitterness that sabotages your efforts to put things in order. But anger also can fire up your resolve, if it's properly directed. Martin Luther, the instigator of the Protestant Reformation, once said, "I never work better than when I am inspired by anger; for when I am angry, I can write, pray, and preach well, for then my whole temperament is quickened, my understanding sharpened, and all mundane vexations and temptations depart."

Turn your anger to good use. Stiffen your spine and increase your self-discipline by getting mad at your superfluous possessions and the situations that tempt you to acquire.

It may seem absurd to get angry with inanimate things, but if that helps you reach your goal, why not put a face on your clutter and tell it who's boss? Does it think it can push you around? Does it want to embarrass you in front of your friends? Does it want to trip you and crowd you and hinder your every movement? Does it blight your thoughts and spoil your mood? Throw it in the trash and slam the lid. Jam it into the recycling bin, where it'll be ground up and transformed into a product that's actually good for something. Kick clutter out the door, and don't let it come crawling back in.

CLUTTER AS A SURVIVAL MECHANISM

"All things are difficult before they are easy."

—Thomas Fuller

Cutting clutter is difficult. Our primitive side sees the accumulation of things as helpful in the battle for survival. The big heap of rocks our prehistoric ancestor piled up in the back of his cave came in handy when the neighbors dropped by to say hello and

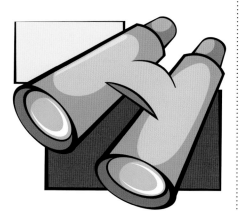

kill him. A closet overflowing with shoes may likewise seem useful to you—although not, presumably, as a stash of missiles.

Acquiring stuff is fun, too. We enjoy the books, the clothing, the art objects, and the furniture with which we fill our homes. The comforting qualities of both food and clutter can overwhelm all our best resolutions.

As difficult as managing a house full of possessions may be, it can be accomplished room by room, shelf by shelf, and object by object. Confucius advised travelers that a thousand-mile journey begins with a single step. Small efforts can be compounded into great efforts, and that certainly is true of attacking clutter. Of course the steps can't be too small, or your thousand-mile journey to an organized life may take a thousand years.

SWEEPING OUT A CLUTTERED MIND

Clutter is more than a physical inconvenience. It can destroy your peace of mind by making every activity more bothersome and distracting. For centuries, philoso-phers have proclaimed the need for simple surroundings conducive to contemplating the grand mysteries of life. To that end, pick up your socks.

6 Ways to Make the Most of Tight Quarters

New Yorkers go to considerable lengths to get the most out of small living spaces, consulting professional "space doctors" to help them. Amy Finely Scott, one such space doctor, has come up with a number of useful prescriptions:

1. Take advantage of a high ceiling to create a loft.

2. Use bunk beds to save space. Furniture stores offer bunk-type arrangements for a single child, substituting a desk and chair for the lower bunk.

3. Add a wall to divide a long room into two smaller rooms, or into a room and a clutter-concealing closet.

4. Replace American appliances with compact European models.

5. Use pocket doors to free up the space allocated to the arc of swinging doors.

6. Replace wide doors with narrower doors to gain a few extra inches of wall space.

TWO

Getting Started:

Some Easy Tasks to Get You Going Fast

"Crash programs fail because they are based on the theory that, with nine women pregnant, you can get a baby in a month."
—Wernher von Braun

We may have accumulated unnecessary possessions for decades. Attacking this clutter monster in our homes can be intimidating, and we declutterers may be frozen in inaction. One way to break this paralysis is to execute a small, easily accomplished decluttering task that's likely to produce success. Such accomplishment will encourage you to do more. This chapter details several such tasks that can get you up out of your chair and on the way to a less cluttered home.

The tasks can also serve as small rehearsals for your larger war on clutter. As you execute them, you'll face lesser versions of the same challenges—motivating yourself, dealing with failure, and maintaining success—that you'll confront in your greater struggle. You're like a knight preparing to face a fearsome dragon by beating up a bunch of straw-filled dummy dragons. The knight winds up better prepared for the main battle against the real dragon.

Of course, there are drawbacks to launching a number of small attacks upon clutter. Multiplying the number of attacks upon a problem doesn't necessarily reduce the time it takes to solve that problem. Crash programs, which convince their followers to rush forward without understanding their problem or having a thoughtful solution in mind, can waste effort. Such followers are a

bit like the hero described in 1911 by Stephen Leacock in *Nonsense Novels*, Gertrude the Governess, who faces a crisis: "Lord Ronald said nothing; he flung himself from the room, flung himself upon his horse and rode madly off in all directions."

Fortunately, reducing your clutter can be accomplished by executing small tasks. In this respect, removing clutter from your home is easier than dieting to lose weight: While a small investment of time can visibly reduce your clutter, a few minutes of dieting won't make a difference in your appearance. So, put on some old clothes, unplug your telephone, and try one of the following short jobs. Think of it as a quickly executed stretching exercise to warm up for more complete decluttering.

3 IDEAS TO FIX FIRST IMPRESSIONS

Go to the front door and turn around to face your home as a visitor would see it. Attack whatever clutter you find.

1. Perhaps you left your coat over the arm of a chair; hang it up.
2. Maybe there's a pile of magazines on your coffee table; clip out any articles you want to keep, then toss the gutted magazines into the recycling bin.
3. Ignore clutter that is hidden or that would take hours to handle. You can attack that when you have more time. Right now, just zip through the obvious and easily handled confusion. Since this is the first area people see when they enter your home, a few minutes of tidying here will have more impact than working elsewhere. If you have time, repeat this procedure for other rooms, attending to the clutter you see as you enter.

CHARITY BEGINS AT HOME

Sheree, a coauthor of this book, has an associate named Megan at her literary agency who keeps a cardboard box in her hall closet dedicated to donations to charity. As she identifies a piece of clothing, a book, or a dish that's disposable, she puts it immediately into this "charity box." As soon as the box is full, she stuffs it into the trunk of her car and drops it off when running errands.

Keep your own charity box in some handy spot, and you'll be more likely to follow through with your intention to donate items to a good cause. By dropping off the box as soon as possible, you'll avoid any second thoughts about holding on to these items. As a quick fix, pull out your charity box and go to your bedroom. Without over-thinking your choices, pull

pieces of clothing from your closet and dresser that you can live without. Don't stop until you fill the box. This simple goal can help you cross the mental line from "I might wear this someday" to "I don't need this."

3 SIMPLE STEPS TO CLEAN A SHELF

Tidying an entire pantry can take hours, but you can get quick results by attacking a single shelf of this space:

1. Choose one you use often, and take every item from it.
2. Discard expired products and anything you aren't likely to use.
3. Wash the shelf, then dry it completely before replacing its contents. (Metal cans may leave rust rings on a wet shelf.)

8 WAYS TO BOX IT UP OUT OF SIGHT

The next time you're in the housewares section of your favorite department store or home center, check out the storage boxes. Plastic boxes with hinged lids are available in a wide variety of sizes and colors. Select a few for organizing small items and storing them out of sight. Most bathroom sink counters, for example, are crowded with toiletries. Put these odds and ends in a plastic storage box and store the box under the sink or in a cabinet. Your things will all be in one spot, neatly out of view but easy to find.

1. Children's lunch boxes, especially those with colorful illustrations, are a cheery form of storage.
2. Old hatboxes make stylish containers.
3. If you like country things, buy a few Shaker boxes. These

oval wooden containers were designed for clutter management in the dormitories of Shaker communities. Although the originals have become high-priced antiques, you can buy reproductions for much less.

4. Cracker or cookie tins, available in any supermarket, can help organize small items on your shelves.

5. Visit a sporting goods store for tackle boxes or a hardware store for toolboxes. These have lots of compartments useful for storing jewelry or sewing supplies. They also have handles for easy carrying.

6. Out-of-the-ordinary tea tins can store small items beautifully.

7. Find quaint biscuit tins at a shop specializing in British goods.

8. Even the plastic boxes that diaper wipes are sold in can be used for storage.

2-STEP BATHROOM BLITZ

Freshly laundered rugs on a clean floor will give your bathroom a crisp look.

1. Wash the mats, rugs, and toilet seat cover from a bathroom.

2. Meanwhile, sweep and then mop the bathroom floor.

CHILD'S PLAY

If you have kids, you can enlist them in your war on clutter with this little game. Set an egg timer for 15 minutes, and send them off to gather items from their rooms for donation to charity. When the timer dings, the child with the biggest pile gets to choose what kind of take-out food to pick up for supper on your way home from dropping off the donations. Just be sure to double-check the giveaways. A kid who loves Chinese food might be happy to donate his or her Sunday go-to-church clothes in return for a pint of Kung Pao chicken.

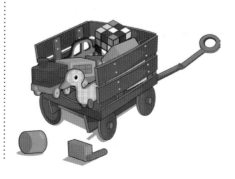

2-STEP COUNTER ATTACK

Kitchen counters are a highly visible part of your home scenery, and cleaning them will produce a greater return for your effort than tidying almost anywhere else.

1. Don't simply wipe off the open spaces—go the extra step of pulling out canisters and appliances and cleaning behind them.
2. A little countertop polish, available at well-stocked groceries or hardware stores, can add an impressive gleam to your kitchen.

HANGER ROUNDUP

"No more wirehangers!"
   —*Mommie Dearest* (1981)

Hangers are like rabbits. When you look away, they get up to you-know-what and before long your closets are filled with them. They're usually a mutant collection including wooden hangers circa 1950, modern plastic hangers, and the ubiquitous cheap wire hangers Mommie Dearest hated. She was a monster when it came to child rearing, but quite right about wire hangers. They pull sweater shoulders out of shape, snag fabric on their pointy hooks, and leave rust marks on damp clothing. Replace them. Plastic hangers are the best choice, and you can find them for as little as a dime apiece in discount stores.

Disposing of wire hangers can be awkward. Rita, a coauthor of this book, returns them to her dry cleaner, which reuses them. Many cleaners don't want them back, however, preferring to use new ones. Thrift stores use a lot of hangers, but they usually have plenty and are reluctant to take more. Ask around, but don't be surprised if you have to throw your cast-off hangers into the trash. The New York City Sanitation Department recycles hangers. Your municipality may also.

MIRROR, MIRROR ON THE WALL

Armed with a bottle of glass cleaner and a paper towel, polish mirrors, appliance fronts, glass-front cabinets, faucets, and of course as many windows as possible. Bright, shiny surfaces and sparking windows will do a lot to enliven your home. Try using:

1. A clean cotton diaper is a popular polishing choice.
2. A clean T-shirt is easy to find.
3. People swear by an ordinary terry cloth towel.
4. Many tipsters recommend newspaper for cleaning glass, but ink can smudge surfaces.
5. Some claim that coffee filters do the trick.
6. The micro fiber polishing cloth, a recent invention, leaves a nice shine with little effort.

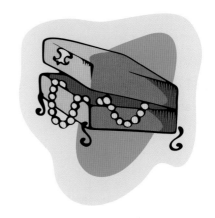

JEWELRY BOX DUMP

"My husband gave me a necklace. It's fake. I requested fake. Maybe I'm paranoid, but in this day and age, I don't want something around my neck that's worth more than my head."

—Rita Rudner

A jewelry box tends to become a microcosm of the clutter found elsewhere in the home. Empty yours on the table with good lighting.

Dump:

1. Inexpensive metal chains
2. Defunct off-brand watches
3. Chipped costume jewelry

4. Earrings that have lost their mates (unless you love them, see below)
5. Novelty jewelry you don't wear

Keep:

1. Jewelry you were regurlarly
2. Singlton earrings that you particularly like (bring these to a jeweler to turn into pins or pendants)
3. Broken items (set aside and taken to a jeweler as soon as possible)
4. Old pieces with sentimental associations, such as a class ring or a merit pin from the Woodland Wanderers (store apart from the jewelry you use every day)
5. Valuable pieces (store in a safe deposit box or a wall safe)

Once you've carried out these steps, your jewelry collections should be manageable—and you may discover a forgotten treasure in the process.

PURSE PURGING

Most women carry purses packed with clutter. If you're among them, dump out your purse on your kitchen table. Throw out any trash. This includes not only old candy wrappers and linty mints, but also less-obvious detritus such as outdated make-up and obsolete business cards. Turn next to your wallet. Weed out expired membership cards, credit cards you no longer use, and photographs that show your teenager at age 2 or your husband when he still sported that 1970s perm.

3 WAYS TO USE IT OR LOSE IT

"You don't have a pitcher for tomorrow. Tomorrow it may rain."
—Leo Durocher

Most of us set aside our nicest household items for special occasions or important visitors. These things rarely, if ever, see the light of day and just eat up storage space. By making daily use of them, you can clear your shelf and cabinets of the mundane items you use instead of "good stuff." You'll enjoy the psychological lift of treating each

day as special occasion, and you'll feel like a respected guest in your own home. Some ideas to consider:

1. Those special china cups that you're saving for company can replace your discount store mugs.
2. The fancy quilt that's hidden away in a closet can be spread across your bed, replacing an old afghan.
3. The crystal vase tucked in an attic chest can replace the jelly jar you've been using for bouquets on the dining table.

6 WAYS TO HANDLE AN EMERGENCY CLEANUP

We all have moments when there just isn't enough time to put our homes in order for unexpected guests. To rise to these occasions, you have to shift into high gear, skipping housecleaning tasks that aren't crucial to the impending visit.

Let's say the president of the United States is touring your town, and his people call to say that he'd like to stop by to talk to a genuine, average American—namely you—while television crews beam your home's interior into three or four billion other average people's homes. Oh, and the prez is due by your place in 45 minutes. As you put down your phone on the pile of old newspapers that you use for a table and rise from the heap of laundry that adds extra softness to your sofa, do you panic? Do you call the White House back and ask the President to drop by next week instead? Of course not, because you're a patriot and you can meet the challenge.

1. The key to presenting an orderly home is quick conceal-ment of obvious clutter. Grab a box, laundry basket, or even a garbage bag and look for the most obvious mess. Whatever it is, shove it into the container and then move on to the next mess and do the same. When the container is full, stick it out of sight in a closet or in a room that won't be visited by your guests.
2. The next step is to tidy the bathroom, a spot guests are

likely to visit. Gather up all the shampoo bottles, combs, razors, and cosmetics, and stow them in a container you can hide. Don't shove them in your medicine cabinet. Curious guests may peek inside, and it could be quite embarrassing for them and you if all that junk cascaded out.

3. Soap scum and bathroom grime can be quickly and adequately wiped up with a fistful of slightly damp bathroom tissue, which is right at hand. Bathroom tissue is particularly good for cleaning up the stray hairs and dust that accumulate on surfaces and in corners. Clean your soap dish

Uncluttered Ambience

When whipping your home into shape for guest, take a moment to create a pleasant atmosphere. Brew a pot of coffee. Slide a tray of slice-and-bake chocolate chip cookies into the oven. The aromas will be so inviting that visitors may overlook an untidy corner here and there.

For evening guests, light candles and build a fire. Candlelight and a flickering fire create a welcoming mood, and the low light level hides imperfections. If it's daytime, go to the opposite extreme. Open all the blinds to fill your home with light. In clement weather, open your windows. Sunlight and fresh air create a healthy, brisk mood that helps to mute disorder.

How a Husband Drove His Wife Nuts By Being Too Tidy

Rita's friend Susan had a pet peeve about the cleaning tactics of her husband, Bob. When visitors were coming over, she'd enlist Bob to help straighten up the place. But instead of vacuuming the carpet or tidying the kitchen counter or doing some other practical chore, Bob would find an obscure area to clean. He'd line up the paint cans in the garage or dust the back of the refrigerator or empty the ashtray in his car.

When Susan suggested he work on something more visible, Bob defended his approach as more comprehensive, insisting that the house isn't really clean if there is disorder *anywhere*. Making matters worse, Bob often made *more* mess in the process of getting to the hidden mess. Before one dinner party, he emptied the pantry onto the kitchen floor so he could reorganize the shelves. There were still towers of canned vegetables and stacks of cake mix on the unwashed floor when the guest arrived.

Susan solved her Bob problem by having him devote his energies to cleaning the bathroom—a small area that he would be able to exhaustively clean in fairly short order. Now he can be entrusted to straighten out the medicine cabinet, clean under the sink, refold the towels–and still have time to clean the highly visible tub, sink, and floor before their guests ring the doorbell.

If you're sharing your home with others, you've probably observed that one person's intolerable mess can be trivial to someone else. By indentifying the decluttering tasks that each person considers most important, you may be able to come up with a complementary blend of approaches for putting your house in order.

and put a new bar of soap in it. Hang fresh towels and a new roll of toilet tissue.

4. On to the living room! This is probably where you'll entertain your guest. Dust surfaces that immediately meet your eye. Don't bother about the high surfaces. Vacuum high-traffic areas after dusting.

5. The next room to declutter is the kitchen, especially if you expect to feed your guest. Empty the sink of dirty dishes by loading them into your dishwasher. Give your counters a quick wipe and dump any relics from earlier meals. Empty your trash bin. Don't worry about items that are neatly ordered on your counters: A stack of clean dishes or folded dish towels will show that yours is a home where people actually live, not a set for a segment of a "gracious living" television program.

6. When you finish your emergency home cleanup, tidy up your person.

If you look scrubbed and well-dressed and all obvious clutter is out of sight, you and your home will project a positive image. The president will be impressed and will never know that your dishwasher is full of dirty dishes or that there's a bag of junk mail bundled away in your closet. Once he and the cameras are gone and you recover your composure, you can do a more complete cleaning job, emptying and sorting whatever you hid away. Don't delay. We hear the Prince of Wales is coming to town next week.

3 WAYS TO EMPLOY OLD WISDOM

"A place for everything and everything in its place" is an old American adage that remains the best, most concise expression of how to create order in your home. Establish a storage spot for every commonly used object.

1. Hang hooks for your dustpan and broom

2. Designate a shelf by the cellar door for a flashlight.

3. Find a drawer for kitchen wrap.

Then return each item to its spot after you use it. It only takes seconds. Your home will look neater, and you'll avoid those explosive blood pressure spikes of frustration when you can't find something you used just yesterday.

THREE

Clutter Triggers

"Lead me not into temptation; I can find the way myself."

—**Rita Mae Brown**

If clutter is a challenge, you may find yourself highly susceptible to acquiring certain objects, even when your possessions are spiraling out of control. Here are our top clutter temptations.

5 WAYS TO ORGANIZE CLUTTER COURTESY OF THE POSTAL SERVICE*

"When I die, my epitaph should read: 'She Paid the Bills.'"

—Gloria Swanson

The daily hubbub of life is made more hubbly and bubbly by the arrival of the mail, with its many enveloped demands upon your bank account and your time. The water department wants your money. Uncle George wants to hear from you. A catalog offers fantastic bargains that will disappear forever if you don't take advantage of them now. Some bank wants to give your dog a credit card. Your monthly issue of *Croquet Illustrated* magazine tempts you with the inside scoop on mallet wax. To complicate things, the mail is often addressed to more than one person: you, your spouse, your average 2.3 children, your above-mentioned dog, and that mysterious roommate who never pays his share of the rent—Occupant.

The key to making sense of this maelstrom of mail is sorting.

1. Buy a basket large enough to handle your daily mail, and use it as an "in" basket.

2. You'll also need several stacking letter trays, so that you can sort the mail as soon as it arrives. These trays are available at office supply stores in wire mesh, plastic, steel, and even nicely finished wood. Put labels on trays for family members and also for specific types of mail such as magazines or catalogs.

3. When going through the day's mail, place bills and important correspondence in the top tray, where they'll be hard to ignore.

* Calling the Consumer Data Industry Association (888-5OPTOUT; www. optoutprescreen.com) can block preapproved cards. This organization will notify credit-reporting agencies that they shouldn't give your credit information to credit card companies seeking new customers.

For help in getting your name removed from junk mail lists, contact the Direct Marketing Association at www.dmaconsumers.org, or DMA Mail Preference Service, P.O. Box 643, Carmel, New York 10512.

4. Immediately throw out unwanted mail, taking care to shred items that may carry private information.

5. When you receive unwanted, preapproved credit cards in the mail, don't simply throw them away. Play it safe by cutting up the credit card and the paperwork sent with it.

7 WAYS TO DEAL WITH BILLS: CLUTTER YOU CAN'T IGNORE

1. Choose a single spot for handling bills. This might be a corner of your kitchen counter or an ornate 18th-century desk. The important thing is to use the same location so you'll always know where your bills and bill paying records are.

2. Keep your bill handling supplies (such as stamps, envelopes, and folders) close at hand in order to save steps.

3. If you don't have time to handle bills as they come in, designate a particular day for bill paying. Identifying a date will help you avoid forgetting to pay a bill.

4. Don't file bills before paying them. Keeping files for expenditures is a good idea, but putting unpaid bills in these files makes it easy to forget them. Keep a basket or other special spot for unpaid bills. After you've paid them, file whatever account statement came with the bill with a notation of when you paid.

5. Many banks offer online bill paying services that will pay your regular bills from your account. This can save you bother and assure prompt payments.

6. Consider using bill-paying software. A program such as Quicken can speed the process and organize your payment records, helping you when it

comes time to prepare your tax return.

7. If you like to delay payment until the due date approaches, you can label the bill's envelope with that date, minus however many days it will take your payment to be delivered. Put the dated envelopes where you'll be sure to check them each day, and mail them when their dates arrive.

OUTGOING MAIL

Outgoing mail needs to be carefully handled to assure it doesn't get misplaced. Set an "Out" basket where you'll see it on your way out in the morning. If you don't have a great deal of outgoing mail, you may choose to mount a pocket mail holder on the wall near the door or on the door itself. Even just a strong clip attached to the wall may be adequate. The key is visibility. You don't want the water company sending its thick-necked goons to break your dishwasher's kneecaps, or its parts equivalent thereto. See Chapter 11, "A Lean and Efficient Home Office," for more details about handling business mail, including e-mail.

NEWSPAPERS: ALL THE CLUTTER THAT'S FIT TO DUMP

Stacks of newspapers always seem to figure prominently in stories about obsessive pack ratism. That's probably because, for some of us, old newspapers have potential value. The newspaper clutter addict will eagerly tell you that, in addition to their literary content, they can be used for packing breakables, soaking up spills, lining shelves, lighting fires, making paper hats, and countless other marvelous things. None of these purposes, however, is a good reason to burden yourself with mounds of newspaper.

First, hundreds of easily searched newspaper archives are available on the Internet. And if you can't find what you're looking for, most libraries have newspapers on microfiche.

The utilitarian value of newspaper is also overrated. Newspaper ink easily rubs off and is difficult to remove, making newspapers a less than ideal choice for packing, cleaning, or shelf lining. Contact with newspaper can stain porcelain or silver.

Instead of packing with inky newspaper, use the plain newsprint available at moving supply stores and truck rental companies. It's cheap, and when you're done with it, it can go into your recycling bin. Plain newsprint is also better for the other functions advanced for newspapers, including making paper hats. It won't smudge your forehead.

Finally, if you ever do find yourself in need of newspapers, given human nature you can count on your neighbors to have mountains of them lying around.

MAGAZINES: STACKS OF GLOSSY CLUTTER

Magazines are another favorite item for clutterers to hoard. Nearly every attic has a stash of *National Geographic* magazines moldering in an unexplored corner.

2 Reasons to Toss Magazines:

1. If you're keeping magazines for their information, any good library will have back issues of most popular magazines and an index to help you find what-

ever you want. You simply can't do a better job of archiving periodicals than a librarian.

2. If you're hoping to retire on the proceeds of your attic stash, think again. While some old magazines can be valuable, setting aside current magazines for resale is a poor investment. It may take years for them to acquire value—years during which you'll have to protect them from deterioration. If you must collect, limit yourself to issues dealing with popular media figures or special events. An issue of *TV Guide* describing the cast of the latest incarnation of *Star Trek* or a copy of *Time* dealing with a remarkable historic event might be worth a few bucks in a decade if you keep it in mint condition.

If you already have a cache of old magazines, you can determine its potential value by consulting the Internet. A few moments' work, for example, can tell you that an undamaged copy of the rare Saturday Evening Post for August 5, 1916, which features a Norman Rockwell cover of boys playing baseball, is worth about $450 as of this writing.

Treating Comics Seriously

Old comic books can be valuable—if they haven't turned into dust. Comic book expert Gary Chisholm Jr. at www.comicbooks. about.com recommends storing comics in Mylar sleeves with cardboard "backers," sold in comic book stores. The inexpensive paper on which comic books are printed contains acids that cause it to yellow and become brittle. Heat, humidity, and sunlight accelerate the process, so store your sleeved and backed comics with these threats in mind.

4 Things to Do with Old Magazines:

1. Drop them off at nursing homes or hospitals.
2. Rita's neighbor Toni donates recent issues to her local library, where extra copies of holiday craft issues are especially welcomed because they tend to disappear from the shelves.
3. Bring a magazine to the dentist's office to entertain yourself, then leave it behind for others to read. You might spare your fellow patients from having to browse Carter-era issues of *Popular Dentistry*.
4. Set up a magazine trading table at your workplace, so that you and your coworkers can drop off issues and pick up others that look interesting.

When giving away magazines, clip off your address labels. You needn't share this personal information—share only the magazines.

7 WAYS TO AVOID BIBLIOMANIA

Books are a particular danger to clutterers. Most of us have grown up with the notion that books are the foremost repositories of knowledge and to throw one out is equivalent in spirit to the torching of the library at Alexandria. Nonetheless, books can easily become a burden. They're bulky and heavy and hard to dust. They can become outdated or simply no longer of

The Magazine-Passing Game

It used to be that when Ed or his wife Laurie finished a magazine, he or she didn't throw it out in case the other hadn't had a chance to read it. So magazines tended to accumulate, adding to their home's clutter. The solution was simple: Now when they finish a magazine, they initial a corner of the cover to let each other know they're done with it.

interest to you. Look through your shelves with a critical eye and cull, cull, cull.

There are two basic types of book: those for work and those for pleasure. They should be shelved separately. If you have a home office, put your work-related books there. Keep only those professional books you expect to use, which contain information that can't

easily be found on the Internet or elsewhere.

Pleasure books are evaluated differently. They criterion for keeping them is the enjoyment they give you. There's nothing wrong with holding onto favorites to reread again and again. But pleasure books become a problem when you fail to establish limits on their numbers. You don't want to accumulate enough reading material to last four or five lifetimes. Here are several tips to help you prevent your home from resembling a used-books store:

1. Are there duplicates in your library? Dump the extras.
2. If a volume is likely to be found in your local library, consider getting rid of your copy. The

library has more shelf space than you do.

3. Be your own book reviewer. Cut poorer works from your library.

4. If you have books that you're sure you'd like to reread some day but not anytime soon, store them in a dry and vermin-free place. There's no reason to burden your shelves with these books now. Someday you'll re-discover them and they'll seem like a small, unexpected treasure trove.

5. When disposing of books, a used-books store is a logical place to start, but don't expect top dollar. As with pawnbrokers and estate buyers, used-book buyers are professionals who can't make a buck unless they get their stock cheap. Some stores will offer you credit toward books on their shelves. If you like their stock, this can be a better choice than cash, as it commonly provides more buying power than the cash offered.

6. You might donate books to libraries, nursing homes, schools, or hospitals. They can use the books in good condition and of general interest, either to expand their collections or to sell to raise money. There are also charities that send books to economically depressed areas in the United States, to overseas literacy programs, or to troops posted far from home.

7. Some of your books may interest collectors. A clean copy of a first edition by a popular author, especially if autographed, may be worth

---

QUICK FIX

USED BOOKS MAKE GOOD GIFTS

If you have trouble disposing of a favorite book, consider giving it to a friend. This is more generous than loaning it, and the gift can deepen your friendship as you share a literary experience.

---

selling. Again, a quick search of the Internet can give you an idea of how valuable your book is. Keep it in as original a state as possible.

4 WAYS TO AVOID THE MAIL-ORDER MENACE

If you're clutter-prone, catalogs appear to be useful resources that should be saved forever. But unless you find the time to browse them, before long you'll have stacks of out-of-date offerings. Another potential clutter problem is that once you do place an order, the company may pass on your address to other eager retailers, who then place you on their mailing lists, swelling your catalog burden. Here are a few suggestions for keeping up with catalog clutter.

1. Keep only the most recent edition of a company's catalog.
2. When you receive a catalog, take a quick look and, unless you immediately spot a possible purchase, recycle it.
3. If you get a catalog from a company that doesn't interest you, call its toll-free number or send a postcard asking to be cut from its mailing list. Cata-

logs are expensive to print and mail, and many companies will comply with your request.
4. Products offered through catalogs may also be available through the Internet, sparing you the need to keep catalogs.

3 WAYS TO CUT WASH DAY CLUTTER

"Now they show you how detergents take out bloodstains, a pretty violent image there. I think if you've got a T-shirt with a bloodstain all over it, maybe laundry isn't your biggest problem. Maybe you should get rid of the body before you do the wash."

—Jerry Seinfeld

The need to do laundry never ends until you die, and even then you'll probably leave a hamper full of dirty duds for your heirs to wash out. For cluttery folk, laundry can quickly pile up, becoming offensive in appearance and smell. In Chapter 13, "Laundry Room Remedies," we'll look in detail at decluttering and organizing this part of your home. Meanwhile, here are some ideas to set you on your way.

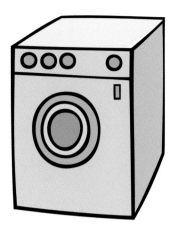

1. Keep a hamper in every laundry-producing area. Your bedroom will probably generate the most laundry, but bathrooms amass piles of damp towels and your kitchen adds still more washing. If you have a hamper handy in each room, it'll be easier to stow dirty laundry there instead of kicking it into a corner.

2. To keep your hampers fresh, empty them often, spray occasionally with a disinfectant, and routinely wash them out.

3. Use plastic hampers that have plenty of ventilation holes. While plastic may lack eye appeal, it can be cleaned easily. Vents reduce mildew by helping damp laundry dry a bit inside the hamper. Some hampers have handles that make them easy to carry to your washer.

5 WAYS TO AVOID DIRTY DISH CLUTTER

"You make the beds, you do the dishes, and six months later you have to start all over again."

—Joan Rivers

In the 1950s, a "Home of the Future" designed by a plastics manufacturer suggested that all tableware should be made of plastic so that it could be cleaned in a novel way: When soiled, the dishes and utensils would be tossed into a machine that melted and remolded them into a new set. Unfortunately, that technology was never perfected, and the only way for you to convert dirty dishes into clean dishes in your primitive home is to wash them.

Dirty dishes pile up in even the neatest home. After eating a meal, you may feel too torpid to deal with them or just lack the time. If you have kids, the problem isn't confined to the kitchen—dirty dishes have a way of migrating to every corner of the house that your kids can reach. If they had a ladder, there would be crusty plates on the roof.

Try the following to ease dish clutter.

1. Make it a rule to wash your dishes as soon as possible.
2. If you have a dishwasher, empty it as soon as a cycle is finished. That way you'll have a place to conceal your dirty dishes.
3. Run the rinse-and-hold cycle to wash off gunk likely to harden. Put a refrigerator magnet on your dishwasher door when you run a rinse-and-hold cycle to indicate the dishes are still dirty. When you get around to running a full wash, remove the magnet.
4. As soon as the dishwasher is full, run its full cleaning cycle and empty it. (See tip #2.)
5. Whenever you wash your dishes, evaluate their condition.

Are they worthy of your table? Chipped or cracked dishware is unattractive, and the imperfections can harbor bacteria. Dump damaged dishes.

6 SUGGESTIONS FOR LIMITING YOUR COLLECTIBLES

Nearly everyone has had a brush with collecting, whether it's the childhood gathering of rocks found in the backyard, or the folk art connoisseur's collection of Laplander antler figurines. Collections can be art objects or wannabe art objects. Some are souvenirs, kept as reminders of a person, place, or event. And collections may come unbidden, as when your mom decides to give you ceramic bunnies on every gift-giving occasion for decades on end because you once admired a Bugs Bunny bank as a toddler. In time, collections can fill every nook and niche and shelf until your home resembles a museum at best—or a flea market at worst.

Ed and his wife, Laurie, once house-sat the home of a fellow who collected Kurdish carpets. Rugs covered the floor, hung from the walls, draped over chairs and

sofas, lined the bookshelves, served as tablecloths, and even hung from the ceiling. Every room was adorned with rugs. The refrigerator had a rug magnetically attached to its face. The shower curtain was a rug with a liner attached. Even the windows were draped with rugs. The overall effect was claustrophobic, not cozy. One didn't feel as snug as the proverbial bug in a rug.

To keep your collection from taking over your home, try to be objective about your devotion to rugs, figurines, or whatever your weakness is. These suggestions might come in handy.

1. Even the most beautiful object loses its allure if you see it day after day. To ensure that your ceramic rabbit collection keeps its eye appeal, pack away half and display the rest. When the visible items have grown familiar and stale, swap them with those you've stored.

2. If items in your collection have been viewed to death, you might try trading them with an antique dealer for a single object of more value. You can reduce a large collection of modest items to a smaller collection of more precious items.

3. Check the value of your collection with a professional or against similar collectibles online. If your collectibles are valuable, consider selling them rather than bearing the burden of storing them safely. If they turn out to be worth little, this may be the impetus to part with them.

4. Donate or loan your collection to a local institution. A collector of Santa Claus figurines gave her collection to a children's hospital, where it was put on display to please the ill children and to solicit donations

for a Christmas charity. Such a gift can serve as a psychological conclusion for obsessive collectors. By turning their treasures over to a worthy purpose, they can stop collecting.

5. Give heirlooms in your collection to relatives. Your granny's old bud vase may have some value on the open market, but it will certainly have more value to your daughter as a family treasure. Instead of willing it to her, give it to her now, while you're alive and can enjoy her thanks.

6. If you must collect, choose something that takes up little space. A collection of stamps, miniature portraits, postcards, or coins can be stored in a single drawer. The same can't be said for a collection of national flags, department store mannequins, circus posters, or manhole covers.

CARING FOR COLLECTIBLES

A collection isn't worth keeping if you don't protect it from deterioration. Handle and store it carefully. Wear cotton gloves; oil and dampness from your fingers can

---

QUICK FIX

MEMORIES, NOT MEMENTOS

Do you collect souvenirs? Are you tempted to buy a suitcase full of them on your trip to Mexico? Put down that sombrero with the dangly pompoms. Instead, memorialize your experience by taking photographs, perhaps trying on that sombrero. Or better yet, invest your time and money in an interesting side trip, and make a memory that creates no clutter whatsoever.

---

cause damage to fragile objects. Airtight storage is only appropriate when the air being trapped with the collectibles is dry; otherwise, mold or mildew can form. Use desiccant packs and check periodically for moisture. Store delicate collectibles where they won't be exposed to insects, mice, sunlight, water, or temperature and humidity extremes. Textiles should be cleaned before storage. Soiled cloth can attract insects and stains

can become harder to remove. To clean delicate items, consult a fabric expert. Cedar chests can discourage moths but unvarnished wood surfaces, such as the boards in a cedar chest, exude oils that can damage fabric.

Amateur collectors commonly rely on plastic bags to protect their collectibles, but plastic bags, while useful for short-term storage, can emit gases that can harm their contents with prolonged exposure. Plastic can also trap moisture. Archival-quality cardboard boxes, with acid-free, archival tissue paper to separate and cushion where necessary, are safer.

For guidance for your particular type of collectible, ask experts in that field. Your local historical society or museum is a good place to start.

KIDS' CLUTTER

"Cleaning your house while your kids are still growing is like shoveling the walk before it stops snowing."

—Phyllis Diller

Children have a habit of acquiring all sorts of clutter. They receive gifts from family and friends, borrow stuff from pals, and gather curious debris from their favorite haunts. And of course there is a steady supply of school projects. The result tends to be disordered mounds that defy organization. What can you do?

3 WAYS TO LIMIT KID CLUTTER

1. Soon after your kids come home from school, have them unload their backpacks and show you their papers. This is the time to weed out the superfluous stuff while keeping an eye out for important forms and notices. Most kids love showing their drawings and writings. You can cull out the less remarkable efforts, then store the better work as souvenirs of your child's development.

2. Encourage your children to donate extra toys and clothing to charity. It helps them develop empathy and a charitable nature.

3. To get your children to put away their possessions, use a "penalty box" for things left out of place. If the kids don't put away their stuff when told to do so, place the items in the box for them to reclaim. At the end of each month, any contents still left in the box are locked away for the next month. Circle the lock-up date in red on your family calendar, and when the day comes, follow through. Setting a specific time, say 3:00 p.m. on every Saturday, for a regular sweep of the house to find out-of-place kid stuff may help. You can call this time the "Hour of Doom," to fix it vividly in your child's mind.

QUICK FIX

BLACK-BAG IT

Parting with possessions can be painful for kids as well as adults. Ed's friend Pat found that her children's artwork was overwhelming her home's storage space. She winnowed out the lesser efforts and was putting them into a clear trash bag when she heard her kids playing in the next room. Realizing that they might see their work discarded and feel hurt, Pat used a black trash bag instead. It was a simple precaution that spared her children's feelings.

You can use the same black-bag technique when disposing of your own possessions. A glimpse of a once-beloved blouse being dispatched to a thrift store or a mystery book that filled an evening with suspense now bound for the library's book drive can tempt a pack rat to rescue an item.

THE MAGIC MIRROR REALIZES THAT HE'S NOW THE "FAIREST OF THEM ALL."

FOUR

Your Entry Area

Making a Good First Impression

"My life is pretty boring. Last week some Jehovah's Witnesses came to the door and I wouldn't let them leave. They snuck away when I went into the kitchen to get some lemonade."

—Marge Simpson

The first space every visitor to your home encounters, be they census-taker, Girl Scout cookie salesperson, or your one true love's mom and dad, is your entry area. It's here that your home makes its first impression. Just as you wouldn't want to meet a blind date with spinach snagged in your front teeth, you don't want visitors to enter your home and see piles of clutter. The entryway is also important for another reason. Not to malign census-takers, Girl Scouts, or your true love's parents, but most of the dirt and clutter from the outside world enters here as well. Consequently, a well-managed entry can help keep your entire home cleaner and less cluttered.

Traditionally, homes have had transition places where visitors could hang up their coats and remove muddy boots. Older houses had vestibules, where there might be an elephant leg umbrella stand in which to stow a bumbershoot or cane, a coatrack with china knobs, and maybe a table bearing a silver tray where visitors could leave their calling cards. A nifty combination coatrack, mirror, and chair was a common feature of 19th-century vestibules. Executed in polished oak and bright brass, perhaps with a bevel-edged mirror, these are beautiful pieces of functional furniture.

A more recent variation on the vestibule is the mudroom, an informal entry where wet and dirty articles of clothing can be shed before entering the home proper. If your home has neither of these amenities, your living areas are apt to be littered with hats, scarves, and gloves. Carpets may grow dark with tracked-in mud. Still, there are ways to protect your home from the dirt and clutter of the world beyond your walls.

5 WAYS TO KEEP THE OUTSIDE FROM COMING INSIDE

1. The first line of resistance is to place a runner of outdoor carpeting, the longer the better, outside your entry to help clean visitors' footwear.

2. Just in front of your door, place a good-quality mat with lots of aggressive bristles to brush off crud. Country homes once had boot scrapers or brushes near the door so that people could clean their boots without bending. These are still available from firms selling reproductions of old hardware and from home-and-garden retailers. They range from cast-iron ducks with scraper blade backs to cement cats sporting brushes instead of fur.

3. Place a second, thinner mat inside the door and vacuum it frequently. This will catch much

of the dirt that otherwise would make it farther into your home.

4. A clear plastic runner will help protect the carpet in the high-traffic area of the entryway. They're inexpensive and don't add another color to your home decor. Buy a runner with nubs on the bottom to anchor it to the carpet and prevent non-comedic pratfalls.

5. A boot tray for wet footwear will spare your home the insults of muck and slush. To encourage people to use the tray, place a bench or chair nearby so that they can comfortably sit and remove their shoes or boots.

Once you've made the arrangements necessary to keep the entry area clean, you need to take measures to control the clutter that naturally accumulates there. Ed built a simple bench with a boot shelf for his entry area. After removing footwear, his family can neatly shelve it.

QUICK FIX

If your family likes to romp in the snow, keep a folding wooden drying rack by the back entry, where you can dry your snowing clothing.

---

3 ENTRY STRATEGIES

1. Look at the pile of shoes and boots that has accumulated by your entry. Chances are some will be disposable—either redundant or just worn out. If

your superfluous footwear isn't in bad shape, donate it to a thrift shop or homeless shelter.

2. A row of wall pegs or hooks by your door can be a great asset. Use them to hang coats, gloves, and scarves. To suspend wet gloves and mittens, use clothespins that have a hook, similar to the hook on a hanger. These can be found with laundry supplies in hardware stores and home centers. Be sure to place a boot pan under any hooks that are going to support items that will drip.

3. As you hang your winter wear, review it. You're apt to receive gloves or scarves as holiday gifts that duplicate stuff you already own. Warm clothing is especially needed by the unfortunate during winter. Donate any spare items.

DEALING WITH KIDS

When children arrive home from school, they tend to dump their books and backpacks as soon as they step inside. Schoolwork can get scattered, and that nice, nutritionally complete lunch you packed for Bobby, of which he ate not a single

bite, can turn rather ripe spending the night in his backpack.

3 WAYS TO HELP YOUR CHILDREN—AND YOU!—PUT STUFF AWAY

1. Assign wall hooks to each at convenient spots by the door for backpacks and coats. Make sure the hooks can handle the weight of heavy backpacks and bulky coats. Mount each one into a stud in the wall, or attach several to a horizontal board that is screwed into studs.

2. Sheree's friend Margaret, a teacher, has two boys in elementary school. To help them keep their things orderly, she bought a pair of "cubbies" from a children's furniture catalog and put them by her front door. Like the cubbies assigned to children in school, these units have a

deep shelf for backpacks, hooks from which to hang coats, and a space at the bottom for shoes and boots. Because everything is put in its place each afternoon, it's easier for Margaret to get her boys out the door in the morning.

3. Adults also bring lots of junk home from their sojourns in the outside world. Briefcases, purses, shopping bags, cell phones—all of them have a way of getting dumped in the entry area. Consider adding an attractive table with a drawer and shelf underneath. Large items, like briefcases and purses, can be set upon the shelf, while small items, like keys and sunglasses,

EASY DOES IT

Adding a Mudroom

If your home doesn't have a mudroom, considering adding one. A contractor can build a small, enclosed room around your front door. This space doesn't have to be as plain and frumpy as the name suggests. Ed spotted a home with a mudroom that doubles as a small greenhouse. It has walls of glass, with shelves for potted plants. Outside, it's surrounded by a wooden framework, allowing vines to creep over it in summer. The result is a mudroom that looks more like a garden pergola than a dumping spot for dirt-clotted boots.

You may prefer a simpler mudroom. Perhaps one side can sport rows of pegs for hanging garments, while the other side features a built-in bench with storage under its seat. A mudroom that shelters a side or back door can be more utilitarian than one at the front of your home. You can equip it with shelves, lockers, bins for outdoor toys, and even a bulletin boards for your family to use to coordinate your activities. You can merge the mudroom function with the functions of a pantry by equipping it with cupboards and a small freezer. Or, create a mudroom/laundry room by placing your washer and dryer here.

can go in the drawer. To be certain your cell phone won't go dead, place its charger on top of the table. If you have a lot of clutter to conceal, try using a decorative bureau. Its drawers will hide your daily "chains."

3 POINTERS FOR DECLUTTERING THE HALL CLOSET

"Gotta clean out that closet one of these days."

—Fibber McGee

There's apt to be a closet near your entry. This closet, usually identified as a hall closet, is likely to be jammed with clutter. Indeed, this clutter-y state is an American tradition. Your grandparents were probably fans of the radio show Fibber McGee and Molly. It featured a running gag about Fibber's ridiculously overburdened hall closet. Each time he opened it, sound-effect technicians went nuts rattling pots, dropping sand bags, and jangling cymbals to convey an avalanche of junk tumbling forth. Fibber never conquered his closet, but you can.

1. There's no point in having a full inventory of winter and summer clothing in your hall closet at the same time. Store off-season items elsewhere.

2. The hall closet tends to accumulate sports equipment—a bowling ball and bag, golf clubs, tennis rackets, a basketball. There is some logic to this, because it's convenient to grab these things as you rush out the door. As with your outerwear, be guided by the seasons. You won't need your golf clubs if there's 4 feet of snow in the yard, so stash them out in the garage until fair weather returns to the fairways.

3. The hall closet is a natural spot to store your vacuum cleaner. Trouble is, it's apt to disappear behind layers of coats and piles of boots, so that you'll be less inclined to go after your dust on a regular basis. A smaller vacuum may fit better into these tight confines. Some manufacturers now offer models that can be folded into more compact forms or can be hung from a hook. Alternatively, you can store your vacuum in a less heavily used closet, reserving the hall closet only for items that are apt to be used frequently.

12 HINTS FOR SELECTING A VACUUM CLEANER

Not all vacuum cleaners are created equal, and no single model may be appropriate for an entire home. Ed, perhaps in penance for being a tax collector in a previous life, once sold vacuum cleaners and offers some pointers on purchasing them.

1. Ask for a demonstration of the vacuum. To test the machine, bring along a bag of the type of crud you commonly find in your home. If your dog sheds, for example, try the vacuum on some of Fido's cast-off hair. If the vacuum won't pick this up from the store's carpet, it won't pick it up from your carpet.

2. Is the vacuum's cord long enough to reach every corner of your largest room?

3. For vacuums that use bags, how easy are they to replace? How much do they cost? Visit a dollar store or discount chain and see which bags they carry. You'll buy hundreds of bags for your vacuum, so a machine that uses cheap, easily-found bags can save you money. Vacuums that don't use bags avoid this cost but may be messy to empty. Ask the salesman to show you how it's done.

4. Many vacuums have rotating brushes that use small belts to link the brush to the motor. Ask the salesman how to replace these. This process may prove frustratingly awkward.

5. Ask the salesman to explain the vacuum's attachments. You can't fully utilize a vacuum if you don't know what it can do.

6. Lift the vacuum. Is it too heavy? Run it across the floor. Does it move easily? Are its switches convenient to use?

7. Can the vacuum clean uncarpeted floors? This is a handy capability.

8. Will the vacuum clean close to walls, in corners, and under furniture?

9. While you may prefer an upright to a canister, or vice versa, there are vacuums that combine the two types. They are essentially uprights with a detachable canister. This allows you to vacuum a carpet, then pull off the canister, attach a hose, and clean spots unreachable by an upright.

10. In an ordinary vacuum, fine dust often passes right through the machine. This fine dust is particularly bothersome to allergy sufferers. Some vacuums are equipped with a special high-efficiency particle arrestance (HEPA) filter that can catch this dust.

11. While vacuums today are made mostly of plastic, stressed parts such as handles or hinges should be made of steel for durability.

12. How noisy is the vacuum? A machine that makes your ears buzz for an hour after you shut it off won't get used often.

EASY DOES IT

3 Vacuum Options Small Homes

If you live in a small home or apartment, you may find it difficult to store a vacuum—there just isn't enough room.

1. One solution, if you have just a bit of carpet to keep clean, is an old-fashioned carpet sweeper—the human-powered kind. It can pick up dirt and is similar in size to a broom or mop.

2. Another alternative to a large vacuum is a handheld model. While they tend to be modestly powered, they can handle the occasional cleanup of cracker crumbs from your sofa's nooks and crannies. Purchase one that plugs into the wall; battery-powered vacuums are very weak.

3. If you have a friend in a neighboring apartment, share a vacuum. You no only can split the cost but also we be storing it only half the time.

4 Reasons to Use a Central Vacuum System for Large Homes

If you're tired of lugging a vacuum cleaner around your house, a central vacuum system may be what you need. This is a powerful vacuum cleaner located in your basement or garage that sucks dirt through pipes that run throughout your home's walls. While it's easier to install a central vacuum in new construction, installers can put a system into nearly any home.

To use the system, you just plug the specialized hose into its outlet, and the vacuum automatically starts. Since the hose is a lot tighter than an ordinary vacuum cleaner, the task of vacuuming takes less effort. There are other advantages, as well:

1. Standard vacuums need high-efficiency particle arrestance (HEPA) filters to eliminate fine dust that can bother a sensitive nose. Central vacuums avoid this problem by venting fine dust outside of your home, where it can make the neighbor's dog sneeze instead of you.

2. A central vacuum system with a "power dustpan" can also help when you sweep uncarpeted rooms. When pushed with a broom, this floor-level hatch activates the central vacuum, sucking in sweepings.

3. Central vacuum systems don't use bags. They deposit dirt in a large outdoor bin that doesn't have to be emptied nearly as often.

4. The motor is located in a remote spot in the home, so that you hear far less noise while vacuuming.

Customizing a "Generic" Storage Cabinet

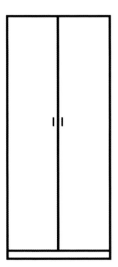

Generic

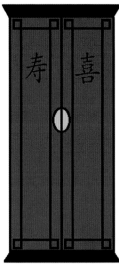

Chinese with characters for "Long Life" and "Happiness"

"Pop Art" with British Union Jack

Early American with bird prints

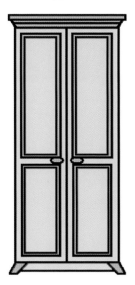

French with gilt trim

Eclectic

FIVE

A Livable Living Room

"I think that someone must have surveillance equipment set up in my living room, because every once in a while, someone on the TV will tell me what channel I'm watching. That really freaks me out, you know?"

—**Pam Stewart**

The living room is the place where you relax, surrounded by the smiling faces of your family—and the heaps of clutter that you and these dear people create. For while the living room isn't subject to major mess-making activities like food preparation or doing the laundry, it tends to fall victim to a relaxed attitude toward clutter. You may not be in the mood to vigilantly clean up every crumb as you snack by the television. Pulling out the vacuum cleaner in the middle of your Super Bowl party wouldn't be very hospitable. The solution is to prepare for messes, limit them without spoiling anyone's good time, and clean up after the mess has been made.

4 STEPS TO A MESS-RESISTANT LIVING ROOM

Like a 19th-century naval commander readying for battle, begin preparing your living room for messy usage by clearing the decks. Eliminate all possible clutter in preparation for the good times you'll have there.

1. Review the room's contents.
2. Can something be tossed out?
3. Does anything belong in another room?
4. Can any clutter be stored out of sight?

3 WAYS TO FIND LIVING ROOM STORAGE

1. A drawer in a coffee table can be cleaned out and used for that stack of magazines you like to spend a Sunday afternoon reading.
2. A section of the bookshelf can be reserved for the week's dvds.
3. Buy an armoire. It'll provide lots of storage and concealment for clutter.

But keep these storage spots orderly. If you've jammed a month's worth of *People* magazines into the drawer, there won't be any room for this week's issue.

EASY DOES IT

A Clutter Taboo

Shree has adopted an incremental decluttering strategy to make the most of the limited space in her apartment. Rather than try to clean it all at once, she declutters spot by spot, as time allows. For the decluttered spots, she mentally imposes a clutter "taboo," forbidding herself from using that location for anything other than its designated purpose. Under her taboo system, her sock drawer accepts only socks, for example. This mental trick helps Shree keep tidied spots uncluttered and reinforces the habit of allocating a place for everything and using that space for nothing else.

THE ENTERTAINMENT CENTER

A home entertainment center used to consist of a TV set and a rabbit-ear antenna. Today, families are apt to be outfitted with DVD player, an advanced sound system, a gigantic TV, and various ports for iPods and such. Without organization, the result can become a disorganized jumble. To save floor space, you can install a flat-panel, wall-mounted television.

An armoire can also provide extra storage space in a room that's typically short on closets. Unfortunately, large armoires may run to a couple of thousand dollars or more. You can save money by painting or staining and varnishing an unfinished piece. An even more inexpensive option is to purchase an unadorned storage cabinet and customize it.

Hardware stores sell a variety of low-priced, armoire-size storage cabinets with two doors opening at the front. Generally, they're made from plywood or a glue-and-wood-chip composite board that's covered with plastic laminate. These cabinets are usually meant for utility areas—the garage, basement, laundry, or closets—and

consequently tend to be as plain as generic white bread. With a little imagination, however, you can turn one into a high-style armoire fitted to your decor.

10 WAYS TO CREATE A UNIQUE ARMOIRE

1. A hardware store will stock a variety of knobs and moldings that you can use to transform a storage cabinet into an interesting piece of furniture.

2. You may also find decorative hinges and closures.

3. A simple coat of paint can dispel the generic look.

4. To simulate the lacquer finish of a Chinese cabinet, spray the cabinet with high-gloss red or black paint. Replace the cabinet's standard pulls with heavy brass pulls (if necessary, use wood putty to fill the holes of the old pulls). If you have some artistic talent, you can brush large Chinese calligraphic characters on the doors, and border these designs with stripes of black or gold paint.

5. Use varying shades of silver paint to suggest the look of an art deco cabinet. Choose a

medium, dull shade of silver to paint the entire cabinet. Then, after the cabinet is completely dry, use painter's masking tape to create stencils for geometric patterns. You can apply the tape in diagonal bands, chevrons, diamond patterns, or parallel lines. Use a different shade of silver paint, either duller or brighter, to fill in these patterns. When the paint is dry, remove the masking tape. A set of chrome or brushed nickel pulls completes the art deco look.

6. If you have a deft hand, faux finishes can give your storage cabinet the look of marble or fine wood. Visit your local craft store or library for information. One way to improve your chances of good results is to cut a sheet of thin plywood to cover each door of the storage cabinet. Apply your faux finish skills to these. If you mess up, start over with another sheet. When you get good results, surround the faux finished sheet with frame molding and attach it to the storage cabinet. This mimics the effect of a panel set in your cabinet's door.

7. A new set of feet can improve the look of your cabinet. You can cobble together a set using post finials, the decorative knobs found on the end posts of stair rails. Turn these knobs upside down, and screw them into the bottom of the cabinet. Take care the feet are securely attached. You don't want your armoire, filled with expensive electronics, to topple.

8. If the storage cabinet is made of unfinished plywood, you can upgrade its appearance by applying stain. Test the stain on some scrap lumber before slathering it all over your cabinet.

9. Give the cabinet a country look by painting it a traditional light blue, cranberry, or hunter green. Use stencils to add country designs, such as autumn leaves, barns, covered bridges, animals, fruits, flowers, or twining vines. Or if you're more ambitious, paint blank squares in the centers of the doors and sides, then paint a country scene in each. Grandma Moses proved that you don't have to be a classical

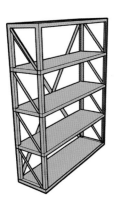

Customizing Utility Shelves

Ordinary steel utility shelves can be modified to be more appealing by spray painting them a color matching your decor then adding a footer and a more decorative top. Suspend fabric panels over the front and sides. Leave an opening in the middle of the front panel and at the front corners.

Ed Morrow

artist to create eye-appealing art. She painted simple scenes from her childhood. You can paint scenes from your life—your home, your pets, and your family. If you have doubts about your talents and suspect you may need multiple tries to produce good results, use the panel approach described above for faux finishes. When you're done painting, replace the original knobs with china or cast-iron knobs to increase the old-fashioned appearance of the cabinet.

10. Once you've customized your cabinet, you can antique it to simulate age. The easiest technique is to use a dark brown stain. Apply it over the painted

cabinet, and quickly wipe it away before it dries, leaving just traces in the cracks and

QUICK FIX

WHERE TO STICK YOUR REMOTE

The television remote is an elusive creature, with a talent for sliding under a sofa cushion or getting kicked under a chair. To keep it handy, uses pieces of adhesive-backed Velcro. Stick squares of it to the back of the remote and to the side of the television. When you finish using the remote, simply press it against the square on the television.

crannies. Your local library will have books describing other techniques. Again, it's a good idea to test a technique before using it on your cabinet. Nail together a few boards, paint them as you did your cabinet, then try antiquing them.

6 WAYS TO LIMIT FURNITURE CLUTTER

Furnishings aren't likely to be the first thing that comes to mind when you think of clutter, but hefty sofas and chairs can easily overwhelm a room and make even a little clutter seem claustrophobic. Some sofas and chairs are designed to be over-plump, with the intent of appearing extra comfy to customers in the furniture store. They're like the chocolate cake at the coffee shop that has an extra inch of icing to make it more appealing to the eye of the potential purchaser. Try to avoid being seduced by such eye candy when you're looking for living room seating.

1. Start with the smallest models. Are they cushy enough for your tush? They'll take up less

room and are likely to be less expensive. Don't park a whale in your living room.

2. Consider a rocking chair. It takes up less room than an over-stuffed recliner, and it's suited to a traditional decor.

3. An ottoman can help make your sofa or modest chairs approximate the function of a big recliner. If you have extra guests, an ottoman can also be pressed into seating service. (It can also serve as extra storage, see below.)

4. Plastic blow-up chairs and sofas might not be quite the look for a Victorian parlor, but they're washable, reasonably comfortable, easily moved, and far cheaper than traditional furniture. And, if you're pinched for space, they can be deflated and stashed out of sight.

5. Office supply firms sell wheeled tables, desks, file cabinets, and even wastebaskets that offer the advantage of being easily repositioned. You can also find sofas, ottomans, beds, side tables, easy chairs, and even entire dining rooms sets

on wheels. When you need a little space, they can easily be moved. If you want the pieces to stay put, the wheels can be locked with just a flip of a catch.

6. Use folding screens. We've all seen the old movie scene in which the detective interviews the glamorous showgirl in her dressing room after her stage act. She slips behind a screen, which just happens to be backlit to silhouette her curves as she changes out of her costume and into a tight dress that isn't much more modest. You can exploit this stock B-movie device to hide clutter. A screen in a corner of your living room, for example, can conceal a file cabinet.

7 THINGS BETTER THAN A COFFEE OR END TABLE

Living rooms often are appointed with elegant, airy end tables and coffee tables that don't offer much in the way of storage space. As a result, books, magazines, coasters, and the other items we place upon them tend to pile

up. Consider flanking a sofa and easy chairs with small cabinets or bookcases, and for the coffee table, use something that provides storage such as a:

1. Vintage blanket chest
2. Carpenter's chest
3. Military foot locker
4. Steamer trunk with stickers from distant lands
5. Wicker chest
6. Spiffed-up old toy box
7. Storage chest that can be stained and antiqued to simulate an old piece

SAFE STORAGE

Storage chests can prove irresistible to children, who just *know* something interesting is hidden inside. To prevent the lid from slamming down unexpectedly and seriously injuring a child, install safety supports. They hold the lid open when raised, and allow it to close slowly with slight pressure. These supports are available at hardware stores and are simple to install.

2 CONSIDERATIONS FOR STORAGE CHESTS

1. You can turn a storage chest into an ottoman by putting a cushion on top of it, securing it in place with strips of adhesive-backed Velcro. Or, if you want a bolder approach, buy some canvas strapping that complements the fabric of your cushion, cut it into lengths, cross them over the cushion, and tack their ends along or under the edges of the chest's lid. Two straps may be enough, or you can go strap-happy and create an interwoven pattern of diamonds or squares.

2. If you're using a wooden chest as a coffee table, it will get a lot of abuse. To protect its surface, apply a few coats of varnish. One advantage of using an "antiqued" storage chest is that any nicks or dents received in the line of duty will only add to its charm. Just revarnish over them.

BASKETS BY THE BUSHEL

Baskets are enjoying great popularity as home décor accessories in every room of the house. Use them in the kitchen to display apples, in the bathroom to contain

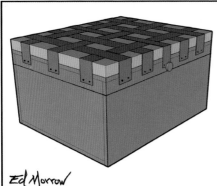

Padded Top Chest

Here, a block of foam covered in a durable fabric is secured to the top of a small chest with straps of similar fabric but different color. They are woven over and under for a decorative and practical design. You could run the straps diagonally or use multiple strap colors.

Ed Morrow

bars of soap and toiletries, and in the living room to hold current magazines.

But baskets tend to proliferate, because they seem too useful to throw away. Eventually they can give your home a cluttered look. As a rule, if you can't think of an immediate purpose for a new basket, don't acquire it.

Some designers position baskets on shelves, to replace furniture with drawers or doors. While this "adds texture" to the appearance of a home, it isn't a great idea in terms of clutter control. A drawer or cabinet hides disorder, while a basket displays it.

QUICK FIX

ADD A DRAWER

To add storage space under a plain table, add a drawer. Hardware stores commonly sell drawers that are pre-assembled and can be attached under a table with just a few screws.

THE HOME GALLERY

"My photographs don't do me justice—they just look like me."
—Phyllis Diller

Most families display a few photographs of family members on their living room walls, but they don't take full advantage of this opportunity. Don't be shy about hanging photographs. The best place to store family photos is on the walls, where people can enjoy them without having to flip through tattered scrapbooks or sift through dusty shoeboxes. Why not display that shot of your great-uncle in his best straw boater, so that you can take pleasure in his company? If you don't wish to risk placing a delicate old photo on your wall, scan or photocopy the original, then hang the copy.

The grouping of framed pictures benefits from a little planning. To try different arrangements of pictures on your wall, cut sheets of paper to match the sizes of the pictures, then stick them to the wall with painter's masking tape. You can move the papers around until you have a pleasing arrangement. On the back of each framed picture, measure from the apex of the hanging wire to the top of the frame. Poke a hole at that same spot on the matching paper sheet, and mark the wall with a pencil through the hole to indicate where you should install a picture hanger.

5 WAYS TO HANG 'EM ALL

Most walls are hollow behind a layer of drywall. Nails or screws driven into them can easily be pulled out. Fortunately, there are special gadgets that will better secure screws into drywall. Some have oversize screw threads that hold more tightly. Some form a plug that won't pull free. The strongest type unfolds inside the hollow area, preventing the bolt from being pulled out.

1. *Molly bolts* are inserted through a pilot hole in the wall, and then turned to cause their side jackets to open within the wall cavity and lock the bolt in place. The bolt is then backed out slightly, and the picture hung on it. The bolt can also be backed out entirely, slipped through a hole in the object to be hung, then reinserted into the jacket and tightened.

2. *Toggle bolts* are similar, but can't be backed out completely (the toggle will fall off and you'll have to insert a new toggle bolt). The bolt is first slid through a hole in the object to be hung, the toggle screwed on, and then the bolt and toggle are inserted into a pilot hole. The toggle bolt's pair of metal wings unfolds inside the wall, preventing the bolt from pulling back out. You then tighten the bolt to hold the object against the wall.

3. Even the best molly or toggle bolt is no stronger than the surface through which it's inserted. Brittle drywall isn't very strong. To support heavy

A NEW LIFE FOR YOUR FADED PAST

A wall may not be the best place to display that precious Civil War daguerreotype of your ancestor in his side-whiskers and Union uniform. Sunlight might make the old soldier simply fade away. But by scanning fragile photos, you can enjoy images that otherwise would have to be stored out of sight. Photo-editing software will allow you to remove dirt and scratches, crop, resize, and adjust the image to best effect. You can also share the image through e-mail with all your relatives—even the ones who live way down south in Dixie.

pictures, you'll have to put a screw into a wall *stud*. Studs run up and down inside your walls at regular intervals. Your hardware store can sell you a *stud finder*, an inexpensive device that uses magnetism to detect these hidden uprights. (The detector actually finds steel drywall screws, which are used to attach drywall to studs.) Studs are normally 16 inches apart, so once you've found one, locating others isn't difficult.

4. Don't use small screws. They may not reach far enough through the drywall to gain a good purchase in the stud.

A 3-inch "decking" screw will usually more than suffice for picture hanging. Slide a washer onto the screw to increase its "hat size" and make it more difficult for a picture's wire to slip off of it.

5. To hang an object from brick or concrete, use an expansion anchor. This is a metal tube that encases a screw. Drill a hole in the brick or concrete using a masonry bit big enough to snugly hold the expansion anchor. Insert the anchor and turn its screw to make the tube expand and grip the hole. You can then suspend a picture from the screw.

When in doubt about which anchoring device to use, consult the staff at a hardware store rather than relying on the weight ratings printed on the anchor's packaging. The packaging may be overly optimistic.

5 STEPS TO HANGING IT ON A DOOR

Doors can be exploited to hang hooks and racks. Secure these devices to a door's crosspieces, not to its thin panels. The doors commonly used today are hollow and have narrow crosspieces hidden inside along the door's edges. To hang something from a hollow door, find out how thin the top crosspiece is.

1. Drill a hole down through the top of the door.
2. Bend a small "L" in a length of wire. Insert the bent end into the hole, all the way through the crosspiece, turn it so that

QUICK FIX

KEEPING IT STRAIGHT

To keep a picture level on your walls, stick two small rubber squares or dots (sold for this purpose in craft and art supply stores) to the bottom corners of the frame's back. The rubber pieces will grip the wall, making it more difficult to jostle the picture. If you can't find these, you can improvise by cutting squares from an ordinary sponge, then gluing them to the frame's back. The rubber or sponge will also protect your wall's surface from being scratched by the picture frame.

"L" will catch, and then pull it up until it does.

3. Mark the length of wire that's in the door and then turn the wire so the "L" no longer catches and remove it. The mark on the wire will indicate the thickness of the crosspiece. You can use this to determine where to drive the screws that will support the hooks or rack.

4. If the crosspiece is too narrow to attach your hooks to it, cut a wider strip of wood to fit the door, paint it to match, then securely attach it to the crosspiece. The wider strip will make it easier to position hooks.

5. Another option is to attach the strip of wood to the door using L-brackets. Screw the back of the brackets to the top of the door. If the door closes too snugly to allow this, you can chisel recesses in the door top into which to nest the L-brackets.

8 WAYS TO EDIT YOUR PHOTO COLLECTION

Your living room is a good place to store family photo albums. Here they can be easily pulled out to entertain visitors. If your family is like most, however, your photographs are a confusing mess. Here are some tips for organizing them and cutting down on your photo clutter.

1. Don't save photos you don't like. Remember that day when you got caught in the rain and wind, and your hair got spun into knots that would shame a troll doll? There's no need to memorialize that moment in your photo album.

2. Don't save blurry or flawed photographs.

3. Record content information on the back of photographs as soon as possible. Don't use a sharp pencil or ballpoint pen, as these can leave an impression that will be visible on the image side of the photo. Use a felt tip pen with ink that won't penetrate paper. If you have doubts about the pen, test it on a photograph you're going to toss.

4. Store your photographs in albums, but not just any albums. So-called self-mounting albums with adhesive pages can damage photos, especially if you later try to remove them. Albums with plastic pockets into which photographs are slipped are far better. Even those old-fashioned corner stickers are superior to adhesive page albums. Never use transparent tape to attach photos to an album page. Tape can yellow and stain your pictures.

5. If you don't have time to put your photos in albums, at least write dates and brief descriptions on their envelopes. Later, when you go through the photographs, you'll have this basic information to help identify them.

6. Organize and protect your negatives by storing them in

negative sheets, available at photography shops. These clear plastic sheets are divided into sleeves, into which you slide your negatives. The sheets fit into three-ring binders, making it easy to organize large numbers of negatives. You can also easily examine the negatives without dirtying them, and you can have *contact sheets* made of them. A photo developer just lays the sheet over a piece of photo paper, exposes it to light, then develops it. This produces negative-size positive images that you can use to evaluate shots.

7. Modern digital cameras lessen photo clutter by storing images electronically. You can download your snapshots into a computer, then transfer them onto CDs. If you don't have a digital camera, many photo processors can transfer pictures taken with an old-style film camera onto CDs for you. A digital photo album only occupies space in your computer or on a digital storage device. Scratches and finger smudges can't damage your

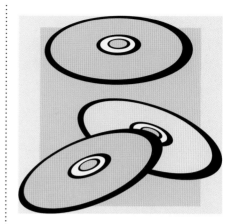

photos there. Digital photos can also be easily shared over the Internet with friends. Be sure to create backup copies of your digital photos on a CD or other digital storage device. Otherwise a computer failure could destroy your photo albums.

8. A good-quality scanner for your home computer can help preserve your old family photographs. Scan them, burn the scanned images onto CDs, and then store the CDs in a safe-deposit box or at the office. This way, if Godzilla stomps down your house or, more prosaically, if it burns to the ground, you'll have copies of otherwise irreplaceable photos.

One over-stuffed fridge plus one midnight snacker equals one extra-long nap under a blanket of decomposing leftovers.

SIX

The Kitchen:

Your Home's Clutter Capital

"Time was when kitchens were big and dark, for keeping house was a gloomy business . . . .But now! Gay colors are the order of the day. Red pots and pans! Blue gas stoves! . . . It is a rainbow, in which the cook sings at her work and never thinks of household tasks as drudgery."
—**Ladies' Home Journal**, **1928**

For many of us, kitchen clutter is the equivalent of a platter of still-warm, double-fudge brownies. The temptation to accumulate cookware and gadgets can be nearly irresistible. What's worse, the kitchen usually ranks as the busiest room in the home. Kitchen clutter is likely to hinder your life every single day, making it all the more crucial to keep it under control.

THE CHALLENGE

Stop to consider everything that goes on in the kitchen, and you can appreciate the clutter problem in this area of the home. Groceries are trundled in and heaped upon the counters. The cabinets are filled with unorganized cooking equipment, dishes, and food. The refrigerator is crowded with aging relics of meals long past, now quietly growing mold and decomposing. Grease coats vertical surfaces, while crumbs can be found on nearly every horizontal surface. Spills on the stove turn into sticky, baked-on glop. Food scraps issue a siren call to scuttling insects and furtive mice: "Come one, come all! Bring your disease-ridden families! It's picnic time!"

Kitchen clutter is compounded by modern family life. Kids come home from school and fix their own meals, without the highest standards of neatness. Husband and wife come in at different times after work, and prepare separate meals. Tired from school, work, and commuting, everyone allows cleanup tasks to slide, and the mess grows like a creature in a 1950s sci-fi flick.

Welsh Plate Rack

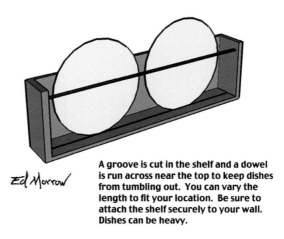

Ed Morrow

A groove is cut in the shelf and a dowel is run across near the top to keep dishes from tumbling out. You can vary the length to fit your location. Be sure to attach the shelf securely to your wall. Dishes can be heavy.

A ROOM OF MANY ROLES

In addition to food preparation, your kitchen is apt to be a center of many nonfood-related activities that add their own detritus and confusion. The phone the family uses most often is in the kitchen. Message taking and appointment making are done here, using the refrigerator as an improvised bulletin board. There may be a TV that the family watches while slapping together snacks. The kitchen table is a favorite spot for reading the newspaper, paying bills, folding laundry, doing homework, or playing a game of rummy.

If your home's back door leads into the kitchen, there's apt to be more traffic here than at the main entrance. Small wonder the kitchen becomes the most coat-cluttered, boot-filled place in the house.

A SAFER KITCHEN

Beyond the confusion, clutter can be dangerous. A knife lurking among the spoons may slice a finger. A mixer perched carelessly on a stack of cookbooks may fall into the sink with electrifying results. A glass tureen can slip from damp fingers and shatter into thousands of razor-sharp shards. The caustic cleansers under the sink can poison a child. If for no other reason, clearing kitchen clutter makes sense because it helps to eliminate these dangers. Here are several ways to ensure that your kitchen is a safe workplace.

6 STEPS TO A SAFER KITCHEN

To get a good idea of the hazards your child's fingers can reach, try kneeling on the floor and looking around your kitchen from your kid's point of view.

1. If you have small children, place safety catches on drawers and cabinet doors. These devices are inexpensive and easy to install. But because most are made of plastic and can be easily broken or bent out of shape, don't put

too much faith in them. Especially dangerous items, such as poisonous cleansers, should be stored in locked cabinets.

2. Your kitchen should have a fire extinguisher. Most extinguishers come with wall brackets, so you can mount them where they're handy and visible to all. Hang your extinguisher near your stove, the most likely source of a fire. Don't hang it too close, though, or a stove fire could prevent you from reaching it. Check your extinguisher periodically to make sure it's properly charged. Don't overestimate your fire-fighting abilities. A fire can spread fast and trap an amateur firefighter. If you suspect the fire might be too big for you to handle, make your escape and call the professionals.

3. Keep your knives sharp. If you need to press hard to cut, a blade is more likely to slip and injure you. Don't mix knives with other items.

4. Don't store heavy jars or pots on high shelves, no matter how limited the kitchen's storage areas may be.

5. Never place flammable objects near stove burners, even when the burners are off. Like guns, burners should always be treated as if they're "loaded"— that means hot and ready to burn.

6. The kitchen is no place for rugs that may slip underfoot. Use rubber-backed rugs, and test them to be sure they won't slide.

CURRENTS IN THE KITCHEN

The kitchen should be wired with ground fault interrupter (GFI) outlets. They shut off the current to an appliance if it develops a short circuit, sparing you a potentially lethal jolt. Over time, GFI outlets may deteriorate, so that they no longer offer protection. The test button allows you to check if the outlet's circuitry is still working. When pressed, this button should trigger the GFI circuit so that the rest button pops out, indicating the current has been shut off. An appliance plugged into the outlet should not operate now. You then can return the outlet to its operational state by pushing the reset button. Test GFIs every month, and replace them if their reset buttons don't pop out.

GET WITH THE PROGRAM

"Most of life is routine—dull and grubby, but routine is the momentum that keeps a man going. If you wait for inspiration, you'll be standing on the corner after the parade is a mile down the street."

—Ben Nicholas

It's been said that love makes the world go round, but a good argument can be made that it's actually routine that makes the world work. We get things done in life by doing them step by step, action by action. But routine can't be fruitful unless we put some thought into the routine we make. We need to plan. With planning, routine can create constructive habits that make household maintenance a source of satisfaction, instead of an endless series of hurried chores.

5 DAILY KITCHEN DUTIES

1. A good daily schedule begins with a quick transit of the kitchen, gathering up trash such as food wrappers, fruit and vegetable peelings, crumbs, and other remnants of a meal now digesting. Work from one end of the kitchen to the other. Do this whenever you clean; it will save steps and keep you from missing tasks you need to carry out.

2. Next, stow away any useful leftovers. Be critical of each item. Is there enough to bother saving? Will anyone actually eat the item? Has it stood on the counter too long to be safe to eat?

3. Move on to washing dishes. Emptying the sink of crud-coated plates and greasy pans will greatly improve the appearance of the kitchen. If you have a dishwasher, empty it as soon as it's run. You can then store dirty dishes in it as they're used, keeping the sink clutter-free.

4. After taking care of the dishes, wipe off the countertops, tables, and stove top. When cleaning the countertops, move aside canisters and small appliances, then clean from the back of the counter to the front edge.

5. Sweep the floor. If the floor still doesn't look clean after you put away the broom, take out the sponge mop.

Steam Cleaning

If your kitchen floor collects lots of sticky spills, consider buying a floor steamer. These use steam to liquefy gummy substances and a fabric pad to wipe them up. There's no need for a cleanser, so steamers are economical. Keeping the kitchen floor shiny and clean provides a lot of satisfaction—it just looks so tidy.

Give Your Kitchen a Chamois Shine

Kitchens are loaded with shiny surfaces, such as countertops and appliance fronts. Treat them to good polishing with a chamois cloth. This is the processed sheepskin used at car washes to wipe away water spots and shine cars. Soak the chamois in clean water, then partially wring it out. The cloth will have a slick feel if it has the correct dampness. Use it to rub away smudges and water marks. Rinse it periodically to wash out dirt and keep it damp. When you're done, wring out the chamois and hang it up to dry. Auto supply stores carry the cloths in a variety of sizes. While they may seem a bit expensive for what look like simple rags, after you've used one, it'll seem like a bargain.

2 WEEKLY FOOD SUPPLY CHECKS

1. A good first step in a weekly decluttering and cleaning schedule is a review of the leftovers in your refrigerator. Leftovers older than a couple of days aren't good for much more than compost.

2. Next, inventory any foods that seem in low supply, and add them to your shopping list. Shopping with list in hand is far more efficient (and cheaper) than wandering from aisle to aisle.

3 ONCE-A-MONTH TASKS

1. Inventory your food stock thoroughly by pulling everything from your shelves.

2. While emptying the cabinets, you also can clean them

and reline them if necessary. Organize your stocks of pantry items as you return them to the cabinets.

3. Undertake heavier types of cleaning: oven, under and behind the refrigerator, under the sink, and wherever the walls are stained. Cooking grease and dust can combine to form oily grime on high, flat surfaces. Wipe it away with a cleaning cloth dipped in warm water and dish detergent. Dry the cleaned areas with an old towel.

EASY DOES IT

Shelf Liners

Ordinary waxed paper makes a cheap, spill-catching shelf liner, or, for a particularly durable shelf covering, use peel-and-stick linoleum floor tiles. They come in a wide variety of colors, can be trimmed to fit your shelves with just a pair of stout scissors, and will last for years. You can even use floor polish to protect them and add shine.

4 FIRST STEPS TO REORGANIZING YOUR KITCHEN

"Some of our most exquisite murders have been domestic, performed with tenderness in simple, homey places like the kitchen table."
—Alfred Hitchcock

Now that your kitchen has been cleaned—or at least you've cleaned around the clutter—you can start reorganizing it.

1. Take a moment to reflect on what you want to accomplish.

2. Form an ideal vision of your kitchen. When you bought your home or rented your apartment, what attractive features did the eager agent point out that won your heart?

3. Consider how you can recover that feeling. Like visualizing success in a weight-loss program, this reflection can help motivate you to endure the travails you are about to undergo.

4. Give yourself time: Don't forget that decluttering the kitchen is a *big* job.

EASY DOES IT

A Computerized Shopping List

Sheree's friend Lori makes her grocery shopping easier by typing up a "standard" list that includes all the items she routinely needs to buy. These include such staples as milk, eggs, bread, and orange juice. Before a trip to the supermarket, she reviews her kitchen's contents and simply checks off those things that are missing. By keeping this list on her home computer, Lori can easily add or subtract items as her needs change. She periodically prints out a few copies for posting on the refrigerator door with a magnetic clip. She also has a pencil tied to a magnet so that it's always handy when another item comes to mind.

ORGANIZING THE CABINETS AND PANTRY

Examine your food stocks, beginning with the canisters on your counter. Check that the contents are fresh. Flour, rice, pasta, and grains can host insects. Sugar can become damp, then turn rock hard. Dump anything you're doubtful about.

6 CANISTER CONSIDERATIONS

1. Metal canisters are unbreakable and may be attractive, but the bottoms of steel containers may rust, staining your countertop.
2. Ceramic containers come in many novelty shapes that can beguile your fancy, but they're not always airtight. That cookie jar shaped like the state of Florida that you received from your aged Aunt Ida in Boca Raton is a pleasant reminder of that dear lady's cookie-baking skills, but it isn't apt to close tightly and your cookies may quickly grow stale.
3. Glass or clear plastic containers with airtight tops will keep their contents fresh, and you can see what's inside.
4. Square containers are easier to shelve than round ones, and waste less space.
5. A potential problem with canisters is that as the contents get low, you may be tempted to top off the container to keep it full. There's something soothing about full containers: Perhaps they suggest abundance and preparedness. However, the habit of topping off can leave you with a layer of old, flavorless, and perhaps unsafe contents languishing at the bottom of the canister. It's better to use up all the contents of the container before refilling

it. If you must combine old and new contents, dump out the old into a bowl, fill the container with the new, then top off with the old.

6. It's useful to put a label on the underside or back of your canisters, where you can record the expiration dates of the materials inside. You can also clip information from their original boxes, such as mixing directions or nutritional information, and tape it to the canisters.

4 MORE CABINET CONSIDERATIONS

1. After you organize your canisters, go through the boxed foods in your kitchen cabinets. Boxes are often poorly sealed and can spill their contents. This is messy and attracts vermin faster than free beer attracts frat boys. If the contents are unspoiled, transfer them to sealable canisters and storage jars.

2. If any boxes have passed their expiration dates, dump them.

If you have doubts and can't find a date on the box, check to see if there's a toll-free number that you can call to learn when the product should be thrown away. If not, the telephone information operator may be able to give you a toll-free number for the company.

3. When you're done with the boxed foods, move on to jars. Jars have the advantage of being clear and relatively immune to bugs, but you may have to deal with hard-to-clean rings of jam, syrup, or oil. Consider storing these jars atop cookie sheets that have raised edges to contain spills and make cleanup easier. In any case, always line your shelves with a waterproof, easily cleaned shelf covering.

4. After jars, move on to canned goods. Again, toss out any out-of-date products. Swollen cans are a telltale sign of spoiled food, so discard them. There's no reason to risk your health to save the cost of an old can of beef stew that has puffed up like an angry toad.

When in Doubt, Throw it Out

Never check food for spoilage by tasting it. Even a small quantity of tainted food can make you sick. If food looks suspect or smells iffy, or you have any reason at all to suspect it's unwholesome, throw it out.

3 WAYS TO RESTOCK AND REORDER

1. When returning packaged food to your shelves, you have a good opportunity to impose order in the kitchen. Place commonly used items on the most easily reached shelves. Your breakfast cereal, for example, should be on a shelf near your counter, not on a high shelf in your pantry. You'll save a couple of steps every morning. To reverse the Confucian proverb, saving yourself from a journey of a thousand steps begins by saving one step.

2. Group like items. All those cans of soup, for example, should be together. The cans in front will hide those behind, but if you organize them by kind, you'll know that more cans of tomato soup are behind the can of tomato soup up front.

3. Once you have an idea of what should go where, label the edges of shelves for what's stored on them. This will help you find things and also impose shelving discipline. If you have a shelf spot labeled for cake mixes, you'll be far

PANTRY PATROL

If grain, flour, meal, or seed moths plague you, you can entice them to their deaths with cardboard traps that use a chemical lure. There are no chemical toxins involved to pose a hazard to humans. The traps are effective for a few months, and then should be replaced.

more likely to store cake mix there. Labels can also guide other family members to correctly shelve items. You won't have to hunt for days for that jar of sweet pickles that someone tucked behind the rolled oats.

3 STEPS TO EASY COMPOSTING

A compost pile is simply a heap of organic waste—grass clippings, leaves, or kitchen scraps—that's allowed to decompose into a humus-rich material that can

be used to improve garden soil. Vegetable peels, tea bags, coffee grounds, and eggshells are good compost ingredients. Meat, dairy products, and oil-rich scraps are not; they're slow to decompose and may attract animals. A compost pile can be free-standing, or enclosed in a wooden box or wire bin. You can buy containers that have carbon filters and tight seals to limit odor, but there's no getting around the smell released when the lid is lifted to add scraps. There's some labor involved in encouraging the decomposition

Practice Safe Refrigeration

Food is best stored at 40ºF. Most refrigerators don't have very accurate controls, so it's best to place a thermometer inside to verify the temperature.

Store opened food in foil, plastic bags, or airtight containers. Newer refrigerators sometime have drawers in which you can adjust the termperature lower than the temperature in the rest of the refrigerator. Meat, poultry, and fish should go in the coldest parts of these fridges, if these foods aren't going in the freezer compartment.

Defrost foods inside the refrigerator. If you defrost on your counter or in the sink, you run the risk of leaving food out long enough for spoilage to start. Finally, keep your fridge clean to minimize bacteria that can attach food.

process, as the compost pile should be turned periodically.

1. Gather your kitchen scraps in a sealable container on a corner of your counter or under your sink.
2. At the end of each day, transfer the waste to your compost pile.
3. If critters get into your compost, consider buying a sealable compost bin. Some models rotate, a bit like a cement mixer, to make it easier to turn the compost.

7 WAYS TO MANAGE LEFTOVERS

Even the most profligate among us pack away far too many leftovers in the refrigerator, allowing some to go uneaten and spoil. Here are some pointers on managing these remnants of meals past.

1. Don't save small portions of food. A couple of spoonfuls of mashed potatoes or a handful of boiled carrots isn't worth the space in your fridge.

2. Don't save leftovers from unpopular meals. If the kids didn't like your Zucchini Surprise the first time, they aren't apt to like it rewarmed.

3. Wrap leftovers carefully, and date them so you can throw out anything more than a couple of days old. You can freeze leftovers to keep them safely for a longer period. But frozen leftovers, like 19th-century Arctic explorers who wandered the icy wastes, are apt to get lost—and then be discovered in less-than-pristine shape.

4. Reserve a particular shelf in your refrigerator for leftovers. When you add more, do what stockers in supermarkets do to avoid hiding old items behind newer stock: Add the new leftovers to the back of the shelf, moving older ones forward.

5. Don't feed leftovers to your pets. "People food" isn't healthy for pets.

6. Before eating leftovers, examine them for spoilage. In Ed's family, he has been designated by custom as the Sniffer of Questionable Foods, because of his acute sense of smell. If your family routinely shoves packages of gray hamburger under your nose and asks, "Does this smell okay?" then you hold a similar position. Take your office seriously. Cast out anything you doubt.

7. The best way to limit leftovers is to simply prepare smaller meals.

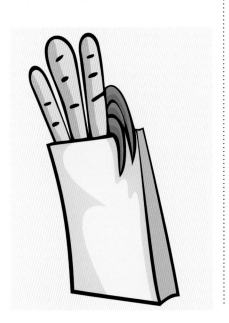

4 STEPS TO CLEANING THE COOLERATOR

1. After you've cleared out all the spoiled food in your refrigerator, set the remaining good food aside and scrub the fridge's inside. For an excellent cleanser, mix liquid dish detergent with baking soda. Don't use abrasive cleansers or sandpapery sponges: A scratched interior can harbor bacteria.

2. After washing, check your fridge's drip tray—the flat pan under the drain in the fridge's floor. In many refrigerators, you can reach it by pulling off the plastic grill on the bottom front of the fridge. Clean out any crud found there. As you pull out the tray, be careful to avoid spilling any fluids that have pooled in it.

3. Periodically vacuum the refrigerator's air vents and coils, which are typically exposed on its back. Clean coils allow the refrigerator to operate more efficiently. Don't neglect vacuuming underneath as well. If you can't roll the refrigerator out to do this, wrap a yardstick in paper towels and sweep it under the fridge. When Ed last cleaned under his refrigerator,

he found enough crud to fill a shoebox. In addition to dust and dirt, his harvest included several pens, 53 cents in change, a toy block, a missive from Ed McMahon, and two dozen cat toys.

4. Finish cleaning your refrigerator by wiping it out with a strong solution of baking soda and water. If you have a mildew problem in your fridge, substitute vinegar for the baking soda. If you've had spills of meat fluids, use a disinfectant. Place an open package of baking soda on a shelf to help keep the refrigerator fresh smelling.

20 ITEMS FOR YOUR CLEANING KIT

Cleaning supplies tend to pile up in the kitchen. You can help manage this mess by creating a cleaning kit containing products that can handle most household cleaning jobs. This will help you avoid duplication, and your products will be handy so you won't create disorder as you root through your supplies. Gather your cleaning tools and cleansers in a plastic carryall, so they can be pulled out together.

1. Cellulose sponge.
2. Mildly-abrasive scouring sponge or scrubber made from plastic loops. Be careful not to rub too hard, or the abrasive will act like sandpaper, removing paint along with grime, and potentially scratching finishes.
3. "Dry sponge." This is a special sponge made from natural rubber that can be used to clean wallpaper, walls coated with flat paint, and other dry surfaces. Just gently rub it against the dirty surface the way you would rub a great big eraser. Never dampen a dry sponge.
4. Cleaning cloths. Old cloth diapers, worn-out towels, and ragged cotton T-shirts make good cleaning rags.
5. Paper towels.
6. Chamois cloths for polishing. (A microfiber polishing cloth can also be useful for shining polished surfaces.)
7. Old toothbrush to scrub narrow spaces.

8. Mild spray cleanser for countertops (you can use dishwasher liquid mixed with water).

9. Heavy-duty spray cleanser for greasy messes.

10. Disinfectant cleaner for controlling germs. To save money, buy concentrated cleansers from a janitorial supply house. Mix them with water and put them in spray bottles. Apply them to dirty surfaces, let them sit for a few moments, then wipe up the loosened dirt. Good cleansers will do the bulk of the cleaning without scrubbing.

11. Plastic putty knife for scraping up tough gunk. This can be purchased in any paint or hardware store.

12. Dust masks to protect your lungs during dusty jobs. These masks aren't effective for fumes or fine particles, however. You'll need an industrial mask to deal with those. And no mask is a substitute for good ventilation.

13. Squeegee to clean windows. Store it carefully, as its rubber edge can be easily damaged and thus cause streaks.

14. Safety goggles. Buy the kind that completely covers your eyes, for protection from splattered cleaning chemicals.

15. Rubber gloves. Most of the gloves available in groceries are thin and short. Hardware stores stock heavier-duty gloves in a variety of styles and sizes.

16. Plastic grocery bags to gather any trash you pick up.

17. Apron with pockets. If it has enough pockets, you can load it up with supplies and tools and skip lugging the carryall.

18. Dust-attracting wipes. Janitorial supply stores sell large versions of these wipes.

19. Clean, soft-bristled paintbrushes to dust baseboards, lampshades, and other odd objects. They're what the Louvre uses to dust off all those expensive paintings.

20. For high spots such as ceiling corners or the top edge of door frames, use a lamb's-wool duster. These are fluffy dusters on long poles. They attract dust and can be cleaned with a good shake outside a window. Vacuum them when they get really dirty.

5 BASIC CLEANING ITEMS FOR EVERY ROOM

You'll also need some larger tools:

1. Broom. An angle-cut nylon broom is especially good for cleaning corners.
2. Bucket.
3. Dust mop. A dust mop treated with a dust-attracting spray is

just the thing for wood floors. Vacuum the mop head when dirty, then run it through the washer and hang it up to dry.
4. Sponge mop. A sponge mop with a pull wringer is good enough for most home use.
5. Feather duster or lamb's-wool duster.

For a large house with lots of floors to be mopped, go to a janitorial supply store for a long-handled floor scrubber. Its business end is a rectangular pad to which different types of cleaning cloths can be attached. This professional tool can be used to dust, scrub, or wax floors.

Spare Your Lungs

When using spray cleaners, don't adjust the bottles' nozzles to make a super-fine mist. Such a mist can be dangerous to inhale. This is especially threatening in confined spaces. Use a large-droplet or stream setting, and open a window for ventilation. Or you can do what Rita does— hold the bottle close to your cleaning cloth and spray the cloth, rather than the surface you'll clean with it.

ORGANIZING A FREEZER

A separate chest freezer is a useful adjunct to your refrigerator's freezer. Ed's neighbor Jane grows a garden and uses a chest freezer to store vegetables for winter use.

She also takes advantage of bulk food sales, as she and her husband feed three ever-hungry boys. She defrosts her chest freezer just before harvesttime, when it's apt to be emptiest. Recently frozen items are temporarily moved to her refrigerator's freezer compartment or to ice chests. Jane then turns off the chest freezer and unplugs it, disposing of spoiled items or those older than 10 months.

To speed defrosting, Jane places a tub of hot water in one of the freezer baskets. (Otherwise, a hot tub set on a cold freezer liner can cause it to crack.) As the water cools, she swaps it for more hot water. Once the freezer is defrosted, she washes it out with a solution of baking soda and water, then leaves the freezer open to dry.

Reloading the freezer is an opportunity to reorganize its contents. Jane groups her frozen food by kind: vegetables with vegetables, meat with meat, and so on. Whenever a new item is added, she makes sure to date its container so she can tell when to throw it out. These dates also let her arrange her food with the oldest placed nearest at hand. Finally, Jane likes to keep

> **QUICK FIX**
>
> ## WAX PAPER TO THE RESCUE
>
> To avoid having to climb a ladder in order to scrub cabinet tops of the top of the refrigerator, cover them with wax paper. When the paper gets dirty, just fold it up and toss it out. Wax paper is cheap, it won't stick, and it's invisible to anyone shorter than a basketball star.

a list of what's in her freezer. She crosses off items as they're removed and adds items as they're placed inside.

3 WAYS TO HELP YOUR DISHWASHER DO ITS JOB

"No woman ever shot her husband while he was doing the dishes."
—George Coote

1. For your dishwasher to work well, the dishes should be scraped and dishes with tough crud should be presoaked. The best dishwasher armed with the most expensive dishwasher detergent can't

remove burnt-on gunk or your baby's rice cereal after it has dried like concrete.

2. Your dishwasher needs hot water. A temperature of 120°F to 125°F is usually recommended, but don't crank the water heater up higher, especially if you have young children. The water heater also serves sinks, bathtubs, and showers, and water hotter than 125°F can scald a child. Fortunately, most dishwashers come with a temperature-boost setting that raises household water to an optimal temperature for cleaning.

3. If you use powdered dishwasher detergent, keep it where it will stay dry. Dampness can cause it to clump, and clump detergent won't dissolve properly. The under-sink area

tends to be humid, so you may need to find another place to store the detergent. Or pour the detergent into a waterproof container before placing it under the sink.

6 STEPS TO A SPOTLESS STOVE TOP

1. A hot stove top can convert spilled foods into a black, hardened crust. To fix this, soak a sponge in hot water, squirt a bit of grease-cutting dish soap on the spot, then cover it with the sponge.

2. Leave the sponge there for an hour. The gunk should soften.

3. You may still need to use an abrasive sponge or a plastic putty knife to loosen it. Be careful not to rub or scrape too hard, or you may damage the stove's surface.

4. Repeat the soaking for stubborn crud.

5. To clean burner pans, soak them in dishwasher detergent in the sink, then run them through the dishwasher. (Ammonia or overly vigorous scrubbing can damage chrome burner pans.)

6. To make stove cleaning a little easier, wrap the burner pans in aluminum foil, molding the foil to their shape. If your stove top opens up, lay a sheet of foil inside to catch spills that evade the foil-wrapped pans.

4 STEPS TO A CLEAN OVEN

1. Cleaning the oven is among the least pleasant household tasks, if you don't have a self-cleaning model. To clean your cold oven, wipe down the inside with ammonia, then leave the ammonia to work overnight. When using ammonia or any caustic cleaner, wear long rubber gloves and eye protection. Proper ventilation is also important. Read the cleaning product's directions and warnings before you begin.

2. By morning, you should be able to wipe away softened gunk. Tough spots may need to be attacked with a mildly abrasive sponge or plastic putty knife. Again, take care not to rub or scrape too hard. If the overnight ammonia treatment doesn't work well enough the first time, repeat it.

3. If the job still isn't done to your satisfaction, you may want to try a commercial oven cleaner. Some brands of oven cleaners are much more caustic than others, so shop around for the least dangerous products.

4. Oven windows often get sooty. If ammonia won't clean them, try white vinegar.

EASY DOES IT

Underfill to Avoid Overflowing

Oven splatters and spills can be minimized by always covering oven dishes with a lid or foil, and by never overfilling them. Leave a margin of at least 10 percent at the top of a dish, to allow for the bubbling and heaving of cooking food.

RATIONALIZING THE KITCHEN ARSENAL

Any kitchen accumulates a varied collection of cooking utensils. If you examine this equipment, you'll probably discover that much of it is damaged, extraneous, or seldom used. Get rid of it.

PURGE THE PLASTIC

Plastic ware is particularly apt to collect in great numbers. Examine all those margarine tubs, microwave meal trays, and fast-food cups that you've saved because they seem potentially useful. In fact, they may not be. Ask yourself, "Have I ever used this item?"

Next, examine the plastic items that actually look like dishware. When you have children, plastic tumblers and dishes are a boon. They don't break, even when your smiling child hurls them across the room at the unsmiling cat. They're often microwave-safe, making it easy to prepare small meals for kids. But as practical as it may be, plastic ware lacks the charm of more substantial materials. If you can get by without them, get rid of these items. Even cheap china is more pleasing to the soul.

4 WAYS TO WEED OUT THE DISHWARE

Most families have two sets of dishes, one for everyday use and another for special occasions.

1. Consider using the nice dishes all the time, but if this isn't possible, pack up your best china. This will make more kitchen space available for items you use every day. Store the china in a sturdy wooden chest in a corner of a closet or another safe spot.

2. Keep your everyday dishes near the dishwasher to save steps in the kitchen.

3. To make better use of your cabinet space, screw cup hooks into the underside of a shelf.

4. Out by the dinner table, a buffet or hutch can be a useful spot for storing items that are used less often, such as your special occasion dishes, while providing extra serving space.

FORKS 'N' SPOONS

Stainless steel cutlery will probably be your everyday choice. Again, it will be easier to replace lost pieces if you buy a popular pattern. Your everyday tableware should be stored near the dishwasher. Any special items that you use only occasionally can be stored outside your kitchen, perhaps along with your special china.

China Shopping

When buying china, purchase a popular pattern, so you can easily replace pieces as they break. One tactic is to choose a pattern that's a solid, popular color, or that has a band of that color. Such china can be paired with similarly colored china, a great boon if you break pieces or want to expand your serving capacity. Ed's friend Ann bought a set of black-banded china that serves four. When she decided to expand her china collection, she couldn't find more of the same, so she bought a set of white china with a black design. When old and new patterns are arranged on her table in alternating settings with alternating black and white napkins, they look rather chic.

Treasure Maps for Your Treasures

Pirates aren't the only ones who can benefit from a treasure map. You can too. When you store valuable items, make a record of where they've been put. That way, when you need your grandmother's tea set, you won't have to rely on your fallible memory to locate it. The map will also help you find items your spouse stored, and vice versa. Post the treasure map on the back of a cabinet door, where you can refer to it easily.

If you're worried that thieves might make use of your map, employ a bit of subterfuge. Make up a code for the items and their locations that strangers won't understand. The tea set, for example, might be listed as "GT-cbg." The first part refers to Grammys' tea set, and the second to the closet "c" in the bedroom "b" with green walls "g." Although your treasure map won't give the number of paces to reach a buried chest, it will be useful in keeping track of the items you value most.

7 WAYS TO DECLUTTER POTS 'N' PANS

1. Set aside a few hours to sort through your cookware.
2. Get rid of duplicates and damaged items.
3. Store items you rarely use. Laurie's cousin Mary has a meat grinder she uses to make Italian sausage on rare occasions, a candy thermometer employed only when making gift fudge, and a flan pan that sees the light of day only at Christmastime. Place items such as these in clear plastic bags, box them up, label the box for each item inside, and then store them away.
4. Consider buying a set of high-quality cookware to replace all your old stuff. With a good set,

you'll get a pot or pan for each of your ordinary needs.

5. Hang your pots: Copper pots look attractive hanging from hooks over your kitchen island, or suspended from S-hooks on a wooden lattice attached to a wall. Avoid suspending cookware where it may fall on someone if a hook fails. Frying pans bounce harmlessly off skulls only in cartoons.

6. While pots can be easily stored by hanging or nesting them together on a shelf, their lids are harder to stash. They don't stack easily, and finding the one you want always seems to involve sorting through a half-dozen wrong choices. Housewares stores sell pot lid organizers similar to dish storage racks that you can store under the sink or in a cabinet.

7. If you don't hang your pots and pans, place them in cabinets near the stove with the most-used ones in front. You may be tempted to tuck items within items and exploit every nook. This allows you to store more stuff in a small space, but it's better to use more space

to organize your cookware so you can easily pull out the pot you need. Otherwise, to reach a deeply nested pot, you may have to pull out all the pots in the cabinet and then have to jam the unneeded pots back. This tedious process invites disorder.

EASY DOES IT

Lighten up!

To make items easier to spot in the far corners of a cabinet, paint the interior a light color.

4 WAYS TO MANAGE GEEGAW

1. Kitchens are the repositories of all sorts of doohickeys—bottle openers, cheese graters, melon ballers, and shrimp deveiners. If you haven't used one of these marvelous inventions in a year, get rid of it. Or store those you decide to keep outside your kitchen and note them on your treasure map.

2. Kitchen utensils that you use regularly should be stored in drawer trays, with the most commonly used ones stored in the handiest drawers.

3. Some utensils, such as spatulas and stirring spoons, can be stored upright in a container on your counter.

4. Metal utensils can also be hung from a magnetic bar secured to a kitchen wall. Avoid suspending utensils where they may fall and injure someone. *Never* hang knives or pointy utensils; they belong in a knife block or a drawer.

COUNTER INTELLIGENCE

Your counter is your work area, and it deserves an especially critical eye as you reconfigure the kitchen. If you have too many objects on it, you'll feel cramped. Allow only frequently used objects to sit there. If you use your toaster every day, it earns its spot. The waffle iron that you use once a month? Find a place for it elsewhere.

4 UNDERSINK STORAGE TIPS

1. The area under the sink is a catchall for cleansers, sponges, and dishwashing supplies. It's a logical location for these things, but don't jam too much under there. You may need to reach your garbage disposal's

reset button or a faucet's shutoff valve in an emergency. And if your sink develops a leak, the things you store there will get soaked.

2. Use a plastic carryall to organize cleaning supplies stored under your sink. This will limit the mess created by dribbly containers.

3. Reuse plastic milk jugs to store spare sponges. Cut a large opening in the jug opposite the handle and shove the sponges inside. The handle makes it easy to pull out the container whenever you need a sponge. Use another jug for pot scrubbers.

4. Reuse liquid washing machine detergent jugs to store powdered cleansers. To do this, clean the jugs, let them dry, and then use

a funnel to fill them with the powdered cleansers. If there's important information on the cleansers' original cartons, tape it to the jugs. The jugs can be sealed tightly, keeping their contents dry while preventing the casual spillage that comes with cardboard cartons. Still another plus: The jugs' caps can help you measure quantities.

ORDERED DRAWERS

The contents of kitchen drawers can become jumbled each time you open and close them. To keep things straight, use dividers to separate each kind of item. You can use silverware trays or even something as economical as cut-down tissue boxes. To keep these dividers from sliding about, secure them to the drawer bottom with poster putty, a claylike adhesive used in schools to attach things to walls without damaging the paint.

6 WAYS TO ORGANIZE YOUR JUNK DRAWER

There's a legend about the sewers of London. Londoners, like people everywhere, lose valu-ables as they live their lives. These items often wind up in the sewers. A diamond ring might slip off in the bath; a dropped coin might jingle and bounce into a manhole. According to the legend, the lost valuables are washed through the sewers till they're trapped in a particular low spot where, through the centuries, a massive knot has formed. Someday, some sewer worker will stub his booted toe on this treasure and retire wealthy.

Something similar occurs in your home in the catchall spot of domestic life: the junk drawer. Here the miscellaneous items of existence accumulate, melding into a lump the opposite in value of the mythical London treasure. Before decluttering, Ed's junk drawer contained a brown shoelace, dozens of bent paper clips,

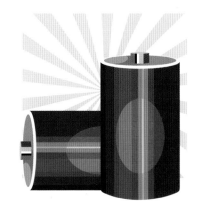

keys to a car he sold 10 years ago, his deceased cat's claw trimmers, and a ballpoint pen an insurance salesman offered him as a bribe to buy a policy.

1. Begin reorganizing your junk drawer by pulling out anything that belongs elsewhere. You may discover objects that are unrecognizable. You may find disposing of such puzzles a minor torture. Is this odd-shaped bit of metal the key to the proper operation of the kitchen stove? Will a repairman charge $80 to replace it?

2. One solution to this quandary is to put all the oddities in a paper bag and date it. Put it aside. If a year passes without your taking anything from the bag, throw it out.

3. The junk drawer should contain only those items you're apt to use—things such as candles with matches for blackouts, pencils and pads for taking notes, and wire twists for trash bags.

4. Organize the drawer using small boxes; plastic egg trays, square plastic storage boxes, or ice cube trays will all work.

The Bureau of Kitchen Accoutrements

Your kitchen may be able to take advantage of a bureau—a chest of drawers usually associated with the bedroom—or a sideboard of the sort used in the dining room. Either will give you a place to put such things as spare dishes, tableware, and kitchen towels. The bureau's top can serve as an extra work space, and is a good spot to park a coffeemaker or bread box. A tall, narrow bureau can exploit a narrow spot in your kitchen that might otherwise go unused. Or you can move a bureau into your pantry to help organize jars and cans.

5. To manage the odd little tools and devices that you know are associated with specific appliances or tasks—which will be useful on rare occasions in the future—attach a tag to each identifying its purpose. Put them in a clear plastic bag or container, and store them in an out-of-the-way location. You don't want to forget where you store them, so add their location to your treasure map.

6. Do spare batteries seem to end up rolling around in the back of your junk drawer? To keep them at the ready, buy a battery rack from a hardware store or home center, and mount it on the back of a pantry door. Some models include a battery tester and recharger.

CATALOGING COOKBOOKS AND RECIPES

"I was 66 years old. I still had to make a living. I looked at my social security check of $105 and decided to use that to try to franchise my chicken recipe. Folks had always liked my chicken."

—Colonel Harland Sanders

6 WAYS TO ORGANIZIE COOKBOOKS AND RECIPES

If you like to cook, you probably collect cookbooks and tear recipes out of magazines. Most likely the resulting food-caked clutter occupies a shelf somewhere in the kitchen.

1. Gather up all your recipes and cookbooks, heaping them on the kitchen table.

2. Go through the pile and cull those cookbooks and recipes you know you'll never use.

3. Discarded cookbooks can be donated to the library or sold at your next garage sale.

4. Stack the remaining cookbooks in one pile, and place the surviving clippings in a second.

5. Once you've pruned your cookbooks, find a place to reshelve

them. Keep in mind that the kitchen can be an unforgiving environment for books. Grease and spatters stain them. Wet countertops dampen them. A shelf near—but not too near—your counter area is a good choice. If you have extra cabinet space, a shelf inside will help keep your cookbooks clean as well as handy.

6. Place clipped recipes in folders, taking care with the labels you use to organize this trove of good ideas. If the magazine is online, you might consider throwing away the clipping and simply searching for the recipe when you have a hankering for that particular dish.

Dual-Purpose Cutting Board

A clear plastic cutting board can serve a second purpose: You can place it over the open pages of a cookbook, keeping your place while sparing the book from splatters.

13 KITCHEN STORAGE SOLUTIONS

Storage is the most important consideration in reorganizing a kitchen. Any space you can find can soon be put to good use. Here are some ideas.

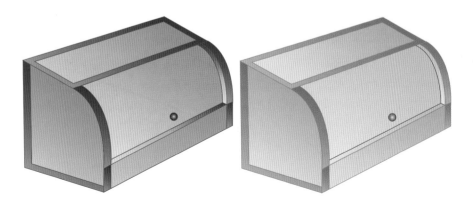

1. Bring back the bread box. Once so common a kitchen object that it became a standard "20 Questions" question, the bread box has disappeared from most homes. Nevertheless, these boxes are as useful as ever for keeping bread and baked goods fresh and in one easy-to-find spot. To track down a source, do an Internet search for "bread box."

2. Paper towels are vital to kitchen cleanup, and some thought should be given to where the dispenser is placed. Don't locate it close to a stove top. A strong tug could spew a streamer of paper towels across an active burner with fiery results.

3. Kitchens tend to collect keys. Store them on a simple board with rows of cup hooks, to spare your family hours of frantic hunting. Never label keys with your name or address, as an unscrupulous finder would know whose doors they opened. If you want to put a phone number on the tag, use your business or cell phone number. To distinguish keys belonging to each family member, choose a colored tag according to his or her favorite hue.

4. A bare section of kitchen wall can be turned into handy storage with shelves. Wooden shelves have a warm appearance. Metal shelves look more institutional, but they're easy to clean. Shelves or racks that are meant to bear a heavy load need to be secured to studs or ceiling joists, which might require a carpenter if you aren't up to locating these framing members.

5. Kitchen specialty stores sell wire shelves that hang under cabinet shelves to make better use of the available space. They're especially useful for stacking different kinds of plates. You can stack dinner plates under a wire shelf holding bread and butter plates.

6. A spice rack on your kitchen wall may look homey, but it isn't the best way to store herbs and spices, which can be damaged by sunlight or the heat and moisture produced by kitchen activity. Instead, hang the rack on the back of a pantry door. You can employ a wire rack

that holds larger jars than the typical spice rack, avoiding the need to transfer bulk spices to smaller containers.

If you use a lot of different herbs and spices, make it easier to find the one you're looking for by storing them in alphabetical order. While you're at

it, stick a label with the date of purchase on each container so that you can discard its contents when stale.

7. A proper wine rack stores bottles with the corks pointing at a slight downward angle, to keep the corks damp and tight-fitting. The rack should

Looking for Mr. Fix-it

In days gone by, most neighborhoods had an amiable handyman who could tinker broken appliances back to health for a small charge. Today, these gentlemen have gone the way of the drive-in movie and gas station pump jockey. Competition has lowered the cost of small appliances so much that a replacement is cheaper than repair. Still, you may be partial to a particular appliance, and prefer to have it fixed. While you may lack the knowledge to repair a motor safely, even the most unskilled person can replace some broken parts, such as  a cracked blender lid or a bent beater. Culinary Parts (www.culinary-parts.com) will help you locate the part that will put your crippled appliance back to work. Or try a search of the Internet using your appliance's name, brand, and the words "replacement parts."

be placed away from heat and sunlight. It can be mounted inside a cabinet or the pantry. Or buy a rack designed to be hung under a shelf, exploiting space that might otherwise go unused. If you go through wine quickly, and don't need to worry about heat and sunlight, you can use a wall-mounted rack that serves as part of your kitchen décor, without taking up conventional storage space.

8. Wine glasses can be awkward to store because they can't be stacked, and are too fragile to mingle with coffee mugs and cereal bowls. Pubs and restaurants suspend wine glasses from overhead racks. Do the same. They can add a decorative touch while providing practical storage.

9. You can suspend smaller appliances, such as can openers and coffeemakers, under your cabinets to free up counter space. Take care not to hang them too near the stove top or sink, to avoid damaging them with heat or moisture. You also don't want to risk damaging *yourself*—by accidentally touching an appliance alive with electricity with one hand, while placing your other hand in a sink filled with water. To make this impossible, install the appliance more than your arm's reach from the sink.

10. To avoid cramping your countertop work area, plan where you should install under-cabinet appliances. To test a location, find a cardboard box similar in size to the appliance, and attach the box to the proposed spot. (Use masking tape to avoid marring your cabinets.) Then you can see how your kitchen activities are affected.

11. Plastic grocery bags come in handy for all sorts of things, but they can be awkward to store. Tuck them in a fabric tube, available in groceries or from mail-order housewares companies. The tube hangs from a loop and is filled by pushing balled-up bags down into it. When you need a bag, you pull it out from the bottom.

12. To guard against the possibility of seeing a valued ring disappear down the kitchen drain,

Cookbooks on a Tray

Housewares stores and mail-order catalogs offer small shelves that slide out from under a kitchen cabinet to hold a cookbook above the counter. There it can be easily read, yet remain above cooking messes.

mount a coat hook near your sink (but not over it) and use it to hang jewelry as you wash dishes.

13. Recycling reduces the amount of waste that ends up in landfills, but it can be irksome. If you're responsible for supplying your own recycling container, give some thought to choosing a convenient model. Look for a lightweight bin with comfortable handles. Or if you expect to have a lot to transport, a better choice might be a wheeled trash can that you don't have to lift. Because a bin left outside may fill with rain if it doesn't have drainage holes, use a power drill with a large bit to put several holes in its bottom.

A KITCHEN CONCLUSION IN 7 POINTS

To summarize, your kitchen can best perform the many tasks that domestic destiny has assigned to it if you:

1. Keep safety in mind.

2. Establish and follow efficient cleaning routines.
3. Reduce and organize your kitchen equipment and dishware.
4. Manage your foodstuffs to assure wholesomeness.
5. Keep your refrigerator and freezer organized, clean, and empty of spoiled food.
6. Put together a set of cleaning products to handle cleaning problems.
7. Maximize your kitchen's storage capacity by storing seldom-used kitchen items elsewhere, and by using novel storage devices.

Over-the-Window Shelf

The dimensions for your over-the-window storage shelf will vary depending on the size of your window. This shelf is about 6" deep with a 3/4" lip around its edge to help prevent objects from falling off. Window shades or drapery hang from the window frame under the shelf. The shelf is securely attached to the wall at its supports and through the back piece into wall studs.

Ed Morrow

Do you dine in serene elegance?

Or something less...

SEVEN

Order in the Dining Room

"Never argue at the dinner table, for the one who is not hungry always gets the best of the argument."

—Archbishop Richard Whately

Chances are you seldom dine in your dining room, not that this part of the house goes unemployed. Your family is apt to use the table for sorting mail, doing homework, stacking newspapers, and so on. The resulting confusion can make it impossible for you to enjoy a meal at your own table. You wind up eating in the kitchen, from a tray in front of the TV, or even over the sink and straight out of the can.

The first step toward redis-covering your dining room is getting rid of clutter. Clear away everything that's disposable—old newspapers and junk mail are likely culprits. Next, remove those objects that belong elsewhere—your kids' toys, Pop's fishing pole, your tennis rackets. Now turn your attention to those things that really do have a place in the dining room.

7 WAYS TO CULL YOUR CHINA COLLECTION

1. Your best—and not-so-best—china is apt to be stored in your dining room. Pull all of it out and inspect each item.

2. Do you have "orphaned" pieces—a single plate or couple of bowls left from what was once a full set?

3. Do you have unneeded duplicates?

4. Are some of your pieces chipped or cracked? Mismatched or broken china add nothing to a meal, so rid yourself of every unwanted piece.

5. Now that you've culled the bad china from your collection, consider whether or not to keep the rest. Do you want to invest years of care and worry in a collection of fragile keepsakes rarely used for a meal?

6. There might be a collector eager to buy it.

7. It might make a lovely gift for someone who would value a good set of dishware.

6 WAYS TO STORE CHINA

If you decide to hold onto your china, you'll want to store it in a way that preserves the pieces and makes them easily accessible. Deep-sea divers have discovered undamaged pieces of china in centuries-old sunken ships, but don't expect your fine dishware to survive rough handling. Here are some tips for keeping your china safe and sound for another generation.

1. If possible, store plates vertically in a plate rack. The weight of a stack of plates, pressing down for months, can snap those at the bottom. When you must stack, stacks shouldn't be higher than 6 to 8 inches.

2. Stack your plates on separators. Made from felt or acid-free paper, these cushions are available in housewares stores and serve to protect glazed surfaces. If you can't find separators, you can use coffeemaker filters or circles cut from felt. The circles should be slightly smaller than the plates.

3. Don't push one stack of plates against another or you may chip the edges.

4. Store cups rim up. The rim is the most delicate part of a cup, and even the cup's own weight

can crack it. Stacking cups should be avoided for the same reason.

5. Don't put fine china or any gilded piece in your microwave.

6. Store your china on a low shelf to ensure that it won't fall far if it slips from your fingers. Stacks of china are heavy, and it's also easier to put them on a low shelf. In earthquake zones, low storage can be an important safety measure.

Zip Up Your Teacups

Padded, zippered fabric pouches are handy for storing fine china. They're a worthwhile investment if you value your settings. Hang a tag from each pouch's zipper so you can identify the contents without opening it; handling increases the risk of breakage.

CRYSTAL CARE

Crystal adds sparkly glamour to any table, but it's even more fragile than china. You can begin your collection with just three basics needed for entertaining: highball glasses, double old-fashioned glasses, and wine goblets. An all-purpose wine goblet will suffice, but if you drink wine regularly, you may want to buy glasses for both white and red wine.

(A wine shop salesperson can explain the difference, or if you have a wine fancier friend, let him or her expound on the subject.)

Beyond the basics, you might want to add three specialty glasses: a tulip shaped or flute wine glass used for champagne; a large-bowled goblet that's the traditional choice for drinking cognac or brandy; and a martini glass, with its distinctively conical shape, for serving cocktails.

When you buy crystal, especially if it's not a standard shape, purchase a few extra pieces as replacements for those broken over the years.

4 WAYS TO KEEP IT CRYSTALLINE

Here are a few points to consider when cleaning and storing crystal to keep it sparkling—and in one piece.

1. Never wash crystal in a dishwasher. Always wash it by hand, after padding your sink with a rubber mat or a dishtowel.
2. Crystal is sensitive to temperature changes. Never put ice or cold liquids in warm crystal. Don't put a hot liquid in a cold glass, either. Gently warm or cool crystal according to what will be poured into it.
3. You may be tempted to store crystal rim down to keep dust from settling inside. But crystal rims are designed to look pretty, not to support the weight of the glass. Store glasses upright, or hang them from their bases in a crystal rack.
4. A lighted, glass-fronted hutch is a great place to display and protect crystal.

SILVER SAVVY

Silver manufacturers advise that the best thing to do with your silver is to use it. Good quality silver is durable, and use helps lessen tarnish. Frequent handling also contributes to developing an attractive patina. Use all your pieces in turn so that the entire set will have a consistent look.

12 HINTS FOR CLEANING AND STORING YOUR SILVER

A set of silver shouldn't be treated as casually as everyday stainless steel tableware. Follow these precautions to keep your silver looking its best.

1. Rinse silver immediately after use. Acidic and salty foods can damage it.

2. Don't soak silver. Long exposure to water can be harmful.

3. Use soap and hot water to clean silver. Clean crevices with a toothbrush. Rinse in clear hot water, then quickly dry with a cotton cloth to avoid spots.

4. Wash pieces individually. If jumbled together, pieces can scratch each other.

5. Check the manufacturer's directions to see if your silver can be washed in a dishwasher, and even then, do so only with care. Use a small amount of detergent and remove the silver before the drying cycle. Silver with hollow handles or intricate patterns can be damaged in a dishwasher. Don't place silverware in the same basket as stainless steel tableware, because the latter may scratch the silver.

6. Silver should be polished once or twice a year with a cotton or flannel cloth and a good-quality paste polish; dip polishes can damage fine details. You should rub lengthwise. Circular rubbing can cause scratches.

7. Don't bundle silverware with rubber bands. The pieces can scrape each other.

8. Wrappings of plastic, aluminum foil, or newspaper may damage silver.

9. Air, dampness, and light make silver tarnish faster.

10. Don't store silverware loose in a drawer, as pieces can jangle about and damage each other.

11. The best way to store silverware is in a silver chest—a wooden box lined with tarnish-proof cloth that provides a slot for each piece.

12. You can also line a drawer with tarnish-proof cloth and install a silverware rack to hold the pieces secure. Drape more of the cloth over the silver. Stores that sell silver also sell fabric bags in which to safely store the silver.

DISPOSING OF ORPHANED DINNERWARE

That odd survivor of a set of china you dropped down a flight of stairs may be just what some other person needs to replace her missing piece. An Internet search can hook you up with dealers specializing in replacement pieces who may be interested in your orphans. There are also replacement dealers for silver and crystal.

LINENS WITHOUT THE LIABILITIES

"A good upbringing means not that you won't spill sauce on the tablecloth, but that you won't notice it when someone else does."

—Anton Pavlovich Chekhov

Table linens are essential to civilized dining, but you don't need enough linen to furnish a restaurant. Limit yourself to a few good quality tablecloths, a table pad, a set of place mats for informal dining, and enough napkins to serve the largest gathering you ever expect to host, plus a few extras for the slob every group of guests is bound to include. Once you've whittled down your stock of linens, take a

little trouble to keep them in good condition.

Most tablecloths and napkins are made of cotton or a cotton blend. To avoid shrinkage, they'll probably need to be washed in cold water. Their care labels will specify how to launder them. Remove any loose food particles before washing. Some tablecloths are stain resistant, but don't confuse this with stain *proof.* Use a table pad under your tablecloth to help protect your table from hot plates, spills, and dings.

5 WAYS TO CREATE DINING ROOM STORAGE

Of all the rooms in your home, the dining room is least likely to have a closet.

1. To provide more space for china, crystal, silver, and table linens, you might add a

sideboard. This piece of furniture can be especially handy if it has a shelf under the main body on which to display large items such as teapots and vases.

2. A sideboard makes a perfect spot to lay out a buffet. A sideboard with a set of shelves on top is also known as a hutch.

3. If you can't find a sideboard to fit your needs, consider employing a bedroom dresser in the dining room. A dresser may provide more storage space, since it's likely to have deeper drawers.

4. Corner cupboards make good use of little-used space in the dining room. They can be freestanding pieces or built-ins. A cupboard with glazed doors can show off your best pieces of china.

5. You also can display dishes on a Welsh plate rack. This is a narrow wall-mounted shelf, with a groove along its base and a wooded dowel across its front to hold pates securely. A plate rack can be extended to run the width of a wall, or even around all four walls as part of the room's trim.

EASY DOES IT

Why Not Rent?

If you rarely stage big parties, why are you keeping that huge punch bowl with 36 punch cups? Or that samovar capable of serving a regiment of the Russian Army? Rental shops stock all sorts of dining and partying items, sparing you the need to store things you seldom use. Drop by the shop to learn what it stocks, and plan ahead when renting. If you want a punch bowl for a Christmas party, for example, reserve one before the holiday rush.

4 WAYS TO PUT THE SHINE ON YOUR DINING ROOM

Dining room furniture needs some care to look its best. Furniture polish comes in three forms— spray, liquid, and paste waxes. Sprays are popular, but they may contain oils that are apt to damage a wax finish or solvents that can eat away at varnish.

1. Liquid polish can be either an emulsion or an oil. Emulsions

are blends of wax, oil, detergent, solvents, and fragrances. They're meant to clean furniture and leave a shine. The shine typically will disappear over time, as the polish dries. Emulsions do little to protect wood.

2. Oil polishes can be either drying or nondrying. Drying oils, such as linseed and tung oil, are meant to penetrate wood to form a hard surface that repels water. Unfortunately, these oils oxidize into an unpleasant brown color and don't dry completely. The result is a hard-to-remove, dark coating with a sticky feel.

3. Nondrying oils, which include mineral oil and paraffin mixtures, don't oxidize but they also remain damp and sticky. Sticky finishes attract dirt and are unpleasant to the touch.

4. Paste waxes provide a water-resistant shine that's durable and doesn't oxidize. They're better for furniture than oil products, but require a lot of rubbing to apply and buffing to shine. Use a clean, soft cloth for this. The better the paste wax, the more effort is required to apply and buff it. Fortunately, because paste waxes hold up well, you don't have to apply them often. Just buff the wood occasionally. When a buffing fails to produce a shine, you know it's time to wax again. The new wax should blend with the old, but if you apply too much, the wax will build up so that it doesn't shine when buffed. You can remove excess wax with mineral spirits. Allow the wood to dry completely before waxing again.

YOU CAN USE IT, INSTEAD OF PUTTING IT AWAY

Sheree's old school pal Rhonda inherited a lot of family silver. She lives in a small apartment and had

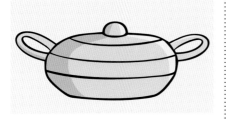

trouble finding places to store it. She was thinking of packing away a covered serving dish meant to keep a roast warm on the table, when she realized that she could use it to store napkins on her sideboard instead. They're kept clean, handy, and out of sight, and the dish looks attractive left out. You can find similar uses for pieces of your silver or china.

Closet Organization

72"

42"

42"

Ed Morrow

EIGHT

The Well-Tempered Bedroom

"Never go to bed mad. Stay up and fight."

—Phyllis Diller

Do you have to forge a trail just to cross from your bedroom door to the bed? Does your search for your favorite silk scarf require an archaeological dig?

Even if you have the rest of your house neat and under control, bedrooms tend to be trouble spots. That's because bedrooms are clutter magnets, pulling in not only clothing and bed linens but also unrelated stuff that ends up here in the flow of daily life. It might be the briefcase that wouldn't fall from your commute-paralyzed fingers until you collapsed on the bed, or the dozen unread books you placed on the nightstand, or a half-finished sweater that you started knitting one sleepless night. If you're in the habit of having a bedtime snack, then dirty glasses and dishes are apt to be part of the scene.

Decluttering the bedroom is a particularly worthwhile investment of time and energy, because the resulting order makes rest more pleasant. You'll start off the day in a better frame of mind, too, because dressing and getting off to work will be less hectic.

4 WAYS TO CASE THE JOINT

1. Take a good look around.
2. Does all that stuff littering the floor, the dresser, the chair have a proper place? If not, you'll have to create a spot for each wayward item.
3. Are there clothes everywhere? Maybe you need a larger dresser or a closet organizer.
4. Are there magazines as far as the eye can see? Maybe a basket will solve the problem. Or perhaps a trip to your recycling bin will be more effective.

8 THINGS TO CONSIDER

You may want to be more ambitious and take the opportunity to completely rethink this part of the house.

1. When you first moved into your home, how did you envision the bedroom? Revisit those dreams, and you may arrive at concrete ideas about how to address the problem of clutter.
2. Maybe you wanted a cozy space, with a nook for reading or an overstuffed chair for watching TV with your feet up.
3. Maybe you wanted a crisp, modern room.
4. Balance your idealized vision with a realistic appraisal of your needs. Obviously, strict minimalism isn't your style if your closet is overflowing with 130 pairs of shoes. Opulent luxury is impractical if your bedroom is closer in size to a walk-in closet.
5. Consider the physical changes you'll have to make to the room to realize your goals. Can you accomplish them yourself? Will you need a carpenter? What investment in

money, time, and effort will be required?

6. Could you improve your situation with simpler measures—adding shelves, buying a larger dresser, cutting clutter?

7. Is dramatic action necessary—sectioning off a portion of the room, or borrowing part of an adjoining room to create more closet space?

8. A simple pencil sketch may be enough to visualize your ideas. If your plan involves moving walls or doors or adding closet space, you'll need a detailed plan, specifying the measurements of the alterations you want. Armed with this plan, you can talk to a contractor about how to proceed.

ADDING A CLOSET

To add a closet, you can frame out one in the bedroom itself, but this will reduce its floor space. Another alternative is to take space from an adjoining room—perhaps the bedroom of a child who has now left the nest. "Cannibalizing" a closet from an adjacent room is an ambitious project. Unless you're very handy, you'll probably need an electrician as well as a carpenter. You may even want to consult an architect to be sure the new storage room works effectively. A building permit and a visit from a building inspector are apt to be necessary as well, depending on the regulations of your municipality.

7 CONSIDERATIONS WHEN ADDING A CLOSET

1. Check that you can get into and out of the closet easily, and that the swing of a hinged door won't obstruct movement in your bedroom. A pocket door, folding doors, or a set of sliding doors may be a good choice in tight quarters.

2. Make sure your closet has effective lighting. You can install door switches that turn on the closet light when you open a door, like the light in a refrigerator, sparing you the need to flick a switch when your hands are full.

3. Although a clothes rod is standard equipment for a bedroom closet, consider adding shelves or drawers as well.

4. A long mirror on the closet door is cliché but useful.

5. You can buy easily assembled shelves and drawer units, adaptable to the height you have available.

6. Coated wire fixtures are lightweight and inexpensive, and they allow you to see what you've stored away.

7. It may serve you better to have the clothes rod extend just halfway across the closet, freeing up space for full-height shelves or drawers. The free end of the rod can be supported by a 2 by 4 that's anchored to the floor with screws and L-brackets and nailed into a joist within the ceiling above.

Stealing Storage Ideas

When planning how to store your possessions, don't forget to consider how professionals store similar items. For example, want some ideas on how to shelve books? Visit a bookstore, and examine how it organizes its shelves. A shoe store may suggest a way to handle your inventory of footwear. A grocery may have a way of storing spices or vegetables or other foodstuffs that you can copy. Those who run these establishments devote a lot of thought to storing and presenting their wares in an efficient way. Use their idea to help make your home just as efficient.

ALTERNATIVES TO ADDING A CLOSET

If you're reluctant to invest in adding a closet, or just don't have the floor area to spare, consider buying an ample armoire. (Chapter 5 described customizing an armoire.) It won't provide as much storage, but it'll be much cheaper, occupy less floor space, involve a fraction of the bother, and if you move, you can take it with you.

Stash It or Trash It

Susan, a meteorological specialist in Port St. John, Florida, blamed her clutter problem on her state's climate. "In central Florida, winter temperatures can bounce from one end of the thermometer to the other in a matter of hours," she says. "That means we can't store our summer clothes in the attic, and only a handful of us have basements. I was tired of battling drawers that bulged with anything from sweaters and sweatshirts to swimsuits and shorts. One day I had had enough, and adopted a new motto: 'Stash it or trash it.' If we don't have room for it, we can't have it. Period."

Susan and her family went shopping at a discount store to buy inexpensive yet attractive dressers that fit into their closets, and left room for hanging garments. They reviewed their wardrobes, guided by their new, stash-or-trash strategy. Then they were done, their reduced supply of clothing was neatly put away. "The battle of the bulging drawers is over in our house," Susan says.

Adding an extra dresser can also increase storage, especially a tall dresser with two or three more drawers than a standard model.

Of course, the best way to create storage space is to reduce the volume of stuff you need to store. Pull a box of old shoes from your closet, and you have that much more space in which to stash the stuff that's now loitering around the bedroom.

A CLOSET PURGE

"There's something about a closet that makes a skeleton terribly restless."
—John Barrymore

The key to bedroom closet clutter is to restrict what gets stored there to those things that are most "closet worthy," and to exploit all the space in the closet to store these items.

Consider the case of Rita's friend Al and his wife, Mary. Al and Mary commute from suburban New Jersey to their jobs in New York. They're busy people, with demanding work and full social lives. Consequently, their home had become little more than a way station.

QUICK FIX

THE NOT-FOR-SHOES BAG

The vinyl multipocketed shoe bag is a classic of closet organization. Unfortunately, it can fall apart under the weight of its burden, and the pockets get dirty from crud that accumulates on your shoes. You'll be better off using a shoe rack. But if you find yourself with a shoe bag, clean it up and use its many pockets for storing small, light items such as stockings, scarves, and jewelry. The clear plastic makes it easy to organize and find things.

Their bedroom was a particular victim of hasty disorder. After years of sleeping in the middle of a mess, the couple decided to set things right. They spent a day removing trash and clearing up clutter that had been heaped on every surface. Next came the more difficult task of decluttering the closet. They pulled everything out, evaluating as they went. Do we need this? Can we throw this out? Does it belong here? Anything unneeded was set aside for disposal. Items better stored elsewhere were trundled off. Al's sleeping bag, for example, which he uses just once a year, was moved to the attic.

6 WARDROBE DECLUTTERING QUESTIONS

1. Does this piece of clothing fit? If it hasn't for the past 2 years, it's not going to fit anytime soon. In the meantime, it'll be a reminder of your unfulfilled hopes for a slender you. Wouldn't it be better to dump it, and when you do trim down, to reward yourself with something new?

2. Is it comfortable? An itchy sweater won't get worn. It'll just waste closet space.

3. Is it flattering? If it makes you look ugly today, it's going to make you look ugly tomorrow. Toss it.

4. Does it need repairs or alterations before you can wear it? Don't return the item to the closet, where it's sure to be forgotten. Stop to consider that a repair can cost more than a piece of clothing is worth. If the article is worth the expense, stick it in a bag and place the bag in your car, ready to be dropped off for repairs.

5. Does it clash with everything else in the closet? If you don't have the matching items necessary for you to wear a garment, give it away.

6. Is it a gift you don't wear but would feel guilty disposing of? Your gift giver didn't want to burden you, so give it away without regret. If the gift giver is curious as to why you haven't been wearing the item, politely lie to spare his or her feelings. You used the wrong iron setting,

you spilled bleach on it, your cat raked it with her claws, or it was filched from your clothesline by rampaging, naked bandits. Of course, the gift giver may kindly replace the unwanted gift with an exact duplicate of the original garment that the bare bandits stole.

Purging with a Little Help from Your Friends

Host a decluttering party. In the same spirit as an old-time quilting bee or barn raising, ask a group of friends over to help you make the difficult decision about what pieces of your wardrobe to discard or keep. Provide beverages, snacks, and music, and allow the guests to take home the discards as party favors. Yes, your cluttered ways will be exposed to your pals, but when it's all over and your closet looks like one in a magazine, the embarrassment will be a small price to pay. Perhaps your friends will imitate your party and you'll get to see their clutter sins.

TOO UGLY TO WEAR, TOO USEFUL TO TOSS

Ed does a lot of work around his yard, and any job that involves getting really dirty—like removing a dead possum from a spiderweb-stuffed crawl space—is his chore. Consequently, Ed keeps old clothing to wear while engaged in these domestic adventures. But in time, his supply of work clothing had grown too large. Ed's torn T-shirts and stained jeans, to his frugal mind, never seemed too worn out to wear during a dirty job. After all, when does an old pair of pants get too tattered to wear while packing off former possums? Ed had wound up with enough work clothing to shabbily attire a dozen possum morticians.

The accumulation of possibly useful things is a classic clutter problem. One solution is to understand that you're unlikely to ever utilize your stockpile of possibly useful junk. Set a realistic limit on how large a supply you keep, and enforce it. Ed decided to dedicate a shelf in his garage to his work clothing. When it fills up, he doesn't steal space from other purposes for more old clothing.

If the "new" old item is worth keeping, he tosses out a garment from his collection to make room for it.

Your "possibly useful" weakness may be for socks or jelly jars or plastic margarine tubs. Treat them the same as Ed's work clothing problem: Set limits, and obey them.

11 WAYS TO UPDATE EXISTING CLOSETS

1. In a walk-in closet, a storage box or low set of shelves with a padded top can give you a seat while providing shoe storage.

2. Wheeled storage carts can be conveniently pulled out to add or remove items.

3. A dresser in your closet can store small items. Drawer dividers can keep their contents sorted. Full-extension drawer runners allow you to pull a drawer out to its very back edge, permitting full access to its contents.

4. Slide-out shelves make it easier to reach items that otherwise would be hard to retrieve.

5. There are battery-powered lights in your hardware store's flashlight section that can be glued to your closet wall to provide light in dark corners. You activate these commonly dome-shaped lights by pressing on them.

6. Pull-out baskets allow you to see your clothing and for air to circulate around it.

7. Folding belt/tie/scarf racks can be mounted on your closet wall. They can be folded out for use, then folded back out of the way.

8. A closet hamper is convenient for soiled clothing, but don't store wet items here. They won't get enough air to avoid mildew. The hamper should be light enough to tote off to your laundry room.

9. A wardrobe lift is a handy device for shorter closet users. It allows a clothing rod to swing out and down to put its burden within easy reach. A lever allows you to lift the clothing back up.

10. Freestanding shelves and dressers allow you to organize your closet without attaching anything to your closet walls.

This method is quicker and allows easy rearrangement. But these shelves generally won't hold as great a load as their wall-attached equivalents and aren't safe for children's rooms.

11. Home centers carry a wide variety of closet organizing devices and complete "systems" to replace all the shelves and

The War on Moths

Cedar is traditionally used to discourage moths. Cedar's scent repels them while its vapor kills small moth larvae. Unfortunately, if closets are opened and shut frequently, they may not hold enough of the scent. Mothballs (and flakes) can also kill moths, but again the moths and mothballs must be in tightly sealed confines.

The best antimoth tactic is scrupulous cleaning. Vacuuming can remove moth eggs, larvae (these are the critters that eat your clothing), and the detritus that shelters infestations. Human perspiration is a lure to moths, so cleaning your clothing before storing is a good preventive. Pheromone traps, which use a chemical to lure moths into a glue-lined box, can help control the pests without using toxic chemicals.

If you develop a moth infestation, don't treat it with ordinary household pesticides. They're ineffective and can

be dangerous. Begin your eradication efforts by destroying any fabrics that are damaged. Vacuum every corner of the infested area and empty the vacuum outside your home. Clean all clothing that has been exposed.

Hot water kills moths and larvae. For those things that can't be washed in hot water, dry cleaning will do the job. For items that can't be washed or dry cleaned, heating at 120°F for 30 minutes or freezing at 18°F will kill moths. You also can fumigate moths with dry ice, which is a useful method for taking care of pillows. Wearing thick gloves to protect your hands, place the moth-infested object in a thick, 30-gallon plastic bag with at least a half-pound lump of dry ice. Keep the bag loosely closed until the dry ice has vaporized (otherwise expanding gas can burst the bag), then seal it tightly for 4 days.

rods in your closet. Many of these are anchored to your closet walls and are very sturdy. They're also flexible in how they can be customized to your needs and to the topography of your closet. You can add more hanging capacity or more pull-out baskets, for example, or arrange shelves around pipes. These systems are designed for the average, somewhat-handy person to install, but a pair of extra hands can be helpful.

TIDYING YOUR DRESSER

After decluttering their closet, Al and Mary turned to their dressers, tossing what could be tossed and relocating items that belonged elsewhere. Before returning things to their dressers,

QUICK FIX

DON'T CRAM YOUR CLOTHES

A properly filled drawer should have room left over. This makes it easier to adjust its contents and to find things. Overstuffing may warp the bottom panel of the drawer so that it won't close easily and may even come apart.

they divided up drawers to organize their wardrobe. Mary, for
example, separated her hand-
kerchiefs and underwear using a
cardboard gift box cut down to fit
a drawer. The couple also used a
packing technique recommended
by professional travelers—they
rolled their clothing rather than
folding it. Rolling doesn't leave
creases; it's faster than folding; and
it allows you to store more in a
limited space.

3 DAILY BEDROOM
DECLUTTER STEPS

Even if your bedroom isn't
much more than a place to lie
horizontally for 8 hours a night,
it requires daily attention to stay
neat and orderly.

1. The first thing you'll need
   to do each day is make your
   bed. This task will go more
   quickly if you use a comforter
   rather than a bedspread over
   blankets. The plumpness of
   the comforter also looks more
   inviting than a flat bedspread.

2. After making your bed, you'll
   need to swap your sleepwear
   for your day's clothing. Some

people stow their pajamas or
nightgowns under their pillows.
It's a convenient, concealed
location that saves space elsewhere. Others prefer to use
their nightstand or dresser.
Sheree's friend Becky keeps an
embroidered pillowcase by her
bed and stuffs her nightwear
into it in the morning. She
can then plop it by her other
pillows on her bed, where it's
neatly camouflaged.

3. When dressing, don't disrupt
   your clothing by pulling out
   item after item, then carelessly
   replacing them or not replacing
   them at all. Rushing in this
   way may save you a couple of
   seconds today, but you'll waste
   minutes tomorrow as you paw
   through your disrupted closet
   or dresser. If your closet and

dresser are well ordered, getting dressed will be easy and quick.

6 WEEKLY BEDROOM DECLUTTER STEPS

1. Do the laundry, including your bed linens.
2. Check over your wardrobe as you return the washed laundry to your bedroom. Get rid of anything that's worn or no longer fits.
3. Dust off surfaces.
4. Sweep the floor or vacuum if you have carpeting
5. Empty your trash can.
6. Put any odd items littering your bedroom back where they belong.

8 WAYS TO DO THE MONTHLY DECLUTTERING

In addition to the weekly cleaning plan:

1. Examine your closet and dressers. Do they need reordering? While you may not want to pull out everything from every storage spot, consider emptying one specific space and reviewing its contents this month, then a different space next month.

2. Dust everywhere, thoroughly.
3. With glass cleaner, spruce up the mirror and any dirty windows.
4. Clean smudged walls.
5. Wax or polish shiny surfaces.
6. After everything is dusted and cleaned, sweep or vacuum. Don't forget to vacuum under your bed and in your closet.
7. You can also vacuum the window treatments, which get surprisingly dusty.
8. Light fixtures also get dusty. Besides being unsightly, dusty fixtures cast less light. Make it a habit to run a dust-attracting cloth over fixtures once a

month. Be sure to turn off the fixture and let it cool before dusting.

SHIFTING WITH THE SEASONS

As the seasons change, you'll want to swap your wardrobe accordingly. Don't store soiled clothing. Time will make the stains harder to remove, and odors from dirty clothing can attract insects and suffuse other items stored with it.

If you place out-of-season clothing in boxes, label them carefully. When the snow starts to fall, you don't want to be forced to explore box after box of summer

---

QUICK FIX

LEGIBLE LABELS

When labeling boxes with descriptions of their contents, write on a side that's sure to be visible. Chances are this will be the narrow end, because boxed typically are stacked narrow end out. To cover contingencies, label two or more sides.

---

sundresses and beachwear to find your favorite sweater.

6 STORAGE SAFETY VALVES

When your closet and dressers become jammed, here are some solutions to make your bedroom livable again.

1. Buy a blanket chest. It's perfect, aptly enough, for storing blankets and other bed linens, but you can also use it for off-season clothing.

2. Put a row of coat hooks on the back of your bedroom door. Be careful to measure the space between the back of your door and whatever it comes up against when opened—you don't want a hook poking a hole in the wall.

3. A jewelry box isn't the only kind of box that can be useful in your bedroom. To help keep order, use a box for the things you empty from your pockets each night. For stylish storage, stack hatboxes or Shaker-style oval boxes. Craft stores sell plain wooden boxes that can be painted to match your decor. Or you can reuse wine crates, cracker tins, and the proverbial

7 Tips as You Resolve to Reorganize

New Year's resolutions are a good device for changing your behavior. They ritualize the effort, and rituals are a powerful social mechanism. Here are some tips to help you keep your resolutions about conquering clutter.

1. Be specific. Decide which rooms you'll declutter.

2. Be realistic. You may want to reduce your possessions to fit into a shoe box, but that won't happen, and failure will make you less inclined to follow through.

3. Put your resolutions on paper. This will make it seem more "legal," binding you to comply.

4. Tell friends. By announcing your resolutions, you'll be more likely to stick to them.

5. Motivate yourself by marking goals on your calendar. You might make February 1st as the day by which you'll have reordered the hall closet, for example, and March 1st as the day by which you'll prune your library of unwanted books.

6. Record your progress. Make a note on your calendar after you reorder that closet. If possible, concoct a measure to reflect your progress. You can keep a running total of the cash value of items you've donated to charity, or of the pounds of clutter you've tossed.

7. Beware of impatience. Remember, it took more than a few days to acquire your clutter, and it'll take more than a few days to get rid of it.

Serious Storage

Steel utility shelving can be used in a bedroom with modern décor, if you spray paint over its garage-gray enamel with a more agreeable color.

For a traditional bedroom, you can dress up steel shelving by hanging fabric panels over its sides and front. First dress up the top with a board that you've stained or painted a pleasing color. Choose a board that's 1 inch wider than the shelves, and cut it 2 inches longer than the shelves. To attach the board, use a power drill to drill a dozen $^{12}/_{64}$-inch holes along the edges of the shelves' top. You don't have to be precise about the hole locations—just space them so they run evenly around the top. Lay the board, top down, on the floor. Turn the shelves upside down and position them on the board so that 1 inch of the board will extend up the shelves' back. With a pencil, mark the board where the holes in the top of the shelves are.

Put aside the shelves, and drill ¼-inch-deep, 9.64-inch holes in the marked spots on the board. These holes will prevent splitting when you attach the board to the shelves. If you have trouble estimating depth, mark ¼ inch on your drill bit with masking tape. Attach the top board to the shelves using #10 ½-inch, sheet metal screws.

If you wish, you can attach 2 x 2-inch boards under the bottom edges of the utility shelves. Cut one board equal to the length of the shelves plus 1 ½ inches, and cut two boards equal to the length of the shelves. Drill holes through the bottom of the shelves' uprights, and attach the boards. Use the same depths and sizes of holes and screws as for the top board. Cut and hem fabric panels to a length that just reveals the bottom edge.

cigar box for clutter organization and storage.

4. Add shelves. Check your hardware store for decorative metal or wood shelf supports. You might look for reproductions of old-fashioned hardware that suits the period of your home. With a dozen supports and a few boards that you paint or stain, you can create an attractive set of shelves for a reasonable price.

5. A folding screen can block off a bookcase, a wheeled clothing rack, or a worktable. Try replacing the fabric in the screen with fabric matching your decor. If the screen has wood panels, you can decoupage them with artwork to suit your taste. Or you can decorate the panels with your own art.

6. Replace your nightstands with bookcases. You'll get more storage without losing a spot for your alarm clock. Unfinished bookcases are inexpensive, and you can stain or paint them to fit in with other furnishings.

STORAGE IN, UNDER, AND AROUND THE BED

You can add storage where it's the handiest with a bookcase headboard. Some headboards have built-in cupboards, and others even incorporate nightstands.

If you're inclined to shove stuff under the bed into the herds of dust bunnies that commonly dwell there, place your things in thin cardboard boxes sold for underbed storage. You even can buy wheeled, clear-lidded boxes made to slide easily in and out of this space.

Another way to make use of the space under a bed is to buy a platform bed that's equipped with deep drawers. Although the drawers are inconveniently low, they can be used to store items that you don't use frequently, such as off-season clothing and even sports equipment.

Ed chose to make his own platform bed. It doesn't have

drawers, but the mattress and box spring can be slid aside for access to seldom-used items. Ed constructed it of 2 x 10-inch boards for the four sides (see illustration). There's no bottom or top to the box; it sits on the floor and the box spring and mattress serve as the top. The planks are held together at each corner with two heavy-duty 8-inch shelf supports. Ed used 1-inch mending plates to secure the box spring to the platform, so that it won't slide around. (Mending plates, available at hardware stores, are small steel strips with holes drilled through them, devised to repair split wood.)

Return of an
Old Storage Classic

If you like silent movies, you've probably seen a hapless comic get fooled up into a Murphy bed. These beds swing up into a wall-mounted cabinet, freeing the bedroom for other uses. Recently, improved versions of the Murphy bed have become popular. They're great for a guest bedroom, where a

standard bed would pointlessly hog the room in between guests' visits. By folding up the bed, you can use the space as an office or family room. The new models feature mattresses and box springs that match standard beds in comfort and far exceed the lump mattresses typical of sofa beds.

To gain access to his underbed storage, Ed shoves the mattress off the box spring. He can then loosen the bottom screws on the mending plates, and remove the top screws. The metal strips swing down, and he can lift the box spring off the platform to reach the stuff stored inside. Since he uses the space inside to store books he seldom uses, this isn't a procedure he needs to go through often.

The result is a large storage area of about 25 cubic feet. The bed is about 26 inches high, 2 to 3 inches higher than a standard one. Ed could've used 8-inch-wide planks and produced a bed of ordinary height, but he preferred to have the extra storage space and a taller bed.

Ed made a simple headboard by securing a row of 2 x 2-inch

uprights to the box using 3-inch decking screws (he predrilled pilot holes), then topping it with a crosspiece. He stained the box and headboard before assembling them in his bedroom. (It's better not to do that messy job inside your living space. Stain is designed to stain, and you'll never get it out of your carpet if you slop some.) You can employ a carpenter to execute more elaborate designs.

6 WAYS TO STORE ITEMS IN FULL SIGHT

1. Knot your silk scarves around a spindle on your headboard.
2. Hang ties over a folding screen in a nice clutch color.
3. Thread your rings on a ribbon, then lay it across your bureau top.
4. Put hooks on the wall and dangle your necklace from them.
5. Love the pattern or hue of a particular piece of clothing? Hang it on a coatrack, in a prominent place that will please your eye.
6. Clothing with sentimental associations can be displayed on your walls in box frames. Your baby's first jumper, your bowling shirt from your tournament year, or that high school letter jacked that Bobby with the sparkling blue eyes gave you after the big game can make a nice wall display. Bobby may be unable to squeeze into that jacket now, but seeing you still think his gift is a treasure can keep the sparkle in his eyes.

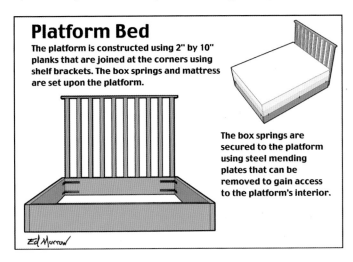

Platform Bed

The platform is constructed using 2" by 10" planks that are joined at the corners using shelf brackets. The box springs and mattress are set upon the platform.

The box springs are secured to the platform using steel mending plates that can be removed to gain access to the platform's interior.

Ed Morrow

The Lone Ranger and Tonto get the drop on the nefarious Bunkhouse Clutter Gang, with the help of the faithful Silver and the stalwart Scout.

Ed Morrow

NINE

Toward a Better Bathroom

"I have absolutely no intention of stepping into a shower. I take baths—only baths."

—Janet Leigh

Bathrooms have become more and more opulent, with elaborate shower arrangements, tubs with massaging jets, double sinks, wall-to-wall mirrors, telephones, heated towel racks, carpeting, marble counters, and televisions. Bathroom clutter has grown, too. Towels, cosmetics, and toiletries crowd shelves and counters. Dirty laundry accumulates here, and mounds of cleansers jam the cabinets. The aggravation produced by this varied clutter is compounded by the daily showering, shaving, and other routines that occur in this busy place.

In the bathroom, the prime hidey holes for clutter are the medicine cabinet and under the sink. Have a couple of cardboard boxes and some trash bags on hand. The boxes can help you sort and organize the clutter you plan to keep, while the bags can provide a repository for cast-off clutter.

A CURE FOR THE COMMON MEDICINE CABINET

"'Tis a sharp medicine, but it will cure all that ails you."

—Sir Walter Raleigh

Your medicine cabinet will no doubt contain lots of half-used cosmetics, ratty first-aid supplies, potions for various portions of your body, shaving supplies, and assorted medicines, both nonprescription and prescription. Of these, the last is the first to consider. It's unhealthful and potentially dangerous to accumulate old prescriptions.

It's tempting to save leftover prescriptions to use when you suffer complaints similar to those for which they were prescribed. Don't play doctor and self-medicate. You may misdiagnose your condition and actually make it worse. For the same reason, never share your medicines with others. Keeping leftover pills can also endanger children, who may tragically mistake medicine for candy. Even a small dose of a drug meant for an adult can have a catastrophic effect on a child.

Throw out old antiseptics, bandages, and other first-aid supplies. With use, exposure to your bathroom environment, and passage of time, these become unsanitary. Anything more than a year old is suspect.

Cosmetics also can become unsanitary, because of frequent exposure to dirty fingers and unclean implements. Dump them every 3 months. If you believe your medications and cosmetics have been exposed to bacteria, dump them sooner. If you've had an eye infection, for example, throw out all your facial cosmetics and their applicators. Cosmetic applicators are often overlooked as an avenue for infection. Replace applicators when you replace cosmetics. Never share cosmetics or applicators.

Many dentists recommend that you buy a new toothbrush every 3 months. Toothbrushes can become contaminated with bacteria, and worn bristles don't clean as well as perky new ones.

After you've culled all the suspect items from your medicine cabinet, scrub it, and then decide what to put back into it. Include only those things you use frequently. Don't place first-aid supplies here. It's better to set aside a special box for them. But you may want to post emergency first-aid instructions, such as how to perform the Heimlich maneuver and CPR, on the inside of the cabinet's door. Also post the phone numbers for your doctor and your local poison control center (the American Association of Poison Control Centers can be reached at 800-222-1222).

3 WAYS TO UPGRADE YOUR MEDICINE CABINET

1. If you have a tiny medicine cabinet, consider replacing it with a larger model to increase bathroom storage and make life a little easier. Newer models also include amenities such as a toothbrush rack and foldout mirror.

2. If your present cabinet is wall-mounted, not built-in, and doesn't incorporate a light or electrical outlet, replacing it is easy. You just take down the old and put up the new.

3. Replacing built-ins can be more involved. A simpler tactic is to place a larger wall-mounted

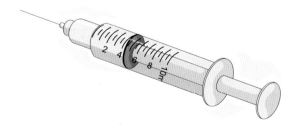

Assembling a First Class First-Aid Kit

Don't store serious first-aid materials in your medicine cabinet. You don't want to have to rummage through cold-cream jars and toothpaste while your thumb is dribbling blood. First-aid supplies should be stored together in a container in a spot that's both visible and easy to reach. After all, on *ER,* the doctors don't keep that defibrillator behind the candy machine in the doctor's lounge.

Resist the temptation to jam your first-aid kit with every Band-Aid and ointment you possess. Stick with a selection of the most commonly used and most important first-aid items, such as:

- Bandages of different sizes and types (include specialty bandages for fingers and knees)
- Sterile gauze pads
- Bottle of peroxide
- Antibiotic cream
- Scissors
- Tweezers
- Adhesive tape
- Petroleum jelly
- Safety pins
- Antibacterial soap or cleanser
- Nonmercury oral and anal thermometers (electronic versions are convenient to use but not always accurate; test them against a thermometer you trust befor adding them to your kit)
- Syrup of ipecac to induce vomiting (use this only when directed to do so by a doctor or poison control center)
- Pamphlet describing basic first-aid, including the Heimlich maneuver and CPR

cabinet over the hole of the old built-in unit. The wall-mounted cabinet will protrude from your wall, but this isn't much of a problem. Indeed, it can place the medicine cabinet mirror that much closer to your face when you're applying makeup or shaving.

To replace a built-in that has light fixtures or outlets, however, you'll need to work with your home's wiring, and that may mean calling on an electrician.

If replacing your medicine cabinet seems too much of a task, it may be simpler to add a second cabinet or install a set of shelves on another wall of the bathroom.

NONEMERGENCY MEDICAL SUPPLIES

Although the medicine cabinet isn't the best place to keep emergency supplies, you can use it for most medicines. This would include headache remedies, allergy pills, and stomach remedies. The prescriptions you're currently using are also good candidates. But with all medicines, take precautions to

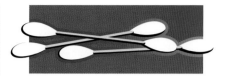

keep them away from children. Even if you have no kids, friends may visit with theirs. Don't rely on childproof bottles or childproof door catches. Use a lockbox for your dangerous pills, or place a lock on the medicine cabinet. Keep the key on the ring with your car keys, so you'll be unlikely to lose it.

4 WAYS TO PERFORM COSMETICS SURGERY

"... [A]ll women, of whatever age, rank, profession, or degree; whether virgin maids or widows; that shall after the passing of this act, impose upon and betray into matrimony any of His Majesty's male subjects, by scents, paints, cosmetics, washes, artificial teeth, false hair, Spanish wool, iron stays, hoops, high-heeled shoes, or bolstered hips, shall incur the penalty of the laws now in force against witchcraft, sorcery, and such like misdemeanors, and that the marriage, upon conviction, shall stand null and void."

—Act of British Parliament

1. Most households keep far too many cosmetics to be stored in the medicine cabinet. The bathroom will run more efficiently if they're stored in a cosmetics bag or case.

2. Most masculine cosmetic clutter has to do with shaving or hair care. Ironically, the traditional shaving kit isn't the best place for shaving gear. Wet and soapy items can't dry properly in it. To store a damp razor, use an old coffee mug with a bit of sponge cut to fit in the bottom. Store the razor with the blade up to help keep the edge dry and sharp. Wipe off the bottom of the shaving cream can before shelving, or it may leave a rust ring.

3. You can install hanging racks in the shower to hold shampoo and soap.

4. If you still need more storage space, consider using a plastic carryall with a handle. You can fill it with shampoos and conditioners, and then place it under your sink. Even an ordinary plastic bucket will serve to store these products in one spot.

3 WAYS TO ORGANIZE BELOW THE BATHROOM SINK

The bathroom's undersink area is a rough neighborhood where miscellaneous bathroom junk tends to hang out. This includes both items used in personal hygiene and products used to clean the bathroom. A plunger may lurk under a pile of toilet tissue, which itself is mixed in with shampoo and tile cleaner.

1. Use one carryall for personal products and another (of a different shape or color) for bathroom cleansers.

2. Before organizing the cleansers, review them for duplication.

Limit cleaning products to those that are used in your bathroom only. Keep in mind that a leak in the plumbing can soak anything stored under the sink.

3. If you're fortunate, you have drawers in your sink cabinet. Bathroom drawers benefit from being divided into compartments, because they're apt to harbor many tiny items that otherwise roll about. Commercial drawer dividers are available at home furnishings stores or office supply stores, or you can make your own using cutdown cardboard boxes.

WHEN COUNTER SPACE IS PRECIOUS

The counter space surrounding the bathroom sink is valuable real estate. Many items could be advantageously positioned here, but there isn't room for all of them. Restrict this space to things you use often or that can't be stowed elsewhere. Most notably, these will include appliances that need to be plugged into the outlets by your counter. An electric toothbrush, for example, will need counter space for its recharger. Keep electrical cords away from water, and make sure each of your bath outlets is equipped with a ground fault interrupter (GFI) to protect you from shocks.

Keep your bathroom counter as clean as possible. It's remarkable how this relatively small space, if it's well ordered, can lift your mood when you visit each morning to brush your teeth or powder your cheeks.

EASY DOES IT

Is Your Hamper a Mold Nursery?

Choose a bathroom laundry hamper that's well ventilated. Wet bath towels end up here, and they'll generate mold if air can't circulate. You also want to choose a hamper that can be thoroughly and easily cleaned. Plastic models are best, while wicked hampers tend to deteriorate when exposed to dampness.

10 WAYS TO STORE MORE

The more storage space you can make available in your bathroom,

the easier it will be to control clutter. Here are several ways to make the most of this room's options.

1. Install two or three towel racks, one over the other, so that you don't have to cram towels into your linen closet.

2. Install a sturdy wooden strip of pegs or hooks across a wall of your bathroom, anchoring it in the wall's studs. You can hang towels, bathrobes, and other clothing here. Clutter that isn't obviously "hangable," such as soaps, shampoo, and washcloths, can be placed in hangable baskets or net bags.

3. If there's space for it, equip the bathroom with a low chest topped by a cushion. The chest provides storage, and the seat is welcome when dressing. Be sure to choose a cushion that will stand up to moisture and that can be easily cleaned.

4. While using the bathroom, many people add to their education with a little light reading. A conventional magazine rack would take up valuable floor space and impede cleaning. Consider adding a wall-mounted rack.

5. Use liquid soap instead of bar soap. It looks better than a gummed-up soap dish bearing broken, shrunken bars of soap.

6. To declutter the shower, mount dispensers on the wall for soap, shampoo, and conditioner. There'll be no need to juggle slippery containers with the risk of dropping one on your bare toes.

7. Hang a shelf over the bathroom window, and suspend your window treatment from it. A shelf can also be set over the mirror. Although high shelves aren't ideal for items you use often, they're a good home for those soothing bath salts you indulge in four times a year after your boss does your quarterly performance review. To keep items from falling

from these shelves, add a strip of wood as a railing.

8. Some bathroom storage gizmos are secured with suction cups. You might think this would be enough—after all, don't cat burglars use suction cups to scale skyscrapers in old movies? In fact, you need something stronger. Adhesive-backed hooks will do a better job of suspending razors, wash-cloths, and other light bath-room accessories. And when in doubt, secure items with screws driven into studs.

9. The wall over the toilet may look like a good spot to place shelves or a cabinet. But objects stored here have a way

of falling into the bowl. If you miss the splash and the object gets flushed, a large plumber's bill can result.

10. If you have a pedestal or wall-mounted sink that's outdated or worn, think about replacing it with a sink set in a cabinet offering cupboard and drawer space. For an old-timey look, you can cut a hole in the top of a dresser and drop a sink into it. Some of its drawers will have to be fastened shut because of the location of the sink and pipes, but others should be operable.

6 STEPS TO POLISHING YOUR POWDER ROOM

In the bathroom, the dust and grime that soil other rooms

is compounded by soap scum and mold that creeps across your tiles. Mineral deposits crust up your faucets. Rust stains mar your sink. Stray hairs litter your floor. In short, there are a lot of cleaning jobs to do in a bathroom, and these tips may come in handy.

1. Hair can be easily cleaned up with a fistful of slightly damp bathroom tissue. Alternatively, you can use your vacuum cleaner.

2. Those shower spray cleansers that claim to ward off soap scum on shower doors actually work. A shower squeegee also will do the trick.

3. Kitchen countertop polish will shine a bathroom counter, too.

4. A "swab" toilet bowl brush with a ball of rayon fabric works best. Push it into the bowl to force the water down the toilet's throat. This will lower the bowl's water level so that the water line, where a ring is apt to form, is accessible to cleanser. Soak the brush with cleanser and wipe it around the inside of the bowl. Let the cleanser work for a few minutes, then scrub and flush. Repeat if necessary.

5. Removing bad stains in a sink, tub, or toilet can require strong chemicals. A hardware store may be able to recommend high-powered products, but these should be used only

Ammonia and Bleach Don't Mix

Ammonia and bleach are valuable allies in household cleaning tasks, but they should never be used in combination—or even be stored near each other. When they combine, they can release a deadly poisonous gas.

with care. Wear eye protection and long, thick rubber gloves. Common kitchen gloves can't be relied on to protect you against powerful potions. Familiarize yourself with warning labels before using cleaning products.

6. *Never* skimp on ventilation while cleaning your bathroom with cleaning concoctions. Open a window, leave the door open, and turn on the bathroom exhaust fan. Bathrooms are small spaces that can quickly fill up with chemical fumes.

GET WITH THE PLAN

As with any part of your home, the bathroom will be a more pleasant, less cluttered space if you devise a schedule of cleaning and maintenance activities.

7 DAILY BATHROOM DUTIES

Every day, tidy up after performing your daily cleaning and cosmetic rituals.

QUICK FIX

MAKE YOUR OWN NONTOXIC TUB AND TILE CLEANER

The Chittenden Solid Waste District, which services the area around Burlington, Vermont, provides its patrons with this recipe for a nontoxic household tub and tile cleaner.

1 2/3 cups baking soda

1/2 cup liquid soap

2 tablespoons vinegar

1/2 cup water (add more if you want a more liquid cleaner)

A few drops of an essential oil of your choice for aroma (optional)

Mix the baking soda and soap. Add the vinegar and water, then the oil if using. Store in a bottle and shake before using. Rinse after use to remove residue.

1. Put the cap on the toothpaste.
2. Store your hairbrush in a drawer or hang it.
3. Put your cosmetics or shaving materials away.
4. Return towels to their rack or, if they're soiled, toss them in the hamper.
5. Wipe up any water that has splattered on the bathroom counter or mirror.
6. In the shower, use one of the after-shower spray products that reduce soap scum or use the recipe provided.
7. As you use your toiletries and other items, consider casting out any products that haven't earned their place in the bathroom. Can one product do the duty of two?

7 WEEKLY BATHROOM CLEANING DUTIES

1. Clean the bathroom counter.
2. Sweep and mop the floor.
3. Restock towels.
4. Give the bathroom mirror a good polishing.
5. Give the toilet a scrub.
6. Choose a shelf or drawer, and rid it of unnecessary clutter.

7. Return all items to their place.

3 MONTHLY SCRUB-DOWN DUTIES

1. Every month, do a complete scrub-down of your bathroom—the counter, tile, floor, toilet, tub, and/or shower.
2. Spray the shower curtain with a mold-removing cleanser. Don't waste time cleaning a badly stained curtain liner. You can purchase a replacement at a dollar store for less than the cost of the cleansers you'd use.
3. Clean your shower doors with a strong cleanser once a month. Give the cleaner a moment to work, then use a scrub brush. The bristles will help loosen

hard-to-remove scum. Wash off the cleanser with soap and water, then squeegee the glass. Use a towel to wipe away any remaining water.

STAYING ON TOP OF THE TASK

Bathroom disorder can rapidly develop, becoming more difficult to tidy. But if you follow the routines described above, you'll be able to stay ahead of the clutter and mess generated by frequent use of your bathroom. Your efforts will be rewarded with a place where you can prepare for the day—and repair the damages from the day—with grace and ease.

TEN

Kid Clutter

"I'm going to clean this dump—just as soon as the kids are grown."

—**Erma Bombeck**

Children can turn a clean, clutter-free home into a disaster area faster than a Kansas tornado can chew up a trailer park and spit the masticated pieces into Colorado, Missouri, Nebraska, and Arkansas. The problem is compounded by the fact that the average child's room is jammed to the ceiling with toys and electronics that are anxiously waiting to escape and colonize every room in your house.

Part of the challenge of kid clutter is modern childhood itself. Children lead hectic little lives, jammed with schoolwork, sports, and other activities. Too often, parents are also overextended and have

little time to teach their children good habits. Indeed, parents tend to be bad examples, surrounding themselves in clutter of their own making. In some cases, parents even worsen their children's clutter by indulging childish whims.

CHORES ARE A FACT OF LIFE

Young children must be taught to clean up after themselves. Left to his own devices, whenever a kid loses interest in an object, he'll drop it on the spot, whether that spot is the middle of his room, your lap, the toilet, or at the top of the stairs where, one night as you go for a glass of warm milk, it will cause you to pitch down to a cartoonish doom.

Fortunately, there are ways to help kids manage their messes. Turn cleaning into a family game. For toddlers, place laundry baskets wherever they play, and put their toys in them. When they finish with a toy and are about to take another, require them to return the first toy to the basket and praise them for completing this task. Eventually, they'll learn that the basket is the proper place to store toys. You can do the same with

clothing. Later, you can move on from baskets to shelves, a bureau, and a closet.

When your children have outgrown the pleasant, imitative stage, a second motivation comes into play—crass rewards in the form of allowances and privileges. Make a checklist of chores that your children must complete. Photocopy it so children can have a fresh copy each week for checking off jobs. Children who can't read yet can be given a list of pictures associated with cleaning—a shirt for putting away clothing, a toy bear for putting away toys, and so on.

If your children skip tasks, reduce their rewards. If they want larger rewards, add tasks. You can give them a small lesson in business practices by having them "bid" to do certain jobs. You may even get a little price war going if you have more than one child, with the kids trying to underbid each other for a task.

Don't overdo this, or you can fuel sibling rivalry. Good relations between your children are more important than a tidy house. You can foster positive interaction

LABEL IT

To remind a young child of what each bureau drawer is meant to contain, label the drawer front with a picture of its contents—a sock, for example, for the sock drawer. Once your child starts learning to read, remember to add the name of each project.

by assigning chores that require siblings to cooperate. It's surprising how the goal of earning some cash can get children to set aside their differences and scheme together.

FOSTERING COOPERATION

Chores can help build positive family feelings. As mentioned earlier, Ed grew up on a dairy farm in Vermont with lots of chores, many of which required coopera-

tion. Some of his best childhood memories are of haying, picking berries, and fetching the cows home with other family members. Working together provided a good chance to talk and joke. His folks always made it seem that his efforts were helpful, even if he didn't manage to clear the field of every stray bit of hay, or if he ate more than a few of the berries before they got to the pie, or if the cows took the scenic route home. Like Ed's parents, you may also have to settle for less than perfection. Building good habits is more important than having chores executed with four-star results.

Point out mistakes gently, and give your children a chance to rectify their work. Don't set things right yourself—that's the harshest form of criticism. If your child is trying but having trouble completing a chore well, work through the task with him, show him how to improve his work, and be a coach—not a critical boss. If your children are deliberately failing or sloppily performing their chores, take the tasks away from them and reduce their allowance or limit privileges.

6 WAYS TO ENCOURAGE YOUR KIDS TO DECLUTTER

1. Assign chores to your children.
2. Set your expectations to match their capabilities.
3. Reward any good-faith efforts.
4. Give gentle guidance to improve performance.
5. Don't step in to do the task yourself.
6. Penalize slacking off.

Nature designs children to be experts at pushing all of a parent's buttons. Like the baby bird whose chirping sends the parent birds searching for worms all day long, your children instinctively know how to get what they want from you. Whining, pouting, yelling, and throwing tantrums are their ways of chirping to get the worms they hanker after: nutrition-free breakfast cereals, CDs featuring singers who display pierced navels, and hair care products intended to produce hair that looks uncared for.

It can be difficult working out effective ways to encourage diligent chore-doing, but it's a lot easier than living with bad behavior that may spill over into other parts of a child's life. Chores foster a sense of accomplishment and teach responsibility while helping to establish you as the authority figure in your home.

8 TASKS FOR OLDER CHILDREN

As children get older, expand their chores to include tasks they'll have to handle when they eventually go out on their own. Children—both boys and girls— should learn how to:

1. Fix meals.
2. Wash dishes.
3. Do laundry.
4. Make beds.
5. Put away toys and belongings.
6. Clean the house.
7. Do yard work.
8. Care for younger siblings.

12 WAYS TO TAME A CHILD'S ROOM

1. A set of coat hooks at a child-appropriate height can help children put away coats, book bags, hats, and other hangable kid clutter. A net laundry bag will encourage them to hang up toys, shoes, small objects, or even laundry.

2. Open shelves provide lots of easily accessible storage space that kids are likely to use. Make sure that shelves are securely attached to wall studs, so they won't collapse under heavy or uneven loads. Children, like little monkeys, are apt to climb, so shelves shouldn't be set too high on the wall.

3. Storage chests are a staple of kid's room storage. They can conceal a lot of mess. Falling lids, however, have injured more than a few children. Be sure to equip chests with safety lid supports. Also, to prevent suffocation, chests shouldn't be airtight. If you suspect a chest is airtight, drill holes in it for ventilation. Nor should chests be lockable at the risk of trapping a child inside. Imagine the nightmares that could foster.

4. Plastic tubs make good storage containers for children's clutter. They're capacious and can be easily cleaned. Large tubs with latching lids are particu-

Bye-Bye Baby Clothing

Babies grow so quickly that they often outgrow their clothing before it gets much wear. Parents wind up with dressers full of cute outfits that look brand new. Some used-clothing stores specialize in infant clothing and will buy baby's out-grown clothes or take them on consignment. There's a large supply of used baby clothing, however, and you may get little for yours. Clothing that's stained or mended won't be accepted, no matter how serviceable it may be. As an alternative, think about giving children's clothing to churches, women's shelters, and crisis pregnancy centers.

larly practical. Clear plastic storage boxes allow your child to see what's inside, without opening them and tossing the contents on the floor. Plastic milk crates and laundry baskets are handy for storing larger items, but their holes make them inadequate for dealing with toys that have small parts. To store small items such as

crayons or blocks, use plastic dishpans.

5. Bookcases encourage children to develop the habit of organizing their literature—and reading. Use only sturdy cases, and attach them to the wall so they can't be pulled over.

6. Board games are awkward to store. Their boxes are long, and they often have small parts that are easy to lose. Put all of a game's pieces in a sealable sandwich bag, keep the bag in the game box, and make sure the box won't fly open by placing an elastic band around it.

7. Art supplies can also be awkward to store. Paints are messy, and pencils and crayons tend to become scattered everywhere. A plastic toolbox,

with its various compartments, will help you organize art supplies and also will contain spills. The handle will make it easy for your children to carry about their supplies whenever and wherever the muse strikes them.

8. Children's closets can become black holes of toys, clothing, and sporting goods. To make it easier for your children to keep their closets orderly, lower the clothes rod so they can hang up their things. Install shelves below the hanging clothes for shoes or toys, and higher shelves to store objects that your children seldom use. These things should be light—spare blankets, extra pillows, winter coats, snow pants, sweaters— lest they fall and cause injury.

9. Periodically review your children's wardrobe to cull outgrown clothing. If it's in good shape, you can sell it via a children's used-clothing store, set it out at your next yard sale, or donate it to charity.

10. Keep hampers in your children's rooms to make it easy for them to put away dirty

clothing. And don't forget to empty them. The average child will just keep piling clothing into a hamper till it's full, then pile more laundry on top of it till the heap reaches the ceiling.

11. Children should have a specific area in which to do their homework. A small desk with lots of drawers is a good choice. If it doesn't have a drawer large enough for files, buy a plastic file box for storing papers. Set up a hanging folder system and show your children how to file their work. If they learn good organizing techniques at an early age, they'll have an edge later in life.

12. Your children's beds can also provide storage possibilities. Bunk beds, of course, store two sleeping kids in the space of one. A trundle bed opens to accommodate sleep-over pals. There are beds for kids that contain storage drawers in their base. You even can buy an elevated bed, similar to a bunk bed, except that instead of a lower bunk, there's a desk

Policy of Containment

Kids' clutter has a way of spreading throughout the house. Comics wind up in the dining room, a sweatshirt will appear hanging from  a doorknob, and shoes clog the hall closet. This disorder comes at a price, turning Mom and Dad into unwilling custodians of their children's junk. When something gets lost, guess who'll be called on to help? So, when kids leave their things in other rooms, insist they gather them up. Young people need to learn that their possessions are their responsibility.

and possibly bookshelves, cupboards, or a storage chest.

TOY MANAGEMENT

"I knew I was an unwanted baby when I saw that my bath toys were a toaster and a radio."

—Joan Rivers

Most kids simply don't have the time or the interest to play with all of their toys. By encouraging children to give away unused toys, you'll make it easier for them to keep their rooms tidy. Seldom-used things can be boxed up and stored in the closet. In a month or two, pull out the box and ask if the toys really are worth holding onto. The

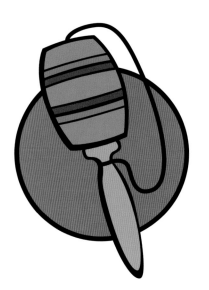

result should be that fewer toys are heaped about your home.

PLAYROOMS

If you're fortunate enough to have a playroom in your home, you can diffuse some of your kids' clutter problem by relegating many

Chalking It Up

Young children love to draw on the walls with crayons and markers. To spare your walls, attach a blackboard at a convenient height. The kids can then doodle with chalk to their heart's content. You can make your own blackboard using hardboard (such as Masonite). You can even extend the chalk-drawing surface all around the room, like wainscoting. Cut the board to wainscoting height, and roll on special-purpose blackboard paint in black or green. Place the lower edge atop the room's baseboard, and attach the blackboard by running screws through pilot holes into the wall's studs. Run molding along the top edge to give the blackboard a finished look.

of their toys here. Don't overburden your playroom, however. The great benefit of a playroom is that it provides your children with space to run about inside your home. If it's choked with toys, romping around becomes impossible.

Storage chests lend themselves to a playroom. In addition to containing toys, they can be used as low tables, or with a cushion as seating. Also consider adding a table for board games, arts and crafts, and homework. A comfortable sofa and chairs will make this a pleasant lounging place, like a second living room of their own. Small children will be happy just flopping on the floor, and you

A Playroom on Wheels

To help preserve the open space that allows kids to really play in a playroom, look for furniture on wheels, or to which wheels or casters can be added. This allows you (or the kids) to roll away chairs, tables, and chests to make way for activities that require room to move.

might want to bring in beanbag chairs and extra-large pillows. If there will be a television in the playroom, you can place it in an appropriately sized armoire. Close the doors, and the TV screen will be protected from airborne toys.

GET YOUR KIDS INVOLVED

Don't be a decluttering martyr. Teach your children to follow a daily bedroom cleaning and organizing plan. Don't step in and perform tasks that they fail to do. Once you start, they'll happily delegate cleaning up their messes to you. You'll become their personal valet or maid—and they're unlikely to be sympathetic employers.

Children like to be involved in adult-level decision making. As you experiment with storage ideas and cleaning techniques, ask your kids to help you evaluate them. They may have ideas of their own on how to organize their possessions—or some objections to your arrangements.

Ed's friend Joan put up a cute coat rack decorated with animals for her daughter to hang her backpack and jacket on after school. The young girl wouldn't use it, dumping her things beneath it. When Joan asked why, it turned out that a neighbor's snarling dog had frightened the girl, and one of the animals painted on the coat-rack was a dog that looked like the unfriendly animal. Joan repainted the rack with ducks because the little girl loved to feed the ducks in a nearby park. The tactic worked, and the girl's backpack and jacket were seldom left sitting about.

6-CHORE DAILY CHECKLIST

In addition to hanging up the day's vestments, there are other small but significant chores to put on your children's list of daily jobs.
1. Keep toothbrushes in their holder, put away toothpaste, and return towels to their rack.
2. Stow dirty clothing in the hamper.
3. Put away toys.
4. Scout the house for things that belong in the bedroom.
5. Make beds.
6. Clean up trash.

The tasks you assign a child will vary according to his or her age, of course. Older children should be entrusted with jobs that are in line with their interests and capabilities.

As soon as possible, include duties beyond those that are centered just on the children themselves. Such tasks might begin with bringing in the mail, sweeping the porch, and setting the table. Gradually introduce jobs that will involve their emerging abilities.

BE A MODEL DECLUTTERER

Children learn most readily by example. Unfortunately, bad examples are often far more influential than good ones. You must strive to be faultless in your household management if you want your children to learn good habits. Otherwise they'll seize upon any missteps you make as justification for their misbehavior. Kids have a very legalistic view of family life, and they're quick to invoke the charge, "That's not fair!" You're apt to hear this message if you ask your children to do chores you don't carry out yourself. If you expect them to be tidy, you too need to be tidy.

5 THINGS TO REMEMBER WHEN DONATING

It's important to teach your children that charitable donations should be clean and in good condition. Workers at charities relate horror stories of donors dropping off dirty laundry, three-legged chairs, pet-stained sofas, and toys that even Santa's elves couldn't repair on overtime. Here are several things to consider when donating toys.

1. Run dishwasher-safe toys through your dishwasher. Other toys can be cleaned in the sink with dishwashing soap and baking soda. Don't use cleansers that might sicken children if they mouth the toy.

2. Wash doll clothing by hand in cold water with a cold-water detergent to prevent it from tearing or shrinking.

3. Check toys for pieces that might come loose and choke a child.

4. Inexpert repairs can be dangerous. Unless, for example, you're a good bicycle mechanic, don't attempt to fix a broken bike. Your repair may be faulty. If a charity accepts a broken but repairable item, attach a label that details the problems so that they won't go unfixed.

5. Don't be tempted to give away toys with missing pieces. How would you like to assemble a 300-piece jigsaw puzzle that has only 299 pieces?

TIDY TEENAGERS?

Decluttering gets complicated when your child hits adolescence. Teenagers are at a stage in life when they begin accumulating larger stocks of clothing and more elaborate devices of amusement. A circus-scene-painted dresser won't suffice for a teenager's wardrobe,

and an old toy box won't contain their electronics, CD collection, and video games. Along with this increase in stuff, there's often a shift in your child's attitudes. The sunny child who wanted mommy and daddy to look at every pebble in her rock collection now gets furious if you glance into her room as you walk by.

KEEP YOUR HANDS OFF TEEN CLUTTER

As for keeping a teenager's room tidy, don't bother. Teenagers are old enough to make their own cleaning decisions and live with the results. The bottom line is, you'll be walking into a lion's den in a steak suit if you enter a teen's room with a vacuum cleaner.

Let them assume responsibility for their rooms. If they can't find an item, it's their fault. If their dirty clothing piles up, they're the ones who will have to scrounge up something clean. If they're not embarrassed to have friends see their mess, why should you be? Don't be tempted to tidy for them. Let them have their rooms just the way they like them—and keep their doors shut when you have guests.

While you can allow your teens the run of their rooms, don't let them treat the rest of your house the same way. Be vigilant to thwart any spread of teen clutter, and demand that they keep their things in their rooms. Fortunately, the parent of a teenager has a few sticks and carrots with which to encourage neatness: expensive items of clothing or electronics, money for dating, permission to spend time with friends, and most important, your car keys.

OFF TO THE REAL WORLD

In the fullness of time, your children will leave your nest. How do you go about making good use of their vacated bedrooms without offending them?

Many kids will want you to keep their rooms unchanged. It's comforting for them to know their old rooms are waiting for them. For you, on the other hand, dedicating a room to a museum of your offspring's childhood may be a rather large burden. A good compromise is to convert this space into a guest room. It will be available to your visiting child, while serving a new, practical function—and give you the opportunity to pack up his or her excess stuff.

When you box up the possessions of children who have left home, you can explain to them that you're operating with a museum curator's concern for preserving their relics. After all, there's a risk some house guest might inadvertently smash the model of Han Solo's Malibu beach house that your child spent days gluing together. If possible, review the room with your child to see just what he or she would like to have you store. A little give-and-take and mature discussion might be all that's needed to persuade your daughter that she won't need her size 4 figure skates, now that her feet are size 9.

Once you've determined what's to be saved, place the items in clearly marked boxes. As the years go by, feel free to periodically remind your children that these treasures are waiting in the attic for them. When you drop by their homes, bring along a box. It'll make a great conversation starter.

To reassure your departing children that they'll remain in your heart even though you're pruning their possessions, keep out a few items as decorations in your guest room—perhaps a piece of their early artwork, nicely framed. The picture may be crude and done entirely in purple Crayola, but it will help both of you recall those youthful days when purple grass and purple trees under a smiling purple sun were perfectly sensible.

ELEVEN

A Lean and Efficient Home Office

"…The person who works with a messy desk spends, on average, one-and-a-half hours per day looking for things or being distracted by things. That's seven-and-a-half hours per week. . . . Like a leaky hot water faucet, drip, drip, drip, it doesn't seem like a major loss, but at the end of the day, we're dumping gallons of hot water down the drain."

—**Dr. Donald Wetmore**

Yᴏu may be the leading expert in your field, but if your client finds you sitting in an office that looks like a drunken magpie's nest, you'll be viewed as unprofessional and possibly incompetent. A person who can't manage to keep his or her workplace organized and efficient may

not be trusted with the affairs of those who want their business handled in an organized and efficient way.

As this book deals with cutting clutter from your home, we'll address your home workplace, but many of the ideas presented here can be carried over to any office.

CLUTTER AND THE HOME OFFICE

Once upon a time, only a few wealthy folks had home offices. The average plutocrat, for example, would command his enterprises from an oak-lined study, featuring a desk the size of a water buffalo that was slavishly tended by an earnest male secretary with horn-rimmed glasses and a hairstyle parted down the middle. A chattering stock ticker and a candlestick

telephone were the only communication links needed. Today, nearly everyone from homemakers to homebuilders sets aside space at home to do business. According to CNN, half of American homes have home offices.

Setting up and maintaining an efficient, clutter-free office is a challenge. This room often winds up being a catchall for anything that won't fit elsewhere in the home. Maybe you have to find a spot to park an exercise bike. Or you need a place to stack old magazines. If there's a closet in your home office, off-season coats may take up the space better used for office supplies.

Then there's the clutter generated by the work itself. Work clutter is a tough problem for pack rats. Thinking "I'll need it for work" is compelling justification for acquiring and saving. You need pens to write, so you store them away like a squirrel preparing for a Minnesota winter. You need information to guide your work, so you stuff your filing cabinet with reports and journals. You need business receipts to back up your tax returns, so you fill a dozen shoe boxes with little bits of paper from the last two decades. Clutter is compounded by bad work habits that develop when working in an informal setting.

At home, there's no frowning boss if you don't clear your desk by 5 o'clock. No coworkers are on hand to complain if you mistakenly file the Abercrombie account under Z. Instead, you're pestered with domestic distractions. The dog needs in. The cat needs out. The paperboy wants his money. You shove aside your work, deal with the interruption, and then when you return, discover your kids have spread their homework atop your desk or that your spouse has hijacked your computer to check his e-mail.

Human nature is another source of festering clutter. Rushing to make a deadline, you may not bother to properly handle your documents, mixing new paperwork with unrelated items. A book laid on a table becomes a pyramid of books, with the buried volumes as mysterious as the mummified contents of a real, unopened pyramid. On your computer, you make a folder for your current project with a hurriedly created name. Inside are files with similarly smacked-on names. There's "Temp" this, "Junk" that, and the cryptic "Old Stuff." Work done while under duress is apt to foster sloppy shortcuts that are hard to correct, while work done with flexible deadlines, as Parkinson's Law states, expands to fill the time available for its completion. Shortcuts and too much flexibility encourage the generation of clutter, just as fast food and lack of self-discipline add inches to your waistline.

Circumstances can further compound home office clutter. You may have little space in your apartment for a home office and be forced to place it in a room that serves an unrelated function. If you use the kitchen table for a desk, flying grease from your morning bacon might ruin your carefully crafted sales report. And your office supplies might get mixed up with your kitchen supplies. Who wants to find paper clips in the sugar bowl?

The result of all these bad influ-ences, bad habits, and bad circum-stances is that your home office is likely a cluttered mess.

REVIEWING DOCUMENTS

The key to an efficient home office is to process informa-tion promptly, in as few steps as possible. If you delay, items pile up and are apt to be lost. You wind up handling the same documents over

and over. It helps to prioritize the kinds of documents you're exam-ining.

Financial Records for the Computer Age

Financial record-keeping pro-grams, such as Quicken, are very useful for tracking household finances. They're particularly good for categorizing expenses, which can be handy at tax time. Since the programs store informa-tion electronically, they can help reduce financial record clutter. It's important, however, to back up any electronic information you store. Some records are also too important to entrust solely to elec-tronic storage, and the originals must be kept.

4 STEPS TO RATIONAL FILING

Your home filing cabinets are apt to become a tangle of docu-ments, some old, some new, some needed, and many unneeded. Into

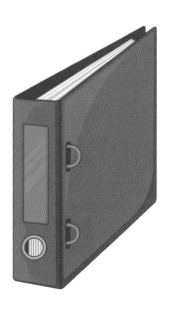

this paper jungle, important documents can disappear like frightened lizards. You may try to deal with this by overcompensating—devising intricate, multilevel file structures with color-coded folders and elaborate indexes. But this only tends to strangle you in your

A Sticky Situation

Sticky notes are wonderful little devices for writing quick notes that you can stick all over your computer, your desk, your walls, and anything else that holds still. They stay there, little yellow signals calling for your attention but easily ignored. Eventually they lose their stickiness and flutter down like aspen leaves in autumn. All too often, we use stickies as a way to convince ourselves that we took action, when we really just put it off.

Use sticky notes only to keep tack of things you'll need to refer to in the *immediate* future. Long-term information should be notes instead on a calendar or tucked into a file.

own system, so that you give up. A simple structure is better for those who don't have a tidy bent.

Here's a simple filing system that Ann, a schoolteacher friend of Sheree's, uses to handle the paperwork in her home office. She devotes the four drawers of her filing cabinet to specific purposes. If you're more inclined to have everything on your computer, you can use similar folder names and file the documents electronically.

1. In "Current Work," Ann keeps copies of her class rolls, grade records, homework assignments, tests, graded work, and current lecture notes. She also uses this drawer to file correspondence, receipts for tax-deductible purchases, insurance records, and other employment-related items for this year.

2. The "Old Lectures" drawer contains past material, which Ann uses to prepare new lectures.

3. In "Background Notes," Ann collects information to use in her classes. For example, she stores her professional journals in this drawer in reverse chron-

ological order. Later, in her few spare moments, she reviews the publications and discards unneeded items.

4. The "Old Work" drawer contains past assignments, tests, grade records, tax returns, employment information, correspondence, and other older items related to her job that she's unlikely to use to produce new work.

Note how Ann designed her filing system to correspond to her job. It organizes the papers she needs in a way that makes them easy for her to use. This works much better than trying to impose some theoretical model out of a business administration textbook.

LABELING IS WORTH THE BOTHER

When filing, either electronically or with hard copies, you'll run across items that don't seem to fall easily under any particular category. You may be tempted to shove these in a folder labeled "Miscellaneous." But it's unlikely you'll remember just what's inside that folder. You might as well stuff your files in a sack and toss it into

---

QUICK FIX

FOLDERS FOR THE SMALL STUFF

Small documents such as receipts can easily slip out of conventional files. Use folders with closed sides or pockets to prevent items from getting lost.

---

the cellar. Take time to compose folder labels that accurately identify their contents. If necessary, use subcategories and sub-subcategories. Don't be afraid to have lots of folders with just one or two items inside each. Being able to find information is worth the cost of a few extra folders.

WEEDING OUT YOUR FILES

If your filing cabinet is stuffed, purge before buying another cabinet. Useless files make it frustrating to find what you're after, so be "throw-out minded." Begin with the oldest files. Subject them to the tough questions listed in "Reviewing Documents."

After reviewing your files, you may still have too much paper in

your filing cabinet. Files that are seldom used but too important to throw out can be archived in a box kept in your attic, at a rental facility, or in another dry, vermin-free place. There's no point storing files that will be ruined. List the contents on the box. Don't spare details. A few extra words can

9 Reasons to Hold onto Old Records

Old records eat up storage space, but you may not want to toss out something a steely-eyed agent from the Internal Revenue Service could demand in the future. Fortunately, there are limits on IRS scrutiny, including a 3-year statute of limitations on IRS audits starting on April 15 of the year you filed, or on the date of an extension. (There are different limits on tax payments made after filing a return.) If you substantially underpaid your taxes, by at least 25 percent, the statute is extended to 6 years. There is no statute of limitations on fraudulently filed tax returns.

So what does this mean for your records?

1. If you're an ordinary taxpayer with an employer and little self-employment income, keeping your tax records for 3 years should be enough. If you file a more complex tax records for 3 years should

be enough. If you file a more complex tax return or are self-employed, 6 years should suffice. Cautious tax experts recommend holding onto all tax records for 7 years. If you think you may have underpaid or suspect you may be subject to an audit, keep your records indefinitely. The IRS may continue to be curious about you.

2. Because of the stiff penalties involved if you owe taxes, and because of the impossibility of re-creating some records, you may decide to save records longer than suggested here. If you have room, keep your tax documents indefinitely. It's a cheap way to soothe your jitters.

3. Many nontax records should also be kept. Documents associated with a real estate purchase or sale should be kept indefinitely. A house sale can generate a substantial capital gains tax. This can be reduced by carefully recording all your expenditures made to improve (but not maintain) the home. Keep receipts for all home improvements indefinitely, as proof that the improvements were made. When you sell your house 20 years from now, your capital gains may be lowered significantly.

4. Legal documents associated with any court case (including a divorce) should be kept indefinitely. You can replace marriage and death certificates, but save yourself the trouble by never throwing them away. Insurance records should be kept indefinitely, too. If you're sued for some past injury, you'll need to know who was insuring you at that time. Records on IRA contributions and all contracts should be kept indefinitely.

5. If you plan to sell your house, you may want to keep monthly electric, heating, and sanitation bills for the year. Buyers often want to know these costs.

6. Receipts for large purchases, such as a car, should be kept as long as you own the items.

7. Keep medical records for serious conditions indefinitely.

8. Keep annual investment statements while you own the investment, and for 6 years after selling it. If the details of monthly statements disappear when they're consolidated in yearly statements, keep the monthly statements.

9. Bank deposit slips, which have been checked against your bank account records and are 6 years old, can be destroyed. Bundles of canceled checks can be destroyed after 3 years, but be sure to save checks with information related to tax deductions, capital gains-reducing expenditures, child support, and legal actions and contracts. Keep credit card statements for 3 years, or long if tax deductions are on them.

As with any tax, financial, or legal matter, you'd be wise to seek professional advice. A good accountant and a clever lawyer will save you money and trouble.

make hunting for a document much easier. These details will also help you purge these off-site files at some future date. If you know when a box's contents will become useless, write that date on the box. Keep a list in your office of the files you've moved off-site.

CLUTTER CRISES

Despite your best efforts, papers will pile up on your desk. Maybe you went on vacation or needed to take off a day for that root canal—or both. You've come back to work sunburned and swollen-jawed, to discover a landfill heaped upon your desk.

For an emergency cleanup, you'll need eight boxes. Sort the papers that have accumulated into boxes labeled "Take Action," "Delegate," "Defer until Future Date," "Defer Indefinitely," "File," "Toss Out," "Extract Info," and "Look at Again."

REVIEW YOUR OFFICE SUPPLIES

Office supplies accumulate until they clog your desk drawers

Store Logically

A key rule for a clutter-free life is to store *like* and *like*. Libraries group books by subjects because doing so makes it easier to find

information quickly. In your home office, store all your link cartridges in the same drawer, keep manuals for office equipment together, and so on. Resist the temptation to tuck something away wherever you see an empty spot.

like cholesterol clogs arteries. Get three boxes—one box for items to discard, the next for items to keep, and a third for things you can donate to charity. Choose a drawer and examine everything in it. Identify items you don't need. If they're in good shape, put them in the charity box. Check for duplication. Have a couple of hundred ballpoint pens? You won't live long enough to use all of them, and they'll make a poor legacy for your descendants. Donate them.

After examining the contents of one drawer, move on to another. Don't put anything back until you've checked all your supplies. That way, you can avoid duplicates, and when you put things away, you can do some organizing—putting all pencils in a drawer near the pencil sharpener, for example.

A LEAN, CLEAN BULLETIN BOARD

A bulletin board is useful only if you actually can see the important things pinned to it. Unfortunately, crucial items are apt to disappear beneath snapshots, cartoons, and your child's Thanksgiving Day traced-hand turkey. Soon, the wall looks like a vertical version of a messy desktop.

Post only items that you need to reference frequently or that are of extra importance. A calendar, a list of significant phone numbers, or a map of your city could be tacked up here. A bulletin board also serves as a highly visible spot to post items that you don't want to forget, such as airline tickets or phone messages.

Bulletin boards are available at office supply stores in a variety of sizes, shapes, and colors. If a standard bulletin board is unappealing to you, you can use a chalkboard or dry-erase board to record information of daily import.

For those who favor old-fashioned things, slate blackboards are still available.

An Internet search will supply you with sellers. Slate boards are heavier and more fragile than modern versions, but their surface is more durable.

Dress Up a Bulletin Board

To give your bulletin board a designer look, place it within an old picture frame. Ornate frames often are available at yard sales and thrift shops. Spiff up the

frame with a little paint or some antiquing. You need to secure the framed board to the wall more firmly than an ordinary picture, because you'll be pushing on it when you tack up notes. Anchor it to studs in the wall.

PRUNE YOUR PROFESSIONAL LIBRARY

Review the books in your office. Has your pleasure reading infiltrated the shelves here? Books by Agatha Christie or Dave Barry may amuse you during an idle moment, but if they won't help you with your work, shelve them elsewhere.

While you're at it, gather manuals for your office equipment, especially any that are computer related. You might want to scan the pages of noncomputer manuals and store them electronically. Don't do this with computer manuals, however. If your computer crashes, you won't have access to the information needed to set things right.

AN OFFICE MAKEOVER

One dramatic solution to a clutter-filled home office is to

move—or, at least, pretend you're moving. Take everything out of your office and put it back in a new, better arrangement.

To add rigor to this exercise, imagine the move is to a remote corner of the Yukon. Every piece of furniture, every scrap of paper, and every file folder will have to be transported by dogsled. Before "packing" an item, ask yourself if it's worth moving. After all, you don't want those poor huskies to needlessly strain in order to haul five identical tape dispensers, 23 boxes of rubber bands, and hundreds of eraserless pencils.

Choose a room near your home office as a staging area into which you'll move its contents. This is an ideal time to reorganize your files.

If you don't have a good filing system, spend a little time devising one. Consider how you'll use the files. Which items will you use often and which seldom? Which are essential to keep up-to-date, and which contain materials you can postpone examining? After you have a strategy, gather and label file storage boxes to reflect this scheme. Then empty your filing cabinet, sorting your documents into these boxes. As the boxes fill, you may need to alter your filing strategy to better suit your needs. Changes are easy when using boxes instead of the drawers in your filing cabinet.

Once the filing cabinet is empty, clean out your desk, then move on to any other documents in the office. When you're done, all your files should be nicely sorted in the cardboard file boxes, ready to be moved back into your filing cabinet.

You can now proceed to "pack" your office equipment, such as your fax machine and computer. If the cables and sockets haven't been clearly labeled, do so as you pull them apart. Ordinary tags with strings, available at office supply stores, can be used to label electrical cords, but their strings can add to the tangle of cables behind your equipment.

Feeding the "Hungry" Discard Box

When clearing out her office, Sheree employs a motivational trick. She chooses a large box for those documents she intends to discard. The challenge of filling the box motivates her to discard more documents. When she evaluates a document that she's unsure about keeping, the waiting "hungry" discard box provides a subtle nudge to throw the document away.

They also aren't very good for labeling sockets and are easily torn off. Instead, use self-adhesive labels. For each socket, write a description of its function on a label, assign it an identifying number, and stick the label by the socket. Write the identifying number on a second label, then wrap it around the appropriate cable. Don't remove the labels after you've made your pretend move—they'll be handy for the next move, be it real or pretend.

After all devices have been removed, consider which pieces of furniture you want to keep in your office. Do you need to replace them with more capacious or comfortable pieces? Do they need repairs or a coat of paint? Move out any that aren't earning their keep. If you don't need to redo your home office's floor, move the remaining furniture into the center of the room and treat the walls to a fresh coat of paint.

8 THINGS TO CONSIDER IN PLANNING A NEW OFFICE

As you declutter and get ready to reorganize your home office, you might find yourself thinking of taking a dramatic step and drawing up plans for a new office, from the floor up. Review the spots in your home where a work center might be established. Perhaps another room has been freed up over the past months. Or you may have the financial resources to expand into an underused basement or attic. Here are some ideas for how to go about setting up a new office.

1. Choose a room large enough to hold everything you need. It should have at least one window. Working in a view-less cube can become depressing—and more distracting than wasting the odd moment watching the occasional blue jay.

2. If possible, locate the office away from the noisier parts of your home. You don't want your work to be interrupted by your children watching a screeching episode of their favorite monster cartoon.

3. Try to place the office away from family foot traffic. An office too close to an outside door may become a dumping ground for junk mail, coats, and hats.

4. You'll need electrical outlets to accommodate your office equipment. Outlets should be grounded so that they'll accept surge protectors. Electronic equipment should always be powered through surge protectors. Unlike Frankenstein's monster, which sprang to life when tickled by a blast of lightning, your electronics can be killed by a small jolt of electricity.

5. You'll need at least one telephone jack. A second line for your computer or fax is convenient. If you plan to use a cable modem, you'll need a cable hookup for your home office.

6. The cables and power cords for your equipment can become a twisty mess. When you lay out your office, keep in mind that you'll need to plan where to put them. It may be possible to simplify matters by bundling cables. Don't use ties that can't be easily released, because you may need to move equipment for maintenance or in emergencies. Electronics stores carry "harnesses" for organizing cables, but you can do better for less money with the double-sided Velcro strips sold at hardware stores.

You can wind these strips around your cables, and release them easily when necessary. If you run cables under a table or desk, you can support them by using the brackets used to secure pipes to walls. Just screw the brackets to the underside of the table, and run the cables through them.

7. Choose a desk adequate for your needs. If you have a "tower" computer, for example, a desk that has a shelf near the floor for the tower will save you desktop space. A slide-out shelf for your keyboard can also help keep your desk clear.

8. If you're going to be meeting with clients in your home office, you'll want your desk, or a corner of it, to face into the room. You'll need a comfortable chair or sofa for your clients. Arrange it so that clients can speak easily with you, and view documents you need to show them.

SERIOUS FILING AND SHELVING

A filing cabinet is an important ally in a home decluttering effort. Avoid cheap models, which soon wear out under the weight of files. Furniture stores are likely to carry

It's All Under There, Somewhere

In 1958, Ray Kostin opened a lumberyard near Philadelphia. His office held two desks, which soon became buried beneath piles of paper—*big* piles. In 2001, Kostin admitted he hadn't seen the desktops once in those 43 years. The *Philadelphia Inquirer* estimated that there were 80 cubic feet of paper on the desks, possibly qualifying them as the messiest in the United States.

the most attractive models, while office furniture stores deal in plain, durable units.

If you aren't set on buying a cabinet in perfect condition, you might look for a bargain at a used office furniture store, an office furniture rental store selling its used inventory, or a government surplus auction.

Find a cabinet with at least one locking drawer for sensitive files. Make sure that its drawers slide freely. Are the rollers plastic or sturdier steel? Some drawers don't even have rollers, relying instead on flimsy plastic strips. Check how easily drawers can be removed. You don't want a drawer that can

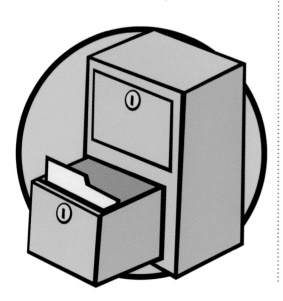

pull free accidentally and dump its contents, but being able to remove a drawer can make cleaning it or sorting files easier.

If a cabinet doesn't come with racks for hanging folders, you can buy these at an office supply store. They can be assembled with just a screwdriver and a pair of pliers.

Filing cabinets come in a wide variety of styles. There are short models, models with wide drawers for larger documents, models that fit under your desk, models with wheels, and "lateral" models with drawers that run alongside a wall instead of extending out from it. The latter have wide drawers in which files are stored from left to right, instead of front to back, allowing the cabinet to fit into narrower workspaces. An oak filing cabinet with brass hardware may make your home office seem more homey and less like a workplace, while a steel cabinet can lend an air of modern efficiency.

As for the denizens of filing cabinets—file folders—a trip to your office supply store will reveal many choices. You can buy simple beige folders, or mixed packs of colored ones that can induce you to organize your papers by category. Because you're likely to end up with too many folders of one color and too few of another, it may be easier to use plain folders and distinguish them with colored labels. Stick a red label on all folders containing bills, for example.

Shelving is the next item you'll need to consider. The simplest solution is to buy a simple open-faced bookcase. Bookcases made from wood will help make the home office look less institutional, or you can shop for metal utility shelving at office supply and restaurant supply stores. Glass-fronted bookcases protect their contents from dust, but they're more costly than open shelves. Barrister bookcases, which feature lift-up glass fronts, are modular. Each shelf is independent of the others, so that you can stack units to fit your circumstances.

Wall-mounted shelving will spare you floor space in a cramped office. The cheapest is composed simply of boards that rest on brackets, which are clipped into vertical metal standards. For a more stylish look, use clear-finished hardwood shelving and decorative supports, such as cast-iron Victorian brackets. You might also want to consider using wall-mounted kitchen cabinets with glass doors. The most expensive option is to hire a cabinetmaker to build and install custom bookshelves to your design.

Credenzas are an office staple. While they offer a lot of storage, a bureau with several drawers will serve the same function while looking warmer and more appropriate for a home setting. All the odds and ends of the workday, such as staplers, paper punches, and spare pens, can be stored here. Use boxes to divide up the drawers for various items. The bureau's top is a good spot for a fax machine or printer.

Wheeled furniture can be handy in keeping the home office's layout adaptable to changing needs. Office furniture stores sell wheeled tables and carts that can be pulled out when needed, then pushed back out of the way. Small plastic cabinets with wheels and multiple drawers can be purchased cheaply at office supply and art supply stores. They're good for storing small office items, which can be pulled over to where they're needed. A rolling file basket can be particularly helpful in sorting documents. Choose one short enough to be rolled under your desk when not in use.

If your office seems cramped, you may want to consider buying a tall storage cabinet to exploit vertical space—similar to the rationale for skyscrapers in crowded Manhattan. Such cabinets are great for organizing and storing office supplies, particularly items that aren't used daily, such as a three-hole punch. Office supply stores offer models made of steel. Home supply stores carry similar items for laundry or garage use, which you can draft into office service. Or if you prefer the look of wood, browse at a furniture store for a cupboard that might suit your home office.

A final piece of office furniture to consider is the "circular file"—the trash can. An ordinary trash can will suffice for nonrecyclables, but your office will produce a lot of recyclable paper, and you'll need a bin for that as well. Consider the space it uses as a tribute to Mother Nature.

EQUIPPING THE HOME OFFICE

The workspace in your home will operate more smoothly and efficiently if you choose equipment

with an eye to ease of maintenance, durability, and compactness.

COMPUTERS

Home computers can be classified by the operating system that they run. The operating system controls how the computer handles information. There are three major systems: Microsoft Windows, Linux, and Macintosh.

Windows is by far the dominant player, being used by 90 percent of home computers. Plenty of inexpensive, Windows-compatible software is available, but computer users often complain about Windows's sometimes "buggy," often cranky performance.

Linux was developed as a free alternative operating system for Windows-running computers. It purports to be more reliable but hasn't yet established itself as an operating system capable of meeting as many needs.

Macintosh computers make up a small section of the computer market but have a deserved reputation for ease of use and stability. They are, however, more expensive, and since they're a minority machine, less software is developed for them. But despite less software, you can find an application to perform any function you're apt to need.

No matter what kind of computer you choose, the choice of computer monitor is important for comfort and ease of use. If you're nearsighted, you'll want a large monitor, but even if you have good eyesight, a large screen is beneficial as it allows the display of more information. Cost rises significantly with size. Flat-screen monitors, which were once an expensive option, are now cheaper and commonplace. They take up less space on your desk, presenting a less monolithic lump. Always try out a monitor before buying to be sure it's comfortable for you to use.

Conventional desktop computers are bulky, and may hog most of the work surface in a compact office. Laptop computers have become remarkably light and easy to use, while keeping pace with desktop computers in power. You can fold up and tuck away a laptop when it's not in use, freeing up your desk for other tasks or lunch. This is particularly advantageous if your office also serves another purpose in your home.

PRINTERS AND SCANNERS

Computer printers have greatly dropped in price, while increasing in quality. For less than fifty dollars, you can buy an ink-jet color printer that can quickly produce

photographic-quality images. The catch is that the ink cartridges for these printers are expensive, and while plain paper can be used for text, the paper necessary for high-quality images is costly.

If possible, buy a printer that has separate ink cartridges for each color. Then when you exhaust one color, you won't need to replace the ink for the other two. Alternatively, if you seldom use color, you should consider a laser printer. They're dependable and fast and produce excellent, black-and-white output. They're usually more expensive than ink-jet printers, but their toner cartridges are cheaper than ink-jet cartridges. If you print a lot of pages, this could yield a lower cost per page.

A scanner is useful for creating computer images of photographs, newspaper articles, and diagrams. You can use a scanner and printer to do copying as well. It'll be a slower process than using a photocopier, but scanners commonly come with software that allows you to edit your copy before printing. You'll also have a digital version of your document in your computer as a data file.

Many scanners come with optical character recognition (OCR) software to turn scanned text into text files ready for your word processor to use. These can work well, but it can take quite a bit of time to scan all the pages of long documents. OCR scanners often encounter documents that they can't handle without lots of user intervention. Don't expect OCR software to work perfectly.

There are multifunction machines that incorporate photocopier, scanner, fax machine, telephone, and answering machine all in one. While this can save desktop space, if one function fails you may lose all the other functions as well. It's also likely that performance for a particular function may be inferior to that available from a machine dedicated to that function.

DATA STORAGE DEVICES

Duplicate computer files may seem to be clutter, but you should always have a secondary storage device for your computer, in addition to its hard disk drive, to create backup copies of your files.

A 3½-inch floppy disk drive used to be the most common device for this, but the new standard is the rewritable CD (compact disk) drive or "CD burner." Another choice is a DVD (digital video disk) burner, but these are more expensive. Designed for storing movies, DVDs have far greater storage than CDs. Both CDs and DVDs are cheap, capacious, and durable.

Another backup option is the miniature USB (universal serial bus) hard drive. About the size of your thumb, it plugs directly into a USB port on your computer. While storing less data than a CD, this type of drive operates just like the computer's hard drive. You can fill it with information, then plug it into another USB-equipped computer to transfer the data simply by copying the files onto the second hard drive.

A traditional external hard drive makes a poor backup choice.

Big-Time Storage

A consortium of six Japanese companies, including Fuji Photo, is busily developing a recordable disc using a holographic technology known as HVD. This will make possible the recording of 1 terabyte of data on a single disc. A terabyte is equal to 1,024 gigabytes. An ordinary DVD disc holds 4.7 gigabytes, and a standard CD disc holds just 700 megabytes (1 gigabyte equals 1,024 megabytes). The new HVD disc will be able to hold more than a month's worth of television programs and will be 40 times faster to burn than a standard DVD. This new disc's capacity and speed will become necessary as digital technology develops. Recording 2 hours of HDTV (high definition TV) programming, for example, could require 25 gigabytes.

While it has a large capacity and can be as fast as the hard drive that came with your computer, you're unlikely to detach the drive and move it to a different location. Part of the purpose of backing up is to produce a copy of your files that can be stored safely away from your computer, so that if your computer is destroyed, you won't lose your data. A backup CD or a miniature USB hard drive can be easily carried to another location.

A recent innovation in backing up computer files is available through the Internet. The provider of this service maintains a massive computer system to which you send copies of your files. The backup is done automatically at intervals you specify. The service claims to be secure from hackers, and since your file copies are stored away from your home or business, they won't be lost if your computer is stolen or destroyed. Restoring files takes just a few mouse clicks.

INTERNET CONNECTIONS

A slow Internet connection can make just reviewing your e-mail a tedious task, and Web surfing seem like you're watching paint dry on a humid day. If you intend to use the Internet with regularity, get the fastest connection you can afford.

The easiest way to get on the Internet is through a modem and dial-up telephone connection. Such a connection can be made wherever there are phone lines. Unfortunately, this is a slow way to access the Internet. While 56 Kbps (kilobytes per second) modems are the standard, these produce far less than 56 Kbps performance. You also need to have a separate phone line dedicated to your modem so that you can easily receive calls while using the Internet.

A faster means of connecting to the Internet is a digital subscriber line (DSL). With a DSL line, you can use your telephone line for voice calls at the same time you use it for the Internet. It's much faster than an ordinary telephone modem connection, but at a typical 260 Kbps, it's not as fast as an average cable modem connection. DSL is more expensive than a dial-up connection.

Cable modems are faster than telephone or DSL connections. Using a special modem, they reach the Internet through the same lines that bring you your cable TV. The service is more expensive than a DSL connection.

A space-age way to reach the Internet is through a satellite.

Satellite connections provide the great benefit of service to rural areas that aren't favored with cable or DSL service. Information is downloaded to your computer via a small satellite disk at a typical rate of 250 Kbps, which is slower than cable. Uploading is generally done through a slower telephone connection. Satellite service requires professional setup, and two-way satellite is the most expensive way to access the Internet. Another drawback is that, on occasion, satellite connections can be interrupted by cloudy weather or thick foliage.

3 SMART PHONE CONSIDERATIONS

Smart phones, such as Black-Berrys and iPhones have become a popular way to automate a day planner, Rolodex, address book, notebook, and phone. They're able to store a lot of data in a small device, and make it readily available. Some people find these gagets streamline their daily lives. For others, they represent mankind's subjugation to the machine. If you're wondering whether to jump on the smart phone bandwagon, consider the following questions:

1. Do you need to get email when you're not at the office? Would you find this helpful or a distraction?
2. How many contacts are you likely to record? If you only keep data on a handful of people, paper can do just fine.
3. Is it difficult for you to enter data into a phone? The tiny keys and touch pad can make it a challenge to enter information.

VOICE MAIL

If you want the appearance of a larger office and a more human touch for your message taking, you can subscribe to a telephone answering service in which a real person answers your phone. But beware: This human touch can include unprofessional operators and mistaken messages. If you do choose a service, periodically have a friend ring it up to check how well it's performing.

5 WAYS TO KEEP YOUR OFFICE COMPACT

If you have only a corner of a room that can serve as a home office, you'll have to reduce your equipment as much as possible.

1. A laptop computer can substitute for a full-size machine.

QUICK FIX

RENT AN OFFICE

If you find your home office is too confining, too noisy, or too accessible to family and friends, you can make a bold move—out of the house. Look into renting office space. If you can't justify the expense or don't need a full-time office, perhaps you can share one with two or three friends.

---

2. Small laser printers are perfectly fine for limited jobs. For larger jobs, you can upload files to a local print shop for a small fee.

3. If you need to do copying, consider using a scanner for both copying and scanning. Small models are available. You can also use this to send faxes.

4. Figure out how to send and receive faxes through your computer.

5. Backup storage devices can be replaced by USB drives for temporary backup.

6 TIPS FOR THE KITCHEN OFFICE

Although the kitchen is vulnerable to cooking messes, its table has long been used as an impromptu office. Joseph Heller wrote *Catch-22* on his kitchen table. With a few modifications, you can make your kitchen suitable for writing your own bestseller.

1. Choose a two-drawer wheeled filing cabinet low enough to slide under a kitchen table.

2. Devote a shelf or two in your kitchen cabinets to storing professional books and office supplies. Try not to mix work items with kitchen stores. You don't want ketchup dripping onto your paperwork or pens mixed in with your cutlery.

3. Consider replacing the chairs surrounding your kitchen table with built-in booth seating, and storage below for files.

4. Use office chairs on wheels as a mobile (and comfortable) alternative to standard kitchen chairs.

5. Add a drawer under the table. Even a shallow drawer can accommodate a lot of small office supplies.

6. Hang a bulletin board on the back of a nearby door.

5 TIPS FOR THE CLOSET OFFICE

A closet can be converted into a small home office. When you've finished the day's work, you simply can close the closet door and all of that clutter disappears.

1. Remove the clothes rod and any hooks.

2. Use existing shelving for books and supplies.

3. The easiest way to provide a work surface is to slide a table or desk into the closet. Or you can construct a desktop (see Quick Fix, page 184).

4. Hang a bulletin board or a pocket-style file holder or consider putting shallow bookcase on the back of the door. You'll want to run a narrow strip of wood along bookshelves as a lip, to keep books in place when the door is opened and closed. Make sure that shelves won't hit the chair or computer when the door is closed.

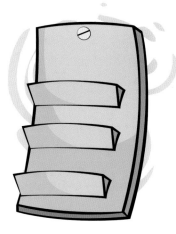

6. Lighting is especially important when you're tucked into
   a closet home office. You can
   supplement the closet's existing
   light with a lamp on your desk,
   but *don't* plug your computer

QUICK FIX

BUILD A CLOSET DESK

1. The best choice of for a closet desktop is ¾-inch birch veneer plywood, because the top ply is smooth. To conceal the raw edge of the plywood, you can glue on veneer tape, or tack on a strip of molding. Varnish will harden the surface so you can write on it with less chance of leaving marks.

2. Cut the plywood to fit the closet. It should be shallow enough so that you can slide your desk chair against it and close the closet door. If you don't have the tools or skills needed to cut a desktop from a sheet of plywood, have the lumberyard or home center do it for you. They'll charge you a small fee for making the cut, and they may expect you to pay for the entire sheet, not just the portion you use. Or you may be able to buy a precut section of plywood that's the right size for a desktop.

3. Support the plywood with L-brackets anchored by screws into the studs of the closet walls. Or if the studs aren't conveniently spaced, rest the desktop on cleats—horizontal boards that you screw into the studs.

4. You can attach a drawer under the desk. Or place a second plywood shelf under the desktop, and slide low boxes or baskets onto it as impromptu drawers. Be sure to leave space for your knees under the desk. A rolling filing cabinet can be placed under the desktop as well.

5. If you want to add shelves above the desk, be sure to allow enough room for cooling air to circulate around your computer. You'll also want the shelves to be shallow enough to clear your forehead when you lean forward over your work.

---

and other devices into an outlet in the closet's light fixture at the risk of dangerously over-loading it. Hire an electrician to add outlets and perhaps a new circuit as needed.

Go with a Pro

Electrical wiring isn't a wise D-I-Y activity for weekend dabblers. Additionally, local codes may restrict this work to licensed electricians, who have tools and skills you probably don't. For example, an electrician will be better able to handle the tricky job of running lines within walls to add new outlets and switches.

3 HOME OFFICE ESCAPE STRATEGIES

You may not be able to carve out enough room at home for a workable work space. If so, here are a few escape strategies.

1. If your day job is in an office outside your home, keep most of your files, books, and papers there, rather than burdening the corner of a room where you keep the family computer. You can transfer files back and forth to the home computer by e-mail. A way to make this easier is to establish a virtual workplace at a Web site, from which you upload and down-load files. Keep backups, so Internet problems or hacker intrusions won't wipe out your labors.

2. If you need space to spread out a large project, pack up your work and go to the nearest library. It will offer big tables, copiers, and lots of reference books. You may be able to plug in your laptop to save battery life. Your library may even

Be a Rebel

Don't limit yourself to standard conceptions of how to organize your home. Custom may dictate that objects of type A be stored in a cabinet of type B, but you may find it better to store them on top of your refrigerator or in a corner of your attic. Your household files, for example, may not be copious enough to justify a file cabinet. Perhaps a portion of your blanket chest would suffice. The important thing is that you handle your stuff efficiently.

allow you to reserve cubicles, where you can work in privacy and store books and papers.

3. Have laptop, will travel: Consider coffee shops, copy centers, and other spots that appeal to you.

SCHEDULING SIMPLIFIED

While a calendar isn't a piece of office equipment, choosing and using one is an important part of setting up your office. If you have only a few tasks to schedule, a simple notebook calendar may suffice. If your work life is more complicated, a stationery or office supply store can provide you with a variety of calendars. Some

incorporate an office diary or telephone and address book. Others have multiple sections with tabs that separate different types of scheduled events.

Most cell phones, so-called smart phones or not, are a highly portable alternative to bound calendars. They store lots of information and manage it so that you can retrieve it easily. Many people now keep a virtual calendar, using a program such as Outlook or a website such as Google. These have the advantage of being easy to update, and available for sharing with co-workers. Virtual calendars usually include "alarm" features that will remind you, sometimes through e-mail, of scheduled events.

BLENDING HOME AND OFFICE

Beyond all the furniture and computer details, the trick to creating a home office is combining the discipline and order of a workplace with the comforts and convenience of home. Try to strike a balance between no-nonsense systems for getting your work done and simple pleasures—looking out a window with a view, or reading the day's mail in a pleasingly broken-in armchair. Your tasks will seem lighter, and you'll find yourself looking forward to stopping by your home office each day.

TWELVE

Managing Cyber Clutter

"A computer lets you make more mistakes faster than any invention in human history—with the possible exceptions of handguns and tequila."

—Mitch Ratcliffe

In January 2004, when the Spirit rover landed on Mars, its Earthly controllers at the Jet Propulsion Laboratory (JPL) eagerly awaited the photographs it was sent to snap. But when Spirit's data began to flow back, it made no sense. For 5 days, JPL scientists desperately struggled to solve the problem. If they couldn't, the multimillion-dollar space probe would be worthless. Finally, the scientists realized that during Spirit's 7-month, 300-million-mile trip to Mars, the rover's computer had gotten fat with clutter. The computer, running routine programs, had generated hundreds and hundreds of garbage files that overwhelmed it. It was only after purging this clutter that Spirit could start transmitting photographs of the Martian surface. Your computer, humming away on your Earthly desk, may look lean and efficient, but its

insides may be getting just as obese as Spirit's computer, barely able to stagger on under its burden of useless files, ancient e-mails, and obsolete software.

IMPOSING ORDER ON COMPUTER CHAOS

Ed has a master's degree in computer science, so his friend George asked for his help in using a computer for record keeping on his dairy farm. While you may not have a herd of Holsteins grazing the back 40, the following steps George took to become better organized will give you ideas for using your computer more efficiently.

Step 1. George began by archiving the present state of his computer. He created a folder on his computer that he named "Old Structure Folder." He copied everything into it and also copied its contents onto CDs as a backup, in case he accidentally deleted a program or document while reorganizing files. For added safety, George made a second copy of these backup CDs and stored them at his cousin's house. This gave him a safe off-site archive of his computer's files. Some programs can't be backed up by copying them on a CD they have to be reinstalled using their original installation disks.

Step 2. As George copied his files, he took notes about their types and purposes to use to design an organizing plan for his computer.

Step 3. With everything now copied into the "Old Structure Folder" and backed up on CDs, George began building a new file structure for his computer, creating folders into which he moved his original files and programs. He decided he needed five basic folders: "Applications Folder" for the software he uses; "Business Folder" for business-related documents; "Personal Folder" for personal files; "Sort Folder" for a central location to store new documents; and "Attic Folder" for items we'll describe below. Some computers arrive with an "Applications Folder" already created. If so, keep and use this folder. This was the case with George's Mac.

The file structure of George's computer now looked like this (we've used indentations to show subfolders and violated alphabetical order for clarity):

Applications Folder
  Applications Programs
Business Folder
  Business Documents
Personal Folder
Personal Documents
Sort Folder
  New Documents

Attic Folder
  Old Structure Folder

George created subfolders and sub-subfolders as needed. For example, George uses two Internet browsers, a program that reports current weather conditions for his region, and a couple of programs that play media, such as streaming audio, that he pulls into his computer using the Internet. George put all these programs in a folder called "Internet Folder," which he put inside "Applications Folder."

Some programs have files associated with them that explain how to use them, or are necessary for the program to run. George's word

Ed Morrow

processing program came with a dictionary file and other associated files. He created a "Word Processing Folder" subfolder in "Applications Folder" and stored the program, dictionary, and associated files in it.

A few programs don't require any associated files. These don't need folders dedicated to them. For example, George has a calculator program that stands alone. He stored this in "Applications Folder" without using a sub-subfolder.

The "Applications Folder" in George's computer now looked like this:

Applications Folder
    Calculator Program
    Internet Folder
        Browser 1
        Browser 2
        Weather Program
        Media Player 1
        Media Player 2
    Word Processing Folder
        Word Processing Program
        Dictionary
        Other word processing associated files
    Other Applications (some grouped in folders)

After organizing his applications programs, George moved on to organize his documents.

COMPUTER DOCUMENT MANAGEMENT

"Plan your work and work your plan."

—American business adage

The secret to good computer document management is to develop a plan that's easy to follow and then stick to it. George began by setting up subfolders for types of documents he put in his "Personal Folder." First, he created a "Letters Folder" for his personal correspondence. He moved all the letters and e-mails of a personal nature that he'd saved into this folder. Next, he placed a "Games Folder" inside his "Personal Folder" for games. George also had documents holding data related to his household. These included lists of phone numbers, scanned manuals for his household appliances, "treasure maps" identifying where he had stored important household items, and other documents associated with the daily operation of his home. He put these in his "Household Folder." George has a digital camera, so he set up a "Photo Folder" to hold the digital photographs he wants to keep on his computer.

George's "Personal Folder" now looked like this:

Personal Folder
> Letters Folder
>> (Letters and e-mails to and from friends)
> Games Folder
>> (Games)
> Household Folder
>> (Household documents)
> Photo Folder
>> (Digital photographs)
> More personal folders

George then moved on to the more complex contents of his "Business Folder." He needed several subfolders inside his "Business Folder" to organize the various aspects of his farm business. These included "E-mail Received Folder," "E-mail Sent Folder," "Equipment Records Folder," "Farm Reports Folder," and other cow biz categories. When he was done, the "Business Folder" looked like this:

Business Folder
> E-mail Received Folder
> E-mail Sent Folder
> Equipment Records Folder
> Farm Reports Folder
> More folders for different business categories

As George uses his computer, he generates new documents. He might write a letter or receive an e-mail. To make managing these documents easier, he created another folder, which he calls "Sort Folder." In George's file structure (see page 209), "Sort Folder" is located alongside "Applications Folder," "Business Folder," "Personal Folder," and "Attic Folder." "Sort Folder" serves as an all-purpose place in which to store new documents, whether received over the Internet or created on his computer, until George can more definitively file them.

Most programs (and most operating systems via a settings file or control panel) allow you to choose a default folder in which to save work. George designated "Sort Folder" as his default folder for all purposes. By using a central folder, George can be certain that new files won't accidentally be placed in the wrong folder or in an obscure folder. It can be hard to find documents that are saved in a variety of folders in different locations, especially if you're unaware that this has happened. Periodically, George goes through "Sort Folder" to review his work, sorting files into the folders matching their content. This is analogous to what he does with actual documents that pass across his desk. A central sorting folder is valuable in decluttering, too. George can easily find files that he doesn't want to keep, such as draft documents, and dump them.

Operating systems often specify a "Documents Folder" as the default folder for newly created documents. The folder generally holds all your other documents, too, which can be confusing when new documents are jammed in among older material. If you decide to use the "Documents Folder" as your "Sort Folder," reserve it just for new documents, which you sort into permanent folders as soon as possible. Don't rename the "Documents Folder," or you'll have to reset the default "Save To" file for your applications. Just mentally take note that "Documents Folder" will contain your new documents, which must be sorted periodically to send them on to their permanent folders elsewhere.

George chose to use his "Sort Folder" and to divide the contents of the "Documents Folder" that came with his Mac among folders dedicated to different purposes. He didn't delete the "Documents Folder," however. Some installer programs store files such as log files or help files by default there for their programs to use. George only uses these files through their programs. He doesn't need to fiddle around with them, so he just leaves them in the "Documents Folder." Because he doesn't use these files directly, that folder isn't shown in the diagrams of his computer file organization. He shouldn't have to move anything into or out of that folder, unless it's sent there by accident.

Let's take a look at George's organizing plan with all its parts:

Applications Folder
    Calculator Program
    Internet Folder
        Browser 1
        Browser 2
        Weather Program

    Media Player 1
    Media Player 2
  Word Processing Folder
    Word Processing Program
    Dictionary
    Other word processing associated files

EASY DOES IT

Top of the List

"Why is the alphabet in that order? Is it because of that song?"

—Steven Wright

When you open a folder from a program menu, the files and folders inside are usually listed alphabetically. It's useful to have frequently used folders at the top of these menu lists, so you don't need to scroll down every time you need to find them. To place a file or folder high on the menu list, give it the prefix "AAA"—just as competitive companies sometimes name themselves "AAA Whatever, Inc.," so that they'll appear first in the Yellow Pages. A folder named "AAA Sort Folder" may look odd, but it can save you a few seconds of hunting every time you open it from a menu.

Conversely, give seldom wanted files or folders the prefix "ZZZ." This will place them at the bottom of the list, so that other, more often used items will be higher in the list and more quickly noticed.

The Mac operating system has a powerful "smart folders" feature that can automatically organize files using portions of their names. If you prefix all your saved e-mails from your mom (using "eim," for example), your computer will automatically group them for you.

Other Applications (some grouped in folders)
Personal Folder
    Letters Folder
       (Letters and e-mails to and from friends)
    Games Folder
       (Games)
    Household Folder
       (Household documents)
    Photo Folder

       (Digital photographs)
    More personal folders
Business Folder
    E-mail Received Folder
    E-mail Sent Folder
    Equipment Records Folder
    Farm Reports Folder
    More folders for different business categories
Sort Folder
Attic Folder

EASY DOES IT

The Name Game

"I don't remember anybody's name. How do you think the 'dahling' thing got started?"

—Zsa Zsa Gabor

As you sort items in the "Sort Folder," any document with a confusing name should be labeled more clearly. Items downloaded from the Internet, for example, often have odd names that aren't readily associated with their contents. Give them meaningful names before they're moved out of the "Sort Folder." (Don't change suffixes, such as ".tiff," as this can interfere with how files are used.) Names should indicate the document's content. For example, George downloaded an image of a cow that a Web site had named "c1934b.jpeg." George changed that name to reflect the cow's actual name: "Cow-Of-War.jpeg." Now when he sees that image file (jpeg is a file format for images) in a folder on his computer, he know what it is without having to open it.

This is a straightforward plan that's easy to understand. Notice that George avoided deeply nesting folders. This quickly routes him to a particular location in just a few steps. It's far better to have a long list of folders shallowly nested, than a shorter list into which you have to delve subfolder after subsubfolder to find a file. But while a well-organized file structure has subfolders only where needed, don't skimp on subfolders when they can improve organization.

George also takes advantage of a feature called "aliases" on his Mac, which is called "shortcuts" on a Windows machine. These are files that "point" to another document, folder, or program. When you click on the alias, the item it points to is opened, sparing you the need to hunt through the file structure for the aliased item. George makes aliases of his most frequently used programs, folders, and files, then places them on his computer's desktop. He has, for example, an alias there for the "Sort Folder" so he can open it in one step.

Aliases for folders are useful for sorting. George created aliases for many of his frequently used folders, positioning them on his desktop. He could then drag e-mail, for example, from his "Sort Folder" to aliases for "E-Mail Received" and "E-Mail Sent."

George's Mac positions a hidden tool bar at the bottom of his screen. When he moves his cursor there, the tool bar pops up. In the tool bar, he can store a pointer to a program, to a folder, or to a document by dragging its icon there. George stores pointers to his most often used programs here, using aliases on his desktop for folders containing documents. Windows machines have a similar feature. In our example, we've ignored tool bars to present a more general organizational scheme, but tool bars can help you keep shortcuts to your programs easily available, without cluttering your desktop.

After George had moved all his files into appropriate folders, had backed up everything onto CDs, and was certain his computer was running correctly, he dumped his "Old Structure Folder." He then made backup CDs of his new file structure to safely document it.

GET YOUR NUMBERS IN ORDER

Your computer's operating system allows you to view files in alphabetical order in folder windows. This can produce oddities. For example, this list is correctly sorted by alphabetical order.

Cow 1
Cow 10
Cow 2

Your computer isn't clever enough to recognize the numerical sequence and place Cow 2 ahead of Cow 10. by placing a leading "0" in front of single digits, these files would be more sensibly sorted.

Cow 01
Cow 02
Cow 10

This works for up to 99 files, when numbered 01 to 99 (999 can be sorted by using 001 to 999, and so on).

A PREFIX FIX

To speed sorting the files in your "Sort Folder," try a presorting trick George uses. When he saves a file, he prefixes its name with a letter or two that gives it a classification. As he receives e-mails about his turkey-raising sideline, for example, he prefixes them with "eit" for "e-mail, incoming, turkey-related." He saves copies of all the e-mail he sends out, and gives an e-mail sent to a turkey buyer the prefix "eot" for "e-mail, outgoing, turkey-related." News items downloaded from the Internet about cows are prefixed with "c." For correspondence that he writes, he saves the files with an "lm" as a prefix for "letter written by me." When these prefixed files are saved into George's "Sort Folder," similar documents will be listed near each other, and he can move them as a group to the appropriate folder. It's a simple, quick tactic that eases sorting.

PUTTING AN ATTIC IN YOUR COMPUTER

George often is 99 percent sure a document is disposable—but not 100 percent sure. Just as the attic of your home can be a useful place to stash possessions that you aren't using now but might need some day, an "Attic Folder" provides you with a mechanism for putting away documents you aren't ready to delete completely. George uses his "Attic Folder" for items such as old e-mails and digital photographs he's not certain he wants to keep. Periodically, he "burns," or copies, the contents of his "Attic Folder" onto an "Attic CD" and then deletes the original files from his computer.

CDs can get ruined. Scratches can make them unreadable. They're made of brittle plastic, not tempered steel, and can snap under pressure. CDs also can't tolerate high temperatures. For safety's sake, George burns an extra copy and stores it away from home.

There are CD cataloging programs that will create a simple database of all the files on a CD, and group this with information about other CDs. These programs make it easy to find an old version of a document that has been moved to an "Attic CD." Such programs can be found through Internet software sites.

COMPRESSION PROGRAMS

You can buy programs to compress huge files to modest proportions in a few seconds, then plump them back up quickly when you want to use them. As hard drives get larger, the need to compress files isn't as compelling as it once was. But by reducing the number of files on your hard drive, you may improve your computer's performance. If you run a compression program on a folder containing a couple of hundred files, then delete the original, your computer will have to keep track of just the single compressed file.

If you're short of hard drive storage space, large programs you seldom use are good candidates for compressing. You can decompress them when they're needed, then recompress them when you're done.

E-MAIL WITHOUT TEARS

E-mail is lightning fast, but as you've probably noticed, it can get out of control nearly as quickly. This is apt to come about in a number of ways. After posting an inquiry on a dairy news group, George found himself getting dozens of junk e-mails for second mortgages, cheap drugs, and dubious methods for improving his manhood. When he sent out e-mails asking to be dropped from the lists of these unwanted message senders, his daily ration of spam tripled.

George's first mistake was posting messages using his e-mail address. This made it available to spammers who "harvest" e-mail addresses from news groups. Responding to spam was his second error. This nearly always invites more spam from the spammers, who now know someone is reading their messages.

Relaxed shoulders

Forearms level

Top of screen at or a bit below eye level and screen positioned to avoid reflected glare

Thighs slightly tilted down

Support for lower back

Feet flat on floor

Ed Morrow

Some Internet service providers allow their subscribers to block e-mail from specific sources. Ideally, e-mail sent to the blocker would simply be dumped. Unfortunately, some services send the spam back to the sender with a notification of its being blocked. Again, this confirms that someone is reading the e-mail sent to that address, and the spammers can route their spam through a new sending address that won't be blocked. This can be repeated over and over.

Many e-mail services provide filtering mechanisms to automatically send certain messages into the trash. Although some purport to learn to identify spam by adapting to its newer forms, the filters may mistake legitimate e-mails for junk. A filter set to identify the suspicious term "XXX" could trash a note from your granny titled "Happy Birthday XXXOOOXXX."

Still, avoiding spam is worth losing a note from Gran. Spam can carry content more malicious than a sales pitch. You might be invited to download software that can launch a virus attack on your computer. Some e-mail viruses just display irritating messages demanding world peace or questioning Bill Gates's parentage. But others attempt to wipe your hard drive, after hijacking your computer and sending copies of themselves to every address stored in your e-mail address book. The senders of these virus-tainted e-mails often give them a subject line that will entice an unsuspecting receiver to open them. You might receive an e-mail titled "Bob said to contact you." Everyone knows a Bob and might be tempted to open the message, especially if the virus-carrying e-mail is sent through a hijacked friend's computer. "Here's the info you requested," "Holiday e-card for you," "Your account expired," and "Notice to all our service subscribers" are other typical spam subject lines.

One classic e-mail scam offers the recipient a share of a colossal international financial transaction—if he allows the sender to use the recipient's bank account, or wires money for bribes to government officials to facilitate the transfer. The recipient's bank account is drained or the wired money disappears.

6 Rules for Reducing Spam

Until the perfect spam blocking program is devised, here are some steps you can take to reduce spam.

1. Don't open email from unknown senders.

2. Don't post your e-mail address in a news group or a spammer may harvest it. The same goes for giving your e-mail address to newsletter or Web sites, no matter what claims are made for respecting your privacy.

3. Several Internet service providers (ISPs) provide free e-mail accounts. You can sign up for one of these and use it whenever you want to post on a message board or are required to give an e-mail address. If this address is harvested and starts to clog up with spam, you can just stop using it and get another free e-mail address.

4. Use the blocking mechanisms provided by your ISP or e-mail filtering programs. They may not be perfect, but they can help.

5. Many ISPs restrict the mailing privileges of spam senders. Report spam to ISP so it can take action.

6. Don't respond to spammers. Never buy any product or service offered through spam. Why reward a seller who's willing to annoy thousands of people? Is such a seller likely to be selling a reliable product?

6 WAYS TO UNCLOG YOUR COMPUTER

1. Computers usually arrive loaded with all sorts of software, much of which may never be used. You may find a solitaire package, a children's encyclopedia, a collection of ugly clip art, and a toddler's game that pits a happy squirrel against swarms of malevolent acorns. If these aren't useful to you, dump them to free up space on your disk drive. You can find these programs by carefully going through your folders. Some installer programs come with an uninstall option. Use this whenever possible, as it will remove all the files associated with a program. Just deleting the program may leave behind many obscure, oddly named files that the program used.

2. Use your generalized uninstall programs, sometimes called "disk drive cleaners," to search out all the files associated with any specified program, then delete those files and the program. These cleaner programs can also identify and delete "orphaned" files—that is, files associated with an application you no longer have on your computer.

3. Delete all temporary files. Many programs use temporary files while they're working. After the program concludes, these temporary files are supposed to disappear. If, however, a program is interrupted, say by a computer crash, those temporary files may go undeleted. Drive cleaner programs can find and delete these useless files.

4. Your computer has "wallpaper" files which can create a variety of screen patterns, most of which you'll never use. Similarly, there may be fonts you won't use, which can slow your system. Delete all unnecessary files, no matter how small. Some users are surprised that the files found by drive cleaner programs are usually very small. They conclude that it's unimportant to purge files that use so little hard drive space. This isn't true. These small files accumulate, and the more files your computer must manage, the slower and less reliably it

will run. Cleaner programs won't detect certain unnecessary files, because using them is a matter of choice. A careful reading of your computer manual and exploring of the folders on your hard drive will help you identify files you don't need.

5. Keep in mind that some files that appear unnecessary may be needed to run vital programs. The wise course is to delete only those items you're absolutely sure you don't need. Even then, keep a written record of what you did and where the file was, as well as a copy of the deleted item on a CD or other removable storage. Then, if your computer starts acting weirdly, you can restore items one by one, in the reverse order of when you removed them, until your machine again purrs.

6. After you've removed all unneeded files, you can further improve your computer's performance by running a "defragmentation" program. As files are deleted, open spots are created on the hard drive. When your computer writes to the hard drive, it will fill in these spots, but may break a file into pieces in order to do so. Over time, as more deletions and additions are made, parts of files and bits of empty space can be scattered all over the drive. The computer may have to look here, there, and yonder to reassemble a file when it's needed. The defragmentation program reorganizes the contents of the hard drive so that all the parts of a file are written in one contiguous section of the drive. The result: Your computer works faster. Farmer George routinely runs a defragmentation program every 6 months. For safety's sake, he makes sure he has backed up his drive before defragging, lest a failure during the process destroys data he can't replace.

COPING WITH CACHE FILES

When you visit an Internet site, information necessary to display it may be loaded into a browser "cache," a section of your hard drive used to store information your browser is likely to use again. For example, if you visit a news page, your browser may download images of a logo and a set of buttons that are used in presenting that page. Your browser may store these images in its cache, so that the next time you visit the Web page, it won't have to download those images again.

Browser caches can save a substantial amount of time when you go to certain sites repeatedly. But if you visit a lot of sites just once, your cache may become filled with information for sites you're unlikely to revisit. Working with this lump of useless information slows your browser, canceling out the advantage of caching. You can go to your browser's control panel, choose preferences settings, and empty the cache, so that your

browser can start fresh, free from the burden of old information. Cleaning out the cache may also improve the general performance of your computer by reducing the number of files your computer must juggle. Disk drive cleaner programs commonly allow you to delete browser cache files while cleaning out other unwanted files.

You may be able to adjust the size of the browser cache using a control panel or settings file. You can experiment with larger or smaller sizes and frequent and less frequent cache clearing until you find a match for your usage habits.

5 COOKIE STRATEGIES

Web sites commonly place "cookies," small files supposedly meant to allow the sites to respond better to your needs, into your computer. If you object to having these put into your machine without your consent, you can configure your Internet browser to block all cookies by opening its privacy preferences or control settings (often listed under "Tools"). Some Web sites, however, won't perform properly without cookies.

You can set your browser to ask about cookies before any are installed, but you'll be amazed by how many times you're requested to allow a cookie. With some browsers, you can enter the URLs of sites you permit to install cookies. Here are several cookie control strategies.

1. Allow cookies, but dump them periodically. This can improve browser performance as can cache emptying, but it doesn't address the issue of whether you want the cookies on your computer in the first place.

2. Allow cookies, but block those for sites you don't trust. This is tedious, as you'll have to enter Web site URLs over and over.

3. Block all cookies, take note of which sites won't work without them, then enable cookies just for those sites. This, too, can become tiresome, and you'll be tempted to give in to the cookie pushers and allow all cookies.

4. Some browsers allow you to block cookies from third-party sites that open when you visit a Web site. This is a good idea, as these are sites you didn't choose to open but were opened for you.

5. Surf through an "anonymizer" site, which acts as an intermediary between you and the Internet. In effect, you ask it to visit sites for you. It passes the Web pages to you without passing on any information about you, such as your Internet Protocol (IP) address, your computer's unique numeric identification—and without storing any cookies from the site on your computer.

If there are legitimate advant-ages to the site's cookies, however, these will be lost to you. For example, a site may record data about your last session and store it in a cookie on your machine, so it can personalize your next visit to that site. The anonymizer site prevents this from taking place, and you won't get the benefit of this feature. You may have to repeatedly enter information that the cookie held. Of course, if you notice a Web site isn't functioning as you wish when reached through the anonymizer site, you can always visit the site directly, skipping the anonymizer and accepting the site's cookies.

Scan Smart

You may be tempted to scan images at the highest resolution. While this stores the greatest amount of detail, the detail comes at the cost of taking up computer memory. All that data may not be needed. The typical computer monitor displays images at 72 dpi (dots per inch). So if an image is meant just for display on your monitor—as part of a Web page, for instance—you needn't scan it at a higher resolution. Scanning it at a low dpi will produce a small file, which will be quickly downloaded from the Internet, improving the Web site's performance. A resolution of 300 to 400 dpi is adequate for images that will be printed out, while images that will be enlarged or viewed close up can benefit by being scanned at higher dpi values.

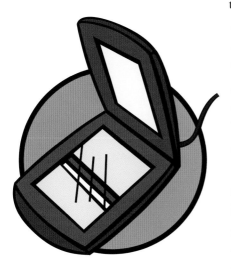

The files for color images are larger than those for black and white, because more information is needed to indentify every dot's color. So if color isn't important to you, scan images in black and white to minimize file size. George is able to take advantage of this when he scans images of his dairy herd for identification purposes. His cows are Holsteins, which by Nature's design are black and white. He pities peacock farmers.

THIRTEEN

Laundry Room Remedies

"It's better to have loved and lost than to have to do forty pounds of laundry a week."

—Laurence J. Peter

Most of the clutter that turns your home into an overweight abode is only visually unappealing. Laundry clutter, however, is both ugly and can be unpleasant smelling if left unattended. And it can quickly accumulate, especially if you have children. Kids dirty their weight in clothing and towels each day. Add your own dirty garments, and the result is a particularly unattractive form of clutter obesity. Dieting it away can significantly improve your home's appearance and livability.

9 GUIDELINES FOR BUYING A WASHER AND DRYER

These appliances come in a range of capabilities, from bare bones to models with more bells and whistles than a circus calliope. Usually the models that fall in the middle of this range are the best buys.

Be sure to get a washer that offers the cycles you need, but don't be beguiled by machines that offer cycles you'll never use. More cycles means a bigger price tag. You need:

1. Regular wash
2. Delicate cycle
3. Permanent press
4. Heavily-soiled loads
5. Temperature setting (cold water option for washer/delicate for dryer)
6. Adjustable water levels
7. Large loads
8. Water-saving options. Front loading washers are popular right now as they usually do a good job of washing while using modest amounts of water.
9. Moisture sensor that automatically turns off your machine when your clothing is dry (for dryer)

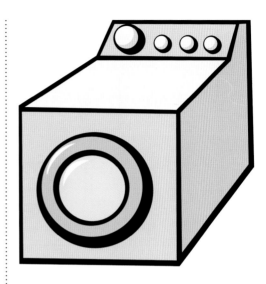

Consumer magazines such as *Consumer Reports* can help you find a good washer or dryer. Be aware, however, that these magazines tend to choose the most capable machines as best, which means they choose machines with features you might not need. Such machines are more expensive than lesser machines that might meet your needs.

HINTS ABOUT LINT

Dryers produce lots of lint, and lint can be flammable. Periodically, vacuum out your dryer vent hose. Metal dryer vent hoses are less of a fire hazard than the flimsy plastic over coiled wire ones commonly used to vent dryers. Don't bend your vent hose into tight coils. This can cause lint to accumulate in bends and block the hose. Be sure your vent hose is securely attached, or it can spew lint that will quickly layer dust over every surface it can reach.

5 LAUNDRY HELPERS

1. Unless you're dexterous enough to fold laundry in midair, a laundry-folding table will be a real boon. If your laundry area is cramped, consider using a folding table that can be closed up and leaned against a wall when not in use.

2. You'll also have to iron your clothing. Ironing boards fold up easily and can be hung on the laundry wall or tucked into a closet. Wall-mounted, fold-away boards are even handier. The best of these include a dampening mechanism to prevent the board from falling precipitously, so that you don't reenact a scene from Tom & Jerry. Foldaway ironing boards come in a variety of types. Some are mounted on your wall, others to the back of your door. These are easy to hang. You need to find two adjacent wall studs, and then securely screw the board's cabinet to them. You also can install a recessed unit that fits into the wall between the studs, so that it doesn't protrude into the room.

3. It's handy to have a drying rack in your laundry room, for those things you don't want to entrust to the dryer. These racks are made of wood, steel,

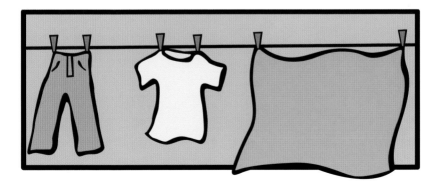

or plastic. Wood is attractive but can warp, darken with use, and harbor mildew. Some wood models avoid this by coating the bars with vinyl, but this reduces their attractiveness to that of a plastic rack. Plastic racks won't discolor but are fragile. Steel racks are stronger but can rust and stain clothing. Probably the best choice is a steel rack coated with vinyl.

4. Retractable clotheslines are also convenient. The clothesline is pulled from a reel and attached to a hook on an opposing wall. A locking mechanism holds the line taut, and a spring-loaded or cranked reel winds up the line when you're done. Most models have a single line, but there are units that run four or five parallel lines. A larger version of this type is available to be hung outside the home, with the lines run to another outer wall or to a post set in the ground. If your laundry has a window, you can use a line hung from pulleys. One pulley is mounted outside the window, while the other is mounted on a pole across your backyard.

5. Plastic laundry baskets make it easier to sort laundry, so that red socks don't turn your white boxers a shocking pink. The baskets can be nested when not in use to take up less space. Hang them from hooks in the laundry room walls or ceiling.

Safety First

Soaps, bleaches, and stain removers can be fatal to curious children, and dangerous to adults as well. To give just one example, a box of powdered bleach might burst into a dusty, eye-burning cloud if dislodged from a high shelf. The best solution is a lockable cabinet. Don't rely on ordinary plastic childproofing locks to secure the cabinet. They break too easily. A good hardware store should carry cabinet locks that can be installed will little difficulty. An ordinary hasp and padlock can also suffice. To control spills, store laundry chemicals in a plastic dishpan. It can do double duty as a soaking vessel for stained clothing.

7 LAUNDRY CHUTE TIPS

If you live in a multiple-story home with a laundry room on a lower floor or in the cellar, consider adding a laundry chute. It will save you many trips up and down your stairs. Here are several points to keep in mind when planning a chute.

1. When hiring a carpenter, get a binding estimate before starting construction. Be sure you and your carpenter agree on a construction timetable.

2. The chute needs to be large enough so sheets and other big pieces of laundry won't get jammed.

3. Don't cut any joists or studs; you can weaken the floor or wall.

4. Pantries and closets are good spots to locate a chute. If these aren't available, you can position a chute in a corner of a room, where you may be able to access it from more than one adjoining room through hatches on corresponding sides of the chute.

5. The chute should be a straight drop. Bends or even slight slanted sections can become clogged with laundry.

6. Plan on placing a basket at the bottom of the chute to catch laundry.

7. Line the chute with aluminum or galvanized steel sheets. Use heavy-duty paneling glue to secure the metal, as nails or screws might snag clothing as it drops.

DUMBWAITERS AREN'T SO DUMB

A dumbwaiter also can be a great convenience, especially for older homeowners. It can carry not only laundry, but also firewood or groceries from floor to floor. A small manual model might not be that challenging to install for an experienced do-it-yourselfer, but a powered dumbwaiter with a heavy load capacity will probably require professional installation.

A manual dumbwaiter is lifted by a rope run through pulleys. The weight of the carriage is balanced by a counterweight to make operation easier. A locking mechanism prevents the carriage from falling when you stop pulling. A powered dumbwaiter is run by an electric motor, so it's something like a little elevator in operation.

Dumbwaiters are most easily installed in new construction, but they can be added to an existing home. As with a laundry chute, try to locate the dumbwaiter where it can be accessed from more than one room.

5 TIPS FOR MAKING A LAUNDRY NOOK

In a smaller home, you'll have to get by with fewer laundry conveniences, so consider:

1. Narrow and/or stackable washer and dryer, or a combination machine, which both washes and dries your clothing.
2. Combining a laundry room with a room of another function—a sewing room, mudroom, or even the kitch-

en—if the intrusion of washer and dryer can be minimized. The stackable set or combo machines might fit into a closet or the kitchen pantry. There are even washers and dryers designed to be installed under the kitchen counter.

3. Foldaway ironing board
4. Retractable drying rack
5. With a small space, you won't have room for mountains of soiled clothing, so you'll need to rely on your bedroom and bathroom hampers to store dirty clothes, emptying them often to keep up.

4 WAYS TO DEAL WITH BAD SMELLS

"If you always stop and smell the roses, eventually you will inhale a bee."

—**Anonymous**

Deodorizing products don't destroy an odor; they only mask it with a pleasant smell until the bad odor fades away. And some odors just won't fade. What can you do to eliminate odors in your house?

1. Locate the spot from which the odor emanates. Scrub the area with laundry detergent, hot water, and a brush. Wipe up the suds with an old towel, then repeat.

2. If this doesn't work, augment the soap with an anti-odor enzyme cleaner. If your grocery rents carpet cleaning machines, it will probably sell this product; and you don't need the machine to use the cleaner. Fill a spray bottle with a 50-50 mixture of water and enzyme cleaner, then spray the smelly area repeatedly. Enzyme cleaners work best when the surface to be treated stays damp.

3. If the enzyme cleaner spray doesn't work, your last option is chlorine bleach. Bleach can only be used where bleaching isn't a problem. Obviously, you won't want to use bleach on carpet. Bleach can also damage wood and other types of flooring.

4. If these treatments all fail, look up "Odor Elimination and Control Services" for compa-

nies that handle environmental and ecological cleaning. They can send out experts who will help you identify and treat problem odors. If these experts suggest an expensive solution, get second and third opinions. Don't delay—odors can become more and more difficult to eliminate as time passes.

2 Steps to Sock Management

1. Sock balling keeps socks matched, but it can stretch out their elastic, especially if the socks are first folded. It's better to lay one sock on its twin, then roll them up. If you must ball your socks, don't fold them before pulling the ankle back over the socks. This will produce a thinner "ankle," which won't stretch your sock's elastic as severely.

2. To avoid having to hunt for a matching sock ever again, settle on a favorite manufacturer and one or two favorite colors that go well with your wardrobe. Then fill your sock drawer with these socks, giving away the rest. Do the same with your athletic socks—plain white cotton suggests itself—in another drawer.

FOURTEEN

Reclaim the Attic, Basement, and Garage

"No person who can read is ever successful at cleaning out an attic."

—Ann Landers

A million muumuus and as many oversize jogging outfits have been purchased by folks anxious to conceal extra pounds. In an overweight home, the attic, basement, and garage are apt to serve a similar purpose as these garments, concealing your excess clutter.

Clutter can pile up for years in these seldom visited spots. In keeping with the "out of sight is out of mind" principle, you aren't likely to impose any order on this stuff, which guarantees frustration when searching for something you've squirreled away. A good decluttering and

cleaning can improve this situation and open up more storage space, so there will be more room under the muumuu.

MAKE A DECLUTTERING MAP

Begin by taking a fresh look at the area to be decluttered. Bring along a pencil and paper on a clip-board. If the area is dusty, wear a dust mask. If there's a low roof to negotiate in the attic, perhaps with roofing nails poking down through it like steel stalactites, wear a plastic safety hard hat. Equip yourself with a pair of work gloves if you anticipate heavy, rough, or less-than-clean items. A flashlight can come in handy, but a shop "trouble light" provides more illumination.

Be mindful of Mother Nature's biohazards. Poisonous spiders love to lurk in dark storage areas. Hornets sometimes nest in attics. The droppings left by mice can carry diseases such as the hanta virus. A dust mask offers some protection against dirt-associated diseases, but only if it's of good quality and fits snugly. If you fall ill after cleaning or have insect bites that turn an unusual color, immediately consult a doctor.

Sketch a simple map of the space to be decluttered. Note any chimneys or flues, to make sure your storage plan won't place flammable items nearby. In the basement, you'll also need to keep a clear path to important household equipment, such as the furnace, water shutoff valves, sump pump, water heater, and circuit-breaker box. Locate these on your sketch, so you can plan around them.

Consider how you'll store your clutter. Note on your map where you hope to put things. Give some thought to the time of year that you'll be likely to use each item, and how frequently you'll want to get your hands on it. Group seasonal items together—all your Christmas decorations, lights, and wrapping paper, for example. Take note of items that will remain unused for long periods, as they can be relegated to less convenient areas. For example, your high school yearbooks won't need to be readily available, no matter how golden those glory days may have been. As elsewhere in the house, be alert for anything that you can throw out or give away. Set these aside, lest you forget about them later.

While you're at it, you may find items that deserve better storage. The attic, basement, and garage can be tough on your possessions. That yearbook could get damp and sprout mold. Do you really want to store your wedding dress under the eaves, where mice might nest in it? An unheated garage can dip to 20 degree below in northern climates, threatening to cause your collection of snow globes, with a measure of irony, to freeze solid and burst.

CLEANING UP AND REORGANIZING

After reviewing the contents of the attic, basement, or garage, sit

down with your map and lists, and plan how you're going to clean and reorganize the area. Consider what cleansers and cleaning tools you'll need, and make a shopping list. Are any of the cleansers caustic? Is there a safer product? Will there be adequate ventilation? If not, find one or more fans to circulate air. Will you need boxes, carton tape, or garbage bags? Will it be necessary to remove items so you have room to clean? Can you create a temporary staging area for the clutter you need to shift? Do you need to add more shelves, hooks, or other storage mechanisms? Note on your map the changes you hope to make.

Ideally, you'll be able to clear out the space completely for a thorough cleaning, using a nearby staging area for your stuff. You can then examine the clutter in the staging area, culling disposable items. If you don't have a staging spot, begin by rearranging your possessions to clear at least a small area in which to assess them. Remove anything you can part with as you discover it, taking it out to the trash or placing it in giveaway boxes. With luck, this will create a space to use for staging.

Be careful when mopping the floor. An attic floor may have gaps, allowing water to leak through and stain the ceilings of the rooms below. Attic, basement, or garage floors may become slick when wet. Wait for floors to dry completely before you start carrying boxes across them.

16-POINT CLEANUP CHECKLIST

An assault on the basement, attic, or garage is likely to require heavy-duty supplies. Here's a list of useful items to have on hand.

1. Dust masks
2. Safety goggles
3. Ear protection
4. Plastic hard hat
5. Work gloves and long rubber gloves
6. Trash bags ("yard" or the even bigger "contractor" bags are less likely to tear when stuffed with your cast-out clutter)
7. Shop vacuum
8. Small-headed broom to reach into tight spots, and a dustpan
9. Heavy-duty cleansers (Murphy's Oil Soap is good for cleaning wood surfaces, and low-sudsing detergent floor cleansers are useful for cleaning floors difficult to rinse. Note that heavily scented cleansers, bleach, and ammonia are apt to become overpowering in small spaces.)
10. Mop and bucket
11. Box cutter
12. Carton tape
13. Markers
14. Hornet spray

15. Mouse and insect traps (date these and note their locations on your map)

16. Pen, paper, and clipboard to annotate your efforts

VACUUM IT

A wet/dry shop vacuum is useful for cleaning attics, basements, and garages. These vacuums are cheap, more powerful than ordinary vacuums, and often have attachments that extend their reach into cramped or high spots. When grounded correctly, they can safely handle water and damp crud. Many models are easily converted into leaf blowers, allowing you to clean areas where a broom can't reach or a vacuum would take too long. By taping plastic over the attic door, for example, you might be able to blow the attic's dust right out an open window, or blow cobwebs, dust, and leaves out the garage door. Blowers have the great advantage of blasting air around boxes, sparing you the need to move all of your stuff around before cleaning. When using a shop vacuum, equip yourself with ear protection—earplugs or headphone-type ear protectors—to prevent its shrill roar from damaging your hearing. If used as a blower, a shop vacuum can fill the air with dirt and debris, so wear a dust mask and safety goggles (safety glasses are less effective, as dirt can blow behind them).

10 ATTIC CONSIDERATIONS

"An antique is something that has made a round trip to the attic and back."

—Anonymous

1. You must be sure the attic floor is strong enough to hold the load you plan to place upon it. If you overburden it, you may create cracks in the ceiling below or, in extreme cases, crash through it. There's also the problem of hauling heavy items up into the attic.

5 Labeling Tips

1. Keep a few markers on hand as you work (they tend to be misplaced), and use them to label clearly boxes as you inspect, reorganize, and pack. A poorly labeled box or a box with unrecorded contents can cause you frustration later.

2. Include a date to alert you to things that have been sitting around unused; these will be likely candidates for discarding the next time you declutter.

3. Different colors of ink can help classify contents—red for important or fragile things, for example.

4. Never label a box "Misc." It's just a waste of ink. You'll have to open the box later to learn its contents.

5. To help you avoid misplacing your markers, store them in a bucket along with your scissors and tape. By keeping these things together in something easy to carry, you won't have to stop work to hunt down these items, a task that can become infuriating on the ninth or tenth repetition.

While some attics are reached via a nice set of stairs, others can only be entered through a hatch reached with a stepladder. Obviously, you can't store items larger than the attic entry, and heavy items, even if they're small enough to pass through, may be too difficult or dangerous to lift or lower through a cramped opening.

2. A leaking roof can destroy your stuff. Before filling your attic with valuables, examine both the exterior and interior sides of its roof. A rainstorm will give you a chance to observe your roof in action. Bring a flashlight up to the attic and look at every part of the roof, especially areas around chimneys or vents where rain may sneak around flashing.

3. Be careful of all belongings that might be affected by temperature changes.

4. Candles can turn into dribbling goo in a hot attic.

5. Plastics and rubber can become brittle or crack in cold attics, while they can ward or become deformed in hot attics.

6. Containers of liquid can freeze and burst.

7. Foodstuffs are a tempting lure to vermin.

8. Electronics contain temperature-sensitive components, which can prematurely age in a hot attic (electronics are also dust magnets).

9. Clothing can host mildew if it becomes damp, and high temperatures can damage delicate fabrics.

10. Paper can dry out during a hot summer and then dampen in the chill of winter, in a cycle that speeds decay.

3 STEPS TO A TEMPERATE ATTIC

The ordinary activities of life—cooking, showering, and washing laundry—generate hot, humid air, which if not exhausted can cause dampness to accumulate in your home. This dampness can damage your insulation, walls, wallpaper,

Don't Be Slowed by Sentiment

When decluttering, you may run into things that have sentimental associations. Before you know it, you're wandering down Memory Lane instead of tidying. More than one attic decluttering expedition has foundered on a box of old photos. A good way to avoid this trap is to deliberately set aside a spot where you can stack sentimental stuff to look through at the end of your work, as a reward for completing the decluttering.

paint, and even your siding. In summer, unventilated attic air is apt to become extremely hot, and high temperatures over time may damage joists, roof sheathing, and roofing. The attic's heat also can warm the rooms below, increasing air conditioning costs. In winter, unventilated damp air can condense on insulation, and cause it to rot and become vulnerable to mold. Proper ventilation will both improve your attic's environment and also protect your home.

1. A remedy is to install exhaust fans in an attic window or through the roof. They can be either operated manually or controlled by a thermostat. Electric fans should be equipped with safety switches to turn them off in case of fire. This prevents them from drawing in air during a blaze that would make the fire more intense.

2. A more permanent solution is to install a vent along the ridge of the roof, drawing cool air from the soffits along the eaves up through the vent using natural convection instead of a fan.

3. Attic temperature extremes can be ameliorated by insulation. Fiberglass insulation, which looks like rolls of cotton candy, can be placed between the rafters of the roof. It's a fairly straightforward job, as long as you take certain precautions. Small particles of fiberglass can damage your lungs, eyes, and skin. Wear a good dust mask, eye protection, gloves, and a long-sleeve shirt during installation. Button the neck of the shirt or tie a neckerchief around your throat, to prevent particles from going down your neck. Shower immediately after working with fiberglass. Keep insulation at least 3 inches away from light fixtures, to prevent overheating. Do not fill the spaces between a chimney and adjacent wood framing with insulation that has vapor-retardant paper attached. Use noncombustible, unfaced fiberglass insulation instead.

FINISHING YOUR ATTIC

You may find it within your do-it-yourself ability to convert an attic into useful storage space, so long as the project doesn't involve electrical wiring or major alterations (be careful to incorporate proper ventilation). You'll probably want to bring in a contractor if the job is more ambitious.

A finished attic will be less dusty, drier, and more moderate in temperature. It can tidily incorporate storage arrangements. Consider using the space where your roof meets the floor at an angle for cupboards or shelves. Spaces that have little headroom can be used for cupboards or cabinets. You can run clothing rods across your attic to hang clothing, or add hooks to joists to suspend items. Be careful that you don't create eye-poking or head-clunking hazards.

5 WAYS TO STOW ATTIC CONTENTS

After cleaning your attic and making any improvements, it's time to neatly stow away your stuff. Using the map you sketched at the start of your attic attack, take some time to plan how you'll store items.

1. Place seldom-used things in first, followed by items you expect to need more often.
2. Possessions that will be used together should be stored together.
3. Keep a list and map of where you're storing things. Post these by the entry to the attic, along with a pencil and some blank paper.
4. Amend your list and map as you add or subtract items from storage.
5. If there are particular features that you may need to find quickly, such as a circuit box or access panel, make a separate, clearly labeled map of where they are, and post it where a repair person can find it in case you aren't around.

A BAG IN A BOX TO FOIL INSECTS

Mothballs and cedar blocks are traditional ways of keeping bugs from damaging clothing. Unfortunately, neither guarantees that your things will be safe. A better approach is to store clothing in clear, tight-sealing plastic storage boxes. They keep their contents dry and bug-free, while allowing you to see what's stored inside. Discount and housewares stores carry a wide selection. A cheaper alternative is to place a clear plastic trash bag in a cardboard box. Fill the bag, press it to expel air, close it tightly with a twist tie, and tape the box shut.

Fur, linen, and leather don't do well in plastic. Antique fabrics may deteriorate, especially if you aren't careful to clean the items before storage. Plastic bags emit chemical vapors that may damage their contents if stored for years. For long-term storage, an ordinary suitcase, trunk, or garment bag used with mothballs or cedar blocks is a good choice. For ordinary seasonal storage, moisture and insects are greater dangers.

When assembling cardboard boxes, use fiberglass-reinforced tape to hold together the bottoms, which will bear the weight of the boxes' contents. Box tops don't need as much strength, so ordinary carton tape should be adequate. Masking tape and old-fashioned gummed tape tend to dry out and fail over time.

Used cardboard boxes can be a source of insect infestations, especially those from groceries. Instead, purchase new boxes from moving companies or storage facilities. In some areas there are box manufacturers who make boxes for commercial use. They often have overruns or seconds that they sell at low prices. These boxes are "one of a kind," so if you find a style that you like, stock up; it's unlikely that you'll be able to buy more in the future.

6 WAYS TO BOX UP YOUR HOLIDAYS

Holiday decorations spend 11 months of the year in storage. Here are several suggestions for keeping everything in good order.

1. Group all of the items associated with a holiday in one place.
2. Dedicate separate boxes to particular types of items—Christmas garlands, lights, and so on. Indoor and outdoor decorations should be boxed separately.
3. Take advantage of the storage process to review your holiday supplies. If things are broken,

over the tubes to keep them dust-free.

FIRE SAFETY

One of the best investments in home safety is a smoke detector. A few bucks and a little vigilance in changing the battery may save your home and your family. Smoke detectors should be mounted near living areas, so your family can hear their alarms. You should also mount detectors in the attic, basement, garage, and other nonliving areas where otherwise a fire might not be noticed until well established.

Your home should also have carbon monoxide detectors. Every winter, clogged flues and faulty furnaces silently kill unwary families. Never substitute a carbon

are unneeded duplicates, or are obsolete, throw them out.

4. Store your Christmas cards and Christmas mailing boxes with your Thanksgiving decorations, so that you'll pull them out early enough to mail in time.

5. As you dispose of each year's Christmas cards, update your Christmas card list. Record not only the address of the senders but also information you might want to refer to in next year's message—the names of family members, important events, and so on.

6. Christmas wrapping paper is awkward to store. Use a tall, clean, kitchen trash can as an organizer, and place a trash bag

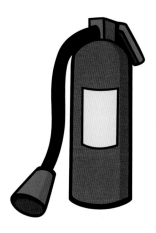

VACUUM BAGS

For some items in your wardrobe, you may want to invest in vacuum storage bags. These are heavy plastic bags equipped with valves, which allow you to extract most of the air inside them with a vacuum cleaner. This compresses the size of bulky items, such as sweaters or blankets, so that you need much less storage space. Note that a down comforter or coat may lose its fluffiness—and its warmth—if compressed tightly for months.

monoxide detector for proper maintenance of your heating system. While it's useful to know if CO is building up in nonliving areas, it's more important to know if it's at dangerous levels in living areas, so install detectors in living areas first.

All detectors should be UL-approved, and you should regularly check that their batteries are fresh and that they're operating correctly. Many homeowners choose the dates when daylight saving time begins and ends as the dates to check their detectors.

8 BASEMENT TIPS

"I told my wife that a husband is like a fine wine; he gets better with age. The next day, she locked me in the cellar."

—Anonymous

Nobody but Uncle Fester enjoys a basement. They're often dark, claustrophobic, and damp, but nevertheless we entrust a lot of what we own to this space.

1. Before going to work on a cluttered basement, examine it for signs of water, such as whitish mineral residue on the walls, rotted wood, or peeling paint. A certified home inspector can help you identify water problems. You then may have to hire a contractor who specializes in solving water problems before you can rely on your basement for safe storage.

2. If you have a sump pump, check to see that it's in working order. You can test it by dumping a bucket of water into the hole that contains the pump. If

the float refuses to rise and turn on the pump, it may be caught in grime. Unplug the pump—to prevent electrical shock—and clear away the grime. If the pump still doesn't work, try repositioning it. If it still refuses to work, call a plumber. It's important to get a faulty sump pump fixed fast before wet weather can flood your basement.

3. Waterproofing paint can help keep your basement dry, as long as you don't have a serious water problem. (If the existing paint has bubbled or lifted up, your basement may be too damp to warrant applying another coat.) Another advantage of painting concrete walls is that they'll produce less dust, making it easier to clean

your basement. Pale gray is a good color, helping to lighten a gloomy basement without showing every bit of dirt that may accumulate. Make sure to buy a paint intended for basements and concrete.

4. Despite inspections and precautions, assume that anything you store in the basement might be exposed to water. Shelving should be elevated a few inches above the floor.

5. Store boxes on shipping pallets, the low wooden platforms that support loads for forklifts. Pallets can sometimes be gotten for free from factories (check the classified ads).

6. Another good basement storage technique is to suspend items from the ceiling using

EASY DOES IT

Seeing in the Cellar

Keep a flashlight near the top of the basement stairs. It can prove handy for probing dark corners and will be invaluable for checking circuit breakers if the power goes out and your breaker box is in the basement.

hooks. Don't place hooks in traffic areas, to avoid bumping your head. Never hang even the lightest items from pipes, heating and cooling ducts, chimneys, or exposed wiring.

7. Dehumidifiers help keep basements dry by condensing moisture from the air. The water either accumulates in a bucket that you empty periodically or runs through a hose to a floor drain.

8. You can use desiccants—a substance that attracts moisture from the air—to help keep your stored possessions dry. You can find these at hardware stores.

STOCKING UP IN THE BASEMENT

Canned and bottled foodstuffs can be safely stored in the basement, as people have been doing for generations. This is an attractive option if you don't have the convenience of a pantry. You can stockpile food on cellar shelves, making fewer trips to the market and taking advantage of lower prices on bulk or sale items. Because basements are apt to be

damp, check cans for rusting, and rotate your stock to ensure freshness. If products aren't labeled with dates by which they should be used, label them with their purchase dates using a marker, so you'll know how old they are in the future.

8 STEPS TO PLANNING BASEMENT STORAGE

1. As with the attic, planning before you declutter and reorganize the basement will produce better results. Sketch a map of the basement. Note the location of the furnace, sump pump, water shutoff valves, and other key features. It's important to plan your storage around these, so that they'll remain accessible. You don't want to have

to move a shelf loaded with pickled zucchini to reach the water shutoff valve when a pipe bursts.

2. After you have a map, lay out where shelves or pallets should go. You want to maximize storage while keeping stored items easy to retrieve. Take a tip from the way retailers shelve their stock. They set shelves against the walls, then cross the remaining space with rows of more shelves. Do the same. You can run the rows right up to the walls in an "E" pattern, with the rows closed off at the back.

3. Keep a list of what's stored where, and draw maps illustrating the list, as you did for the attic. Post the list and map near the stairs, where you can easily find them. Keep them up-to-date. You'll also want to post a map that omits storage details but shows where important basement features are located, such as your water shutoff valve. Post it where service people can see it, in case you're not around when they call.

4. As you compose your basement plan, consider how you'll be cleaning the space. You won't

5 Unhappy Basement Residents

Not all items are suitable for basement storage.

1. Paper can absorb moisture over time, growing dank or sprouting mildew.

2. Boxed foods can be spoiled by dampness or attacked by insects or mice.

3. Metal items may rust in a damp environment.

4. Electric appliances can become dangerous if their wiring deteriorates from corrosion or from the nibbling teeth of mice.

5. Clothing, blankets, and stuffed items such as pillows and teddy bears can get musty.

want to carry stuff upstairs to make room for cleaning, only to bring it back down for storage. It's better to move everything to one side of the basement, clean the vacated area, then move everything to the other side, and clean the remaining space.

5. A shop vacuum can help you clean under and behind objects. Don't neglect the basement's ceiling, where cobwebs invariably accumulate.

6. It's unlikely your basement is well ventilated, so be extra careful about employing cleaning chemicals. Don't use any that emit toxic fumes.

7. Wear a dust mask to protect you from dust and mold that you kick up while cleaning.

8. Improve ventilation by setting a box fan at the cellar door to blow fresh air down the cellar stairs.

FINISHING YOUR BASEMENT

Turning your basement into living space is a popular home improvement project. A finished basement makes a great family room or guest bedroom, while freeing up storage space throughout your home. But basements can retain a dark, damp, chilly atmosphere, even when insulated and finished off with drywall or paneling. To minimize this, give extra attention to lighting and warmth, and resolve water problems before finishing your basement. It can be difficult and costly to correct problems after the renovation has been completed.

Keep in mind that finishing a basement may reduce its floor

space, meaning less room for your shelves of canned goods and that pool table your family wants. You might want to devote only part of the basement to a finished living area, reserving an unfinished section for storage and utilities.

9 STEPS TO GARAGE DECLUTTER

"Only in America—do we leave cars worth thousands of dollars in the driveway and put our useless junk in the garage"

—**Anonymous**

1. Pick a pleasant weekend to tackle the garage. When the weather turns cold, you won't want to wrestle with the clutter in an unheated garage. And the sweaty days of summer also deflate one's decluttering enthusiasm. Your clutter-cutting and reorganization will proceed more smoothly if you can lug everything out to the driveway for inspection, disposal, and repacking. It will also be easier to clean your garage thoroughly.

2. Each season creates its own clutter pressures. Winter requires setting aside space for gear such as snow shovels, driveway salt, sleds, and boots. Summer means the kids' bikes will be put to use. Spring may bring out your gardening gear and lawn mower, while fall means your rake and leaf blower will be needed. If possible, reserve a convenient space for the necessary clutter of the moment. Swap out its contents as the seasons pass.

3. Draw up a map of your garage, noting important features. As you review its contents, make a list of the things that will be stored here. With your map and list, do a little planning to work out how best to store your belongings. Your interests will guide your plans. If you like to garden, for example, you'll need to allocate space for garden tools and supplies. If you tinker with your car, you'll want to dedicate room to your auto tools.

4. Your garage likely isn't heated or air-conditioned, but the things stored there will be in better shape if you can moderate the temperature by insulating the

Chemical Lockup

Paint thinner, insecticides, anti-freeze, pool cleaners, and dozens of other substances commonly stored in garages can sicken or kill a curious kid. Get a lockable cabinet, and store them safely away.

walls and roof. You can then cover these surfaces with sheets of plywood or composite board for a finished appearance.

5. Time to clean. Open the door for ventilation before you begin using any cleansers.

6. If you're able to move most of your possessions out of the way, you can blow dust and debris out of the garage door with a leaf blower. Or use a small-headed broom or shop vacuum to clean corners and under objects, and sweep open areas with a push broom.

7. After sweeping out dirt, wash the garage floor with a strong detergent. Garage floors commonly become oil stained. Some homeowners use caustic cleansers to clean these stains away. This can be very dangerous. If you must use such products, always read their labels before you even open the container, wear protective gear such as goggles and gloves, and be prepared with countermeasures such as baking soda to neutralize acid and a hose to flush skin.

8. To more safely clean oil spots, apply a paste of baking soda and kitty litter or powdered dishwasher detergent. Rub it in with a brush, let it set a few moments, then sweep it up. Wash the spot with dishwasher detergent, then rinse with clean water. Stains can also be diminished by sanding or by scrubbing with a wire brush.

9. To forestall staining your garage floor, place a boot drip pan under your car to catch leaks. Sprinkle kitty litter in the pan to soak up oil.

20 MUST-HAVE FIX-IT TOOLS

Many homeowners keep a workbench in their garage, where they store an assortment of tools for everyday household repairs. It doesn't take long for an amateur handyperson to accumulate a lot of tools, many of which are seldom used. A little organization can simplify this situation. If you're only going to nail up the occasional picture or tighten the odd screw, you won't need many tools. You can buy an inexpensive tool kit and supplement it as necessary so you have:

1. Ratchet wrench set
2. Screwdrivers
3. Pliers
4. Wire strippers
5. Hammer
6. Tape measure

7. Handsaw
8. Hacksaw for cutting metal
9. Cordless electric drill

These tools will carry you through most simple tasks. They also won't need much storage space. The next step up in handyperson equipage is setting up a workbench. Hardware stores sell kits for sturdy workbenches with storage underneath. You'll need ground fault interrupter (GFI) outlets near the workbench to prevent accidental shocks, and good overhead lighting in order to work safely.

If you choose to take on more than simple household projects, add tools judiciously. Here's a suggested inventory:

10. Putty knife
11. Vise to hold objects securely while you work on them
12. Basic power tools, such as a circular saw, sander, and jigsaw
13. Miter box and miter saw for cutting accurate angles
14. Monkey wrench for basic plumbing
15. Sawhorses
16. Extension cord with a built-in circuit breaker

It makes good decluttering sense to rent tools that you don't use often. A tile cutter, for example, is essential to tiling your bathroom, but you're unlikely to do enough tiling to justify keeping one.

17. Framing triangle and carpenter's square for laying out angles
18. Shop light for illuminating dark work areas
19. Heavy-duty snippers for cutting sheet metal and wire
20. Level

10 WAYS TO STORE FIX-IT STUFF

1. If you plan to tackle a lot of fix-it jobs, invest in a special-purpose tool chest.
2. A secondhand dresser can also serve to store tools.
3. If you do a lot of work on your car, visit an auto parts shop for a look at a multi-drawer, rolling tool organizer. When not in use, it can be wheeled out of the way.
4. Peg-Board is a traditional way of storing tools on a wall out in the open, where they can be easily seen. There's a wide variety of Peg-Board hangers designed to support just about any tool, from chisels all the way up to shovels and rakes. You also can buy hangers that will support lightweight shelving.

When putting up Peg-Board, you need to leave a small space behind it so that the hangers can fit through the holes and lock in place. To do this on a finished wall, you'll have to secure furring strips to the wall first, and then attach the Peg-Board to them. Otherwise, hanging Peg-Board is simple—just be sure to securely attach it with screws that will reach well into the wall's studs.

To hang smaller tools, you can place a Peg-Board over a workbench. To store larger tools, you may have to install it along an open section of wall. Don't hang it where you'll be apt to get snagged when walking past.

5. If your carpentry efforts extend to projects using such stationary equipment as table saws, router tables, and other woodworking machinery, you'll need to allocate space for them. They're apt to generate great clouds of dust. There are vacuum systems to collect this, but they won't capture every bit. Drape tarps over things you want to keep clean. You can also install an exhaust fan to help expel dust from the garage. Routinely clean the garage, using a shop vacuum to help collect fugitive sawdust.

6. Nails and screws can be stored in clear plastic jars recycled from your kitchen. Don't use glass jars; they can break and scatter sharp shards of glass (along with your nails) across the garage floor.

7. Odds and ends of hardware, such as wire, door catches, and L-brackets, can be stored in clear plastic storage tubs.

8. Gather smaller items into open-top boxes to organize them.

9. Paint, stains, caulk, and similar supplies are best stored on low shelves where they won't tumble. To keep your shelves clean, you can place paper plates under paint cans to catch drips that run down their sides. The drips will glue the plate to the can, keeping the plate where it can catch future drips.

EASY DOES IT

The Old Suspended Jar Trick

A longtime garage workshop tip is to drill a hole in the lid of a jar, attach the lid to the underside of a shelf with a sheet-metal screw, fill the jar with nails or bolts, and then turn the jar to secure it to the lid. Use plastic jars for safety.

10. In addition to storing small supplies, you may need to

find a way to stash lumber of various lengths and widths. Boards should to be stored flat, with enough support to prevent bowing and warping. You can construct a simple wooden rack to store and organize your lumber. Using 2 by 4s, construct three rectangular frames about 3 feet wide and 4 feet tall, with a horizontal piece crossing at the middle. Place the frames upright, and connect them with 6-foot-long 2 by 4s. Bolt the 2 by 4s together for extra strength; the rack will be supporting a lot of weight. By extending the bottom 2 by 4s of the frames a few inches on one side, you can create a platform for plywood to lean against the rack. Add a short vertical piece at each end, to prevent the plywood from sliding off. If you store plywood this way for an extended time, you may want to turn it in the rack periodically to prevent bowing.

6 SHELVING CONSIDERATIONS

As you consider where to place the things you want to keep in your garage, think in terms of exploiting

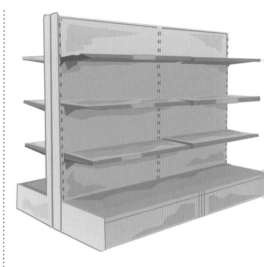

the walls, rafters, and every nook, while leaving room for the main purpose of this part of your house—storing one or more cars.

Shelves provide the best horizontal storage in this limited area, but invest considerable thought in laying out garage shelves and other storage arrangements. You'll have to open your car doors to get in and out, sometimes with bulky parcels in your arms. To make it easier to park your car without banging it into shelves or cabinets, employ the old tennis-ball-hanging-from-a-rope trick. Position the rope so it dangles the ball where it will just touch the driver's side of the windshield when the car is properly parked.

1. Wooden shelves can be customized to fit your garage's corners and nooks and can hold very large loads. But unfinished, rough-surfaced wooden shelving can be difficult to clean, as every crevice traps grime.
2. Painted wooden shelves fare better but may not resist garage spills and rough use.
3. Steel utility shelves are stronger and easier to keep clean, but those that bolt together can become rickety and even collapse if the bolts loosen. They also tend to have sharp edges that can surprise the unwary.
4. A more finished quality of steel shelving, like that used in libraries and stores, won't easily fall apart but will be much more expensive. Steel shelves of all types can rust.
5. Plastic resin shelves hold up well in damp garages, can bear moderately heavy loads, and are easy to clean. They snap together without screws or bolts. As an added ecological boon, these shelves are commonly made from recycled soda bottles. They can, however, be expensive, and like any manufactured storage unit, they may not fit the particular geography of your garage.
6. You can assemble your own shelving using plastic shelving brackets and 2 by 4s for the legs and shelf frames. Plywood is cut to form the shelves. No complicated cuts or joints are needed. The 2 by 4s are held tight in the brackets with screws. You can vary the height of the vertical 2 by 4s and length of the horizontal 2 by 4s to customize the shelves to your location. It's easy to take apart these shelves and alter them to fit changing needs.

4 WAYS TO RACK OR HANG ITEMS

1. To suspend items from the walls, you may be tempted to simply pound nails here and there and use them as hooks. While this may work, it's rather inelegant, and nails are apt to fail under large loads. Instead, attach a horizontal board to the studs of the garage wall

with screws, then screw hooks into the board.

2. Hardware stores sell special hangers for suspending long-handled tools, such as brooms or shovels.

3. Another solution for storing long-handled yard tools is to stand them handle down in a large barrel. An ordinary garbage can will work. To keep the barrel from over-turning, pour a few inches of gravel or sand into it. Garden supply centers often stock used wooden barrels. Junkyards sometimes have old steel barrels you can slap a coat of paint on. Just be sure to avoid any barrels inscribed with "Toxic Waste."

4. You can build a simple rack with 2 by 4s to store hoes, rakes, and such. Make a 4-foot-high,

open-sided box, about 2⅓ feet by 2⅓ feet square. At the top and about a foot from the ground, cross 2 by 4s to divide the box's interior into four. Store your tools by standing them in the open sections. You can vary these dimensions to fit your needs and tools. The rack will be difficult to over-turn, but to make sure, attach it to your garage wall with a few L-brackets. Then if a child climbs on it or your car nudges it, it won't topple.

BIKE STORAGE

Bicycles are bulky bits of clutter that can clog your garage. If they're not in frequent use, you can suspend them from your garage ceiling or walls. Check with a bicycle shop for special-purpose racks. One appealing device uses a rope and catch arrangement like that used to pull up window blinds. The rope is attached to the bike, which is hoisted above the garage floor where the catch locks it aloft. Tug the rope to one side and the catch loosens and you can lower the bike. Be sure to put a cleat on the wall where it'll be handy to tie off the rope. You don't want a failure of the catch to dump your bike.

A LOFTY SOLUTION

To make the most of the space in a garage, you can construct a loft—a raised platform that can provide "floor space" on a level above the garage floor. This works in garages that have high ceilings, or even better, no ceilings. You may even be able to install a full attic. Do careful measuring and planning before you begin, as building a large loft can involve some tricky positioning. To support the load, you'll likely need posts, which may restrict how you can park your car. In a two-car garage, you might reserve one side for a compact car and a loft above, while the other side is left open for a taller vehicle.

The Garage as Your Frozen-Food Section

A separate freezer can save you money by allowing you to buy and preserve foods in bulk when they're on sale. Since this additional freezer is unlikely to be opened every single day, the garage tends to be a good spot for it. This area is easy to break into, however, so put a padlock on the freezer's latch (some models come with locks). Your freezer should always be plugged into a GFI outlet. You don't want to electrocute yourself fetching a bag of frozen peas.

As to which model to buy, manual-defrost freezers typically use 35 to 40 percent less electricity than comparable automatic-defrost models. Automatic defrosters remove moist air to forestall frost, which can dehydrate food and lead to freezer burn. Chest freezers are usually better insulated and don't dump their cold air when opened. They may use 20 percent less electricity than stand-up models, but the food inside a chest freezer won't be as easy to see and touch.

The loft should be provided with a lip, to prevent stored objects from rolling off. If the area is large enough to allow walking around, you'll want to add a railing to keep you from taking a tumble. A ladder may suffice for access, but where possible, build a set of permanent stairs.

An option less involved than building a loft is to construct a large storage shelf that takes advantage of the space above the hood of a parked car. You'll need to either suspend this shelf from overhead joists—this is only suitable for lighter loads—or support it from underneath with posts and strong beams, for heavier loads. While you'll gain storage space, you won't be able to walk around the front of the car or open its hood. Later on, such a loft can be an obstacle if you replace your car with a higher-hooded vehicle.

Garages are such caverns of clutter that a number of manufacturers are producing elaborate systems of cabinets, lockers, and shelving specifically for this area. Visit a few home improvement centers and take a look at what they offer. Even if you find their solutions too expensive or not suited to your garage, they may give you ideas that will be useful when planning your own storage arrangements.

11 WAYS TO DISCOURAGE PESTS

Mice, rats, and squirrels can make a terrible mess of your stored items in your attic, basement, or garage. What to do?

1. If you discover a nest, remove it and clean out the area immediately, as the odor will only worsen.
2. A cat might seem a logical remedy, but many domestic felines prefer a nice bowl of commercial cat food, rather than hunting down an elusive

rodent. Even if your cat is a ferocious hunter, it may not have access to areas where critters have set up housekeeping.

3. Poison can be effective at killing rodents, but a mouse or squirrel may die in a wall or under a floor and create a stink as it decomposes. Also, your cat might be made ill by dining on the deceased varmint.

4. Traditional snap traps can work well, but they may pin a mouse's paw without killing the pest. Newer snap traps place the snapping bar inside an enclosure that makes it nearly impossible for a mouse to avoid being killed.

5. Battery-powered traps now make it possible to electrocute mice.

6. Live-capture traps are another option, but they require you to transport the animal away from your home, where it may just become some other householder's problem. Also, an animal released in strange terrain may quickly fall prey to predators, so your mercy may not be merciful. Finally, an agitated mouse may bite you as

you release it, exposing you to rabies or other diseases.

7. You probably have seen ultrasonic pest-repelling devices on the market, which are supposed to emit a sound frequency that sends rodents running. There's little evidence that these work.

8. Other repellants employ a smellier approach. They use absorbent particles soaked in bobcat or fox urine. You spread the particles outside your house, allegedly to convince mice that predators are near. The more pleasant odors of spearmint and peppermint oils, which mice are said to abhor, are also used to infuse mouse repellants. You can make your own minty sachets by stuffing old panty hose with dried spearmint or peppermint leaves. While many people swear by odor-based repellants, there's little or no scientific evidence that they work.

9. The most effective antirodent measure you can take is to close all the openings rodents may use to enter your home. Mice can squeeze through small cracks, and squirrels are very adept at

chewing through wood. Look for any hole wider than a finger width, and seal it up. A simple tactic for finding openings into attics, cellars, and garages is to darken these areas—tape paper over windows and turn out the lights—and then look for any sign of light from the outside in a crack or hole. Caulk and exterior-grade Spackle work well to close small openings. Larger holes can be stuffed with wire screening and then covered over with Spackle. To close a large hole, cut a piece of wood to fit, then nail it in place. A bit of quick-setting concrete can also be used to close openings, and it will resist rodent teeth better than caulk or Spackle. As a beneficial side effect, you'll be sealing out drafts and increasing the energy efficiency of your home.

10. To block off ventilation openings, use screens or screened caps, which admit air without allowing animals to enter.

11. If all else falls, you'll have to consult an exterminator. Squirrels, in particular, can be diffi-

cult to control. Exterminators have specialized equipment that will do the job effectively.

10 WAYS TO CONTROL CAR CLUTTER

"Never buy a car that's being sold at the bottom of a ravine."

—Joey Adams

Don't overlook your car when attacking clutter. It's apt to be full of old fast-food wrappers, CDs, and unrefoldable road maps. If

12-Point Emergency Car Kit

1. Simple first-aid manual
2. First-aid supplies such as bandages and antibacterial wipes
3. Jumper cables with the instructions for using them
4. Duct tape
5. Reflectors to make your car more visible on the side of the road. (Road flares can do this but eventually burn out, while a reflector remains reflective.)
6. Multi-tool gizmos that has pliers, a screwdriver, and a knife
7. Spare fuses
8. Gasoline funnel
9. If you have room, stow a small, unused, empty plastic gas can. It can prove handy if you run dry of either gas or water and need to fetch some. Never store a gas can with gasoline in it in your car. It can be very dangerous.
10. If you know how to change the signal and brake lights, buy spares.
11. If your car is apt to burn or leak oil, include a couple quarts of it in your kit.
12. In the winter, supplement your emergency kit with a small shovel, a bag of sand or kitty litter for traction on ice, deicer spray, a couple of blankets, some rock candy or granola bars, candles, and matches. Remember to remove the candles in warm weather. They'll melt in a hot automobile.

you have children, you can add toys and a lot more fast-food trash to the list. Clear the clutter from your car on a routine basis.

1. Purge your glove compartment.
2. Remove the sheaf of gas receipts clipped to your visor.
3. Pull garbage out from under the seats.

4. Examine the contents of your trunk, and toss extraneous items.

5. Place sturdy, rectangular laundry baskets in the trunk to hold groceries and other purchases. The baskets will prevent goods from tumbling about and make it easier to carry them into your home.

6. Keep a plastic basket in the backseat, so that your kids can tidily stow the toys they like to take on trips.

7. A zippered portfolio, tucked under your seat, makes an excellent container for maps.

8. To make an inaccessible spare tire easier to get at, place it in a trash bag and store it in the trunk. This will also make it simple for you to periodically check the spare's air pressure. A flat spare won't get you anywhere.

9. Put trash bags in your car to collect refuse. Plastic grocery sacks are good for this. Roll a few up and stash them under a seat. When you generate trash, pull one out and use it to stow the trash. You can dispose of

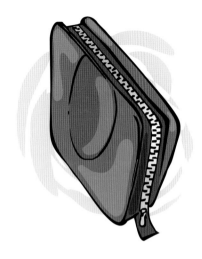

the sack when you reach your destination.

10. Reserve the glove compartment for items that have immediate value, such as your owner's manual, a tire pressure gauge, extra tire valve caps (these are always going missing), an ice scraper for your windshield (a longer snow brush can be kept in your trunk), a change purse for tolls and pay phones, a flashlight with fresh batteries, a pencil and pad for taking notes, sunglasses, a local map—and maybe even a pair of gloves.

Simple Cellar Plan

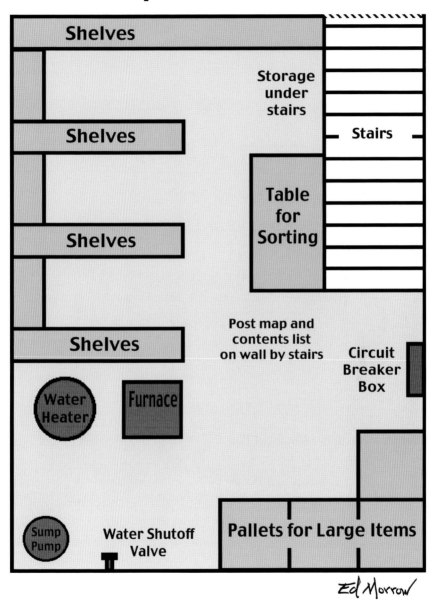

FIFTEEN

The Uncluttered Yard

"I appreciate the misunderstanding I have had with Nature over my perennial border. I think it is a flower garden; she thinks it is a meadow lacking grass, and tries to correct the error."

— Sara Stein

While the clutter in your home is visible only to family, visiting friends, and the occasional service person, your yard is on display to the whole neighborhood. Everyone can see your shaggy lawn, dispirited hedges, and seasick roses. In diet terms, it's a bit like eating tiny meals of cottage cheese and carrot sticks at home, then going out to the county fair where you enter and win a pie-eating contest. To live a truly decluttered life, you need to control clutter outside your home as well as inside it.

4 KEYS TO A BEAUTIFUL YARD

The key to a tidy yard is to plan to make the property easy to maintain during all four seasons.

1. Simplify your yard. Choose a few vigorous decorative plantings that need little attention. Consult a nursery about which plants and trees do best in your area, while needing the least amount of care.

2. Keep in mind the layout of your yard, and how your plantings

will grow. For example, a little Douglas fir on your lawn may look charming when bedecked with twinkle lights at Christmastime, but 20 years down the line, the cute sapling that looked like Charlie Brown's humble tree could be two stories high, blocking your view of anything other than its hulking green mass.

3. A nursery professional will be able to suggest plantings suitable for the spaces in your yard and describe how they will mature. He or she may even come to your home to advise you without charge. You can also consult your county extension agent for gardening advice. While you may think these people work only where the corn is as high as an elephant's eye, they also serve urban areas.

4. Don't overlook experts who may live around the corner. Every neighborhood has a house where all the plants in the yard are hale and hearty, the grass is luxuriant, and the flowers bloom wantonly. Stop by when the owners are outside

puttering around, and ask what they plant and how they nurture it. People who love to garden often love talking about gardening, too, and they'll share their expertise.

Don't Plant Trouble

When you set out plants, don't forget home security. A cluttered landscape can create hiding places for burglars or prowlers. Other plantings can be protective, such as a thorny hedge that discourages intruders.

5 MOVABLE GARDEN TIPS

Most yards feature flower beds to enliven them, but as the summer passes and the glamorous blooming plants of spring become the tired, bare stalks of late summer and fall, your flower beds can become unkempt blocks of yard clutter. Many gardeners forestall this by swapping out plants that have passed their prime for newer, more alluring plants. This can involve a lot of effort and eventually will falter as the growing season ends, leaving patches of your yard that bear nothing but dead, shrunken vegetation.

Potted plants offer an easier, less cluttery alternative. Pots of plants can be removed from view when their contents stop being ornamental, preventing those shriveled spots of dead plants. Potted plants require less weeding, pest control, and fertilizing. Containers can be easily rearranged as their contents bloom or fade. They can be grouped to present a mass of color like a flower bed, or placed out in small clutches wherever you want to add some visual stimulation to your yard. They're especially handy on a deck or porch where you have limited space to devote to plants. Pots come in a wide variety of styles and can be decorative in themselves while providing spatial definition to parts of your yard. A few long planters full of flowers will brighten and delineate the edges of a patio, for example.

Pots and planters also can be arranged to conceal unattractive clutter in your yard, such as a utility access post. Large pots containing shrubs or bushes are especially good for screening, and even these heavy containers can be rearranged with a dolly or forklift. Mix in new elements to keep your yard's appearance fresh and interesting. Here are some planter options.

1. Glazed ceramic pots are available in many shapes and colors, with plenty of designs from which to choose. They tend to be heavy.

2. Terra-cotta containers are attractive and drain well, letting roots breathe. They're porous, however, and the soil they contain can quickly dry out. They, too, are heavy.

3. Another heavyweight is the concrete planter. These are strong and available in many shapes, ranging from simple pot forms to imitations of classical urns.

4. Plastic planters are light and hold moisture well. Some simulate the appearance of traditional containers, while others offer designs only practical to produce in plastic.

5. Wooden planters have an appealingly rustic look, but they can seem nearly as heavy as concrete if the wood becomes damp. Damp wood, even redwood or wood treated with preservatives, will deteriorate. Some planters forestall this with metal liners to protect the wood.

No matter what they're made of, larger planters are better at holding in moisture than smaller containers, and they also provide more root room for your plants. Just keep in mind the back strain that may be involved in moving them.

5 CONSIDERATIONS FOR FLOWER BEDS AND PERMANENT PLANTINGS

While using pots and planters has advantages, flower beds and permanent plantings offer other advantages and possibilities, especially for committed gardeners. Perennials, for example, can be cultivated over a period of years into better and better form. Planters are too cramped to make this easy. Flower beds and plantings can also fill larger spaces, making them more useful for landscaping and clutter concealment. Here are some points to consider.

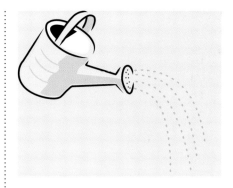

1. Choose the location of flower beds and permanent plantings carefully; they'll be troublesome to move. If you're unsure about how they may fit into your yard, you can lay out cardboard boxes mimicking their size, then stand back to observe the effect.

2. Mulch can provide an attractive, tidy background for your plants. It helps retain moisture while limiting rain-spattered mud, which can begrime your house from foundation plantings.

3. Garden fabric reduces the visual clutter of weeds. The open weave allows water to penetrate, while discouraging weeds from growing up through it. You place garden fabric over a planting bed, cut individual holes for inserting plants, then cover the fabric with mulch.

4. Consider raised flower beds, formed by building frames of rot-resistant logs or boards, then filling them with soil. Raised beds are easier to cultivate, because you don't have to bend over quite as far.

5. When choosing plants, keep in mind how they'll look at all stages of their lives. Too often we're beguiled by a beautiful seed packet picture or by a plant that's displayed on a nursery table at its voluptuous

peak—and then are disappointed when, in its more everyday phases, it appears ordinary and even dull. Consider how long the plant's blooms will last, then block the blooms from your mind and look at the plant's leaves and stems. Are they interesting in hue or do they have a pleasing shape?

USING PLANTS FOR CLUTTER CAMOUFLAGE

The military uses greenery to camouflage troops. You can copy its example to conceal yard clutter such as garden hose reels, swimming pool cleaning systems, doghouses, central air-conditioning units, and other unappealing features. Position shrubbery, for example, to hide your trash can, or use climbing vines and flowers to cover lattice enclosing it.

While you may be tempted to conceal an electric or gas meter, this may not be legal in your area. Fire departments need to find meters quickly so electricity and gas can be turned off before firefighters enter a burning building.

To conceal a central air-conditioning unit, make sure plantings are set at least a yard away to allow space for air circulation. Periodically trim back the plantings.

5 STEPS TO YARD STORAGE

The average homeowner generates clutter outdoors as well as indoors—lawn mowers, rakes, bags of fertilizer, hoses, sprinklers, and sporting equipment. The garage provides storage for some of these, but there are other options.

1. Keep your garden hose on a crank-operated hose reel. Wheeled models can be rolled out of sight after you water the lawn. Some reels even double as a bench, giving you a place to rest between yard chores.

2. Garden benches are relaxing places to park oneself, and there are models that also provide a storage chest underneath for yard tools or other outside clutter. These range from modernistic, backless cedar boxes with vinyl-covered cushions to traditional hard-seated, high-backed garden benches. There even is a bench that hides an ice chest for cold drinks. Several manufacturers offer plastic yard storage benches and cupboards. These provide a waterproof place to keep outdoor odds and ends.

3. Lightweight lawn furniture can be attached to a stout post, an anchoring stake, or to your house itself to keep these pieces from spinning out of your yard in a strong wind. Securing them can also prevent theft.

4. Wheeled storage carts are an especially handy form of outdoor storage. These resemble street vendors' carts for selling pretzels or hot dogs. You can use them to bring barbecue or potting supplies out from your garage for as long as they're needed—then wheel them away when done, leaving your yard less cluttered.

5. Storage sheds come both plain and fancy, both small and big enough to serve as cottages. They can be ready-built, kit-built, or custom-built by a carpenter.

   For all sheds, water exclusion from both above and below is key. You need a watertight roof, a foundation that keeps the shed above the damp ground, and a tight floor. Even a shed that sheds water like a duck, however, shouldn't be used to store things that will not tolerate dampness. Items that don't suffer much from moisture, such as yard tools, can be stored in a shed with a gravel floor. Birdseed, grass seed, and pet food will lure vermin, so store these in tightly sealed containers that can stand up to sharp little teeth.

   Sheds may violate zoning ordinances, homeowners' association rules, or utility easements. Do a little research before erecting any storage structure. Otherwise you may have to move it or even tear it down.

5 DECK AND PATIO CONSIDERATIONS

Some of us tend to use an otherwise pleasant deck or patio to store spillover from garden sheds and the garage, and these leisure-time spaces suffer for it. That set of snow tires should be stored in your garage, not stacked on a corner of your patio. When decluttering outdoors, it may help to think of the deck or patio as another room in your home. Plan how to keep it orderly and attractive. The first step in achieving this is to choose durable furniture that will help make it useful. Here are some options to consider.

Keeping Your Firewood Ready to Burn

Stacks of firewood will attract insects such as beetles, carpenter ants, and spiders, which can infest your home if the wood's too close by. Store wood some distance away. To keep it off the ground, dry, and neatly stacked, you may want to use a sturdy firewood rack made of metal. You can protect the wood from rain and snow with a tarp. There are zippered tarps designed specifically for covering woodpiles. Tie your tarp down, so a strong wind won't send it flapping away like a gigantic bat.

1. Cast-iron lawn furniture is strong and the wind can't toss it about, but it can rust and its weight makes it difficult to reposition.
2. Cast-aluminum lawn furniture won't rust and is lighter than cast-iron, but it's expensive.
3. Wooden furniture, such as the ubiquitous redwood campground table with bench seats, is sturdy but can fade or rot.

4. Furniture made with wood and canvas, or with steel or aluminum tubes and plastic webbing, isn't durable and can be bothersome to use. Nearly everyone can recall a frustrating wrestling match with a multihinged folding chair.

5. To avoid rust, rot, weakness, and wrestling, plastic lawn furniture may be your best alternative. It's light, and while cheap types can be flimsy, the more expensive versions are quite robust and can be easily cleaned. Recently, outdoor furniture has been made from post-consumer, high-density polyethylene resins—more simply said, recycled pop bottles. This helps reduce landfill burdens.

8 WAYS TO FENCE OR WALL

"Good fences make good neighbors."
—Anonymous

Fences formalize the boundaries of a property, providing a visual border as well as establishing a comfortable distance between you and the world. They also provide clutter concealment. Because fences are out in the open and subject to bangs and bumps, they should be installed with appearance and durability in mind.

1. Chain-link "hurricane" fences are strong but ugly, and they don't offer privacy or clutter concealment unless you run unattractive plastic slats through their links.

2. Stockade fencing, made of preassembled wood panels, is

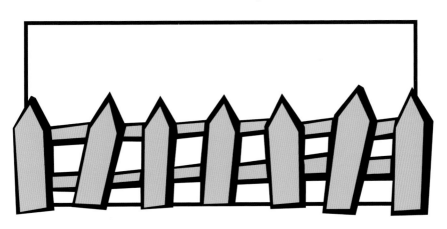

more attractive than chain-link and blocks prying eyes, but it is usually less finished-looking than wooden fences assembled board by board.

3. Preservative-treated wood board fencing is presentable but may not age well.

4. Redwood fencing is more appealing and durable, but this choice is expensive and will eventually deteriorate.

5. Wooden picket fences provide little privacy or clutter concealment. They're primarily decorative while marking property lines. They come in prefabricated sections or can be stick built. Usually they're quite low, but taller versions are available that provide an elegant way to delineate your property. Wood fences may need to be sprayed with preservative, stained, or painted periodically to forestall decay.

6. Vinyl fencing has become a popular alternative to the above types. Good-quality examples look much like painted wood but need little maintenance. They don't rot and can last for decades. They're

available in many styles that offer full concealment or simulate wooden picket fencing.

7. If you fancy something a lot more substantial and durable, you can build a wall. Concrete blocks are the least expensive option. They can be quick to assemble and strong. A simple block wall can be customized with specialty blocks that have interesting textures or cutouts. Blocks can also be laid in patterns to provide variety. Paint or stucco can be applied to further disguise the bland Berlin Wall look of cement block.

8. The next step up in wall construction is brick. Brick is available in far more shades than you may imagine, ranging from traditional red to creamy beige. It's also manufactured in many textures and shapes. There are even bricks that are deliberately made to appear wavy and warped. These "clinker" bricks are popular with builders of Craftsman-style homes. They give a homey, rustic look to any wall in which they're used. There are hundreds of patterns for brick walls.

Both concrete block and brick require that the area under them be firm. The costs of preparing the ground, the materials, and labor make walls far more expensive than fencing.

Be aware of local ordinances, zoning laws, and homeowners' association restrictions that may affect your plans to erect a fence or wall. Your home-owners' association rules, for example, could have been written before vinyl fencing was introduced, and they may require that all fences be made of redwood boards, even though vinyl can be more attractive. If you're building a fence to increase your security, note that there may be local restrictions that require you to keep a gate unlocked for utility access—potentially putting a pretty big hole in your security strategy.

YOUR POOL: 5 WAYS TO KEEP IT NEAT

"My mom said she learned how to swim when someone took her out in the lake and threw her off the boat. I said, 'Mom, they weren't trying to teach you how to swim.'"

—Paula Poundstone

A swimming pool is a delight during a hot July, but maintaining it is a year-round burden. There's the need to keep the water clean, of course, and then there's the clutter of water toys and pool mainte-nance equipment. Add to this the natural debris that the equipment is meant to clean up.

1. Begin by placing a limit on the number of toys in your pool flotilla. Electric air pumps not only rapidly inflate toys, but also can deflate them for easy storage.

2. Leaves are nature's pool clutter. Use a skimmer mounted on a pole to manually remove as many as you can, to lessen the load on your pool's skimmer basket and filter system.

3. Clean the basket and filter on a regular schedule. The day you skip will be the day Mother

Nature dumps a bushel of greenery in your pool. Trim back bushes and trees that contribute leaves. And sweep up leaves before they can find their way into your pool.

4. You're likely to have a variety of pool cleaning implements, such as skimmer poles or hoses, around your pool. These are unsightly and can pose tripping hazards. Young children also love playing with them. A joust between kids brandishing skimmer poles is unlikely to end happily. If you can, store these implements away from your pool.

5. There's one important exception to this put-it-away philosophy: Always keep a rescue hook near your pool. This is a pole with a large, shepherd's-crook-style hook on the end, reminiscent of those used at the Apollo Theater to remove nonstellar acts. You can extend the pole to swimmers in trouble and fish them out. It's a lot quicker than jumping into the water to save them and it enables nonswimmers to make rescues. Make it clear to children who use your pool that the hook is an emergency device, not a toy.

EASY DOES IT

Use a Safety Cover

Come fall, many homeowners spread a tarp across their pool, securing its edges with weights. This keeps leaves and debris out of the pool, but children and pets may mistake the tarp for solid ground and step on it. The tarp won't support them. A safety cover can prevent this. Resembling a trampoline, it's stretched over the pool and securely fastened to the pool's deck. A child can walk out onto it without falling through.

One manufacturer advertises the strength of its safety cover by walking an elephant across it without mishap. So if you install that maker's safety cover and its claim is true, not only will your children be safer but so will your elephant.

10 STEPS TO POOLSIDE SAFETY

Here are some tips to help make your pool safer.

1. Put a fence with locking gates around the pool.

2. Learn how to rescue and revive a drowning victim. Post instructions for artificial respiration near the pool.

3. Have a rescue pole or lifesaving ring handy.

4. If a wooden deck surrounds your pool, paint the deck with nonskid paint.

5. Don't install a diving board. Most ordinary pools are too

Not All Trash Cans Are Created Equal

"Marriage is not just spiritual communion and passionate embraces; marriage is also three-meals-a-day and remembering to carry out the trash."

—Dr. Joyce Brothers

If you're in the market for a trash can, choose one with wheels. Even a rather feeble person can move a lot of trash to the curb easily, if the trash can is mounted on wheels. Recycling bins aren't apt to have wheels and can be heavy. To move them about, use a child's wagon or garden cart.

In many neighborhoods, roaming dogs knock over trash cans, creating squalid messes. Use cans that have latches, or secure the lids with a bungee cord. Racks that hold cans upright and unspilled—even when dogs try to topple them—can also be purchased, or constructed with modest skills. These racks are essentially just a rectangular framework or box secured to the ground. One manufacturer offers a rack that has wheels and holds two cans. It can be moved out to the curb like a cart.

small for a diving board to be used safely.

6. Light your pool. Darkness makes a pool dangerous. Be sure the lighting fixtures and wiring don't pose a shock hazard.

7. Don't operate your pool's filtration system while there are swimmers in the water.

8. Stock a supply of U.S. Coast Guard–approved life vests for children. Small children must wear life vests, even when supervised. "Water wings," inner tubes, or improvised flotation devices shouldn't be substituted for life vests.

9. No one should swim alone. An adult should accompany children.

10. Always keep a rescue hook near your pool.

10 SELF-STORAGE CONSIDERATIONS

Self-storage facilities and storage warehouses now dot the landscape. These garages-away-from-home can be a godsend to households that are full to the bursting point. Here are some suggestions for making the best use of these firms.

1. Before renting storage, try one last bout of clutter cutting. You might not need extra space.

2. Is your stored property insured properly? Self-storage and warehouse facilities often provide little or no insurance coverage for your property. Those that do may charge excessive fees. Ask your insurance agent if your homeowner's insurance will cover items you store elsewhere. You may be able to add an inexpensive rider that will cover your stored property.

3. Is the storage facility clean and dry? If you smell a musty odor, it may indicate a mold or mildew problem.

4. Are your goods packed to resist damage from rough handling and stacking? Can vermin get into your goods?

5. Is the self-storage facility reputable? Call the Better Business Bureau (www.bbb.org) or your local consumer affairs authority and ask if it's had complaints. Is the facility a member of the Self-Storage Association? It promotes standards that protect renters.

6. What security measures are taken by the facility? Does it have fences, gates, lights, locks, alarms, and video cameras? Are staff members on watch? In addition to wanting your stuff to be safe, you also want to be able to use the facility in safety.

7. Does the facility provide climate-controlled storage? Self-storage facilities generally don't, and the stuff you store will be exposed to seasonal temperatures.

8. Storage warehouses are more likely to be climate controlled, but they aren't as easily accessed as self-storage facilities. You'll have to stash your stuff during their working hours, and in the company of a staff member. Storage fees for a warehouse are usually cheaper.

9. A very convenient—but expensive—form of storage rental may be available in your part of the country. A large steel storage container, like those manufacturers use to ship products, is dropped off at your home so that you can place items in it at your leisure. When full, the container is picked up by the storage service, transported to its facility, and stacked with other containers. To access your stuff, you must arrange an appointment to have your container pulled out for you. These services offer the advantage of making it easy to ship your items when you move. The container is just trucked to your new location.

10. Keep a list at home of what you've stored. Photographs can document your belongings' original condition. You'll need an accurate professional appraisal of any valuable objects. Your own estimate may not be accepted if you need to file a claim for damages, or if you deduct a loss on your taxes.

SIXTEEN

Clutter Disposal

"There's cash in trash."

—Anonymous

As you whittle away every extra ounce of unwanted stuff from every closet and shelf, you face another challenge—getting rid of all that junk. The easiest way is to hand it over to the guys in the garbage trucks. While this is convenient, just dumping clutter isn't environmentally friendly. It also fails to address one of the biggest psychological hang-ups that cluttery folks have.

Clutter collectors save things for years because they think the items might be useful, so they're unlikely to waste "valuable" stuff by sending it to the dump. The solution is to dispose of your clutter in such a way that you feel it isn't being wasted. If you can get a little cash or a nice tax deduction on top of this, you'll actually be rewarded for your clutter cutting. Here are some disposal options you might want to explore.

FREE STUFF

To get rid of most of your unwanted possessions, you need do nothing more than place the things by the curb and post a big "Free" sign by them. You'll be surprised how quickly passersby carry off your clutter. They may even take your sign. Any leftovers can be turned over to the garbage men in good conscience.

A modern version of this strategy is to give away clutter through the Internet. The Web site www. freecycle.org allows people to post their free stuff. Another group, NY Wa\$teMatch (www.wastematch.org), provides recycling and reuse alternatives in a free Internet-based marketplace, where surplus or used but still usable castoffs can be sold, traded, or donated. You can always post on www.craigslist.org as well.

HAND ME DOWN MY HAND-ME-DOWNS

Children from big families have long benefited from hand-me-down clothing from older relatives. Maternity clothing is another kind of clutter that's passed down through families.

Look for opportunities to pass on your excess clutter to friends and family. What you don't need may be useful to someone else.

REGIFTING AND PRETEND CHRISTMAS

All of us get gifts that we can't use. While kindly meant, they might be all wrong, like a blouse that makes your complexion look like a bowl of tomato bisque. One low-guilt way to dispose of unwanted gifts is "re-gifting"— passing on a gift to someone else. Take the precaution of giving the present to a person who isn't likely to encounter the original giver, and avoid the major gaff of re-gifting a gift to its original giver.

Re-gifting can be done unilaterally. Keep a box dedicated to gifts you decide to re-gift. When the box is full in July or September or March, celebrate a Pretend Christmas. Wrap up these gifts and pass them out to friends and family. If a receiver offers you a gift in return, politely insist the gesture is not necessary. Just explain you had a gift on hand that you thought he or she might like, and say, "Merry Christmas!" or "Happy Hanukkah!" or "Joyous You-Fill-in-the-Gift-Giving-Holiday-Here!"

RECYCLE IT

Recycling is another way to ease any regrets you might have about parting with clutter. Everything from plastic milk jugs to empty cornflakes boxes can be recycled, although municipalities vary in what they'll accept.

Vermonters have a tradition of making do and reusing, which lives on in that state's small-town recycling programs. Some towns have "Reuse Zones" at trash drop-off sites, where castoffs are available free for the taking. At some of these sites, there are drums to receive leftover paint—oil or latex, interior or exterior. The resulting free paint is a mongrel brown that's perfect for painting the back steps, the inside of your garage, or (aptly) a doghouse.

Your municipality may collect potentially dangerous trash, such as dead batteries, pesticides, used motor oil, and old tires. This lessens the likelihood that toxic

substances will be dumped in alleys or sewer grates. Some cities designate a drop-off site, while others send out special trucks to gather this toxic clutter.

EASY DOES IT

Stackable Recycling Bins

Multiple recycling bins can hog floor space, but stackable units take up less room and put some storage containers at a more convenient height. Look for bins that have hinged lids, which allow you to add contents easily. Be sure to put heavier recyclables in the bottom bins to make the stack more stable.

ACTS OF CHARITY

Throughout the country, charities such as the Salvation Army, Disabled American Veterans, and Goodwill welcome donated household goods. Some will send a truck around to your house to pick them up. They'll also give you a receipt that will allow you to deduct the items' value from your taxes.

To schedule a pickup or to find a drop-off location for the Salvation

Army, visit its Web site at www.salvationarmyusa.org. Branches of the Disabled American Veterans can be found at www.dav.org. To find the nearest Goodwill, check www.goodwillindustries.org. Local charities and churches collect items for rummage sales, thrift shops, or for relief efforts. To find charities, search the Internet under "Charitable Organizations."

EASY DOES IT

Do-It-Yourself Charity

Consider setting up your own charity. In Vermont some years ago, a retired woman cleaned out her bookshelves, then instead of selling or donating her books, she set up her own lending library in an old roadside vegetable stand. Stocked with her surplus books, augmented by yard sale purchases and donations from other book lovers, her one-room library provided local families with lots of free reading material. There woman turned a bit of clutter removal into a fulfilling charitable hobby, which kept her well connected to her neighbors who remember her fondly as "The Book Lady."

SELL YOUR GOODS

If you have items that might fetch a reasonable price, run a craigslist.org or a newspaper classified ad. Don't overlook "penny shopper" newspapers that are given away free and are scanned by people looking for bargains. You could pay more to have your ad run in bold type, to set it apart from others on the page. Someone looking for a particular item, however, will peruse all the ads, so spend the money on another ad in another paper instead.

If you don't want to get involved with haggling, indicate in the ad that your price is firm. To avoid having to deal with unhappy buyers, be sure you make all sales "as is," and don't exaggerate the quality of your merchandise.

27 YARD SALE TIPS

A yard sale can be an excellent way of ridding yourself of an amazing amount of stuff, including your old goat-milking stool, while picking up a bit of money in the process. The curious thing you'll discover about your junk is that other people won't consider it junk. They'll get up early in the morning, drive for hours, then elbow through a crowd of other elbowers to get a look at your chipped plates and warped Tupperware.

There are several key points to consider when planning a yard sale.

1. Find out if you need a permit from your municipality.

2. Check the weather forecast for a weekend with good weather. Include a rain date in your advertising, in case the weather turns bad.

3. Generally, schedule your sale for a weekend that isn't a holiday, when buyers might be out of town (although some communities have a tradition of holding yard sales on Memorial Day weekend).

4. Invite your neighbors to join in your sale. The more help

and the more merchandise you have, the better.

5. Run a newspaper ad for your sale, giving your address, the date, and the rain date. Be sure to mention attractive items you'll be selling. Antiques and baby items are favorites. If more than one family is involved in your sale, make sure your ad mentions this. Veteran yard sale customers know this means better pickings.

6. Double-check items that you think may be worth more than a yard sale price. Have a look at what these potential treasures are bringing on eBay.

7. While you don't want to price your merchandise too low, high prices can drive off customers. Price things to sell. You don't want to have to lug your clutter back into your garage.

8. To move more merchandise, price items as a group. Seven paperbacks for $5 will clear out your old romance novels fast, especially if you also price them singly at a dollar each.

9. Tidy up your wares. Would you buy a rusty rake with dead leaves caught in its teeth? A few

moments with a wire brush may triple the price you can fetch.

10. Display your merchandise in an orderly, attractive way, with like items grouped together. Use any tables and clothing racks you can round up. A couple of sawhorses and a sheet of thick plywood can be used as a simple table.

11. If you have appliances or electronics for sale, run an extension cord to your sales area, so you can demonstrate that they work. For safety, use an outlet equipped with a ground fault interrupter (GFI) to power the cord. Have batteries on hand for battery-operated items.

12. Leave flyers in the library, laundromat, drugstore, waiting rooms, and anywhere else people congregate. Use tear-off address tags on flyers that you post on bulletin boards, so a prospective customer won't pull down the flyer just to get the address.

13. If local laws permit, post signs on corner telephone poles to advertise your sale. Use colored poster board and write legibly with a black marker. A clutch of balloons or a knot of crepe paper will attract attention to your signs. Post your signs far enough away from your sale so that drivers will have time to slow down for a look at your stuff. Use arrows to indicate where your sale is. Even if a motorist misses other details, that arrow will point them toward your sale. Check your sign for visibility by driving by. After the sale, be sure to take down your signs.

14. Set up a "Free" box for items you know you can't sell or which will fetch just pennies. This will help clear out that clutter and create goodwill, while fueling your customers'

acquisitive mood. Old children's toys make particularly good giveaways, as they can keep children occupied while their parents ponder purchases.

15. Some yard sale aficionados try to skunk their competition by showing up hours before the time you advertise for your sale. Include a "No Early Birds" line in your ad, and place a sign on your front door repeating the time the sale will start with a declaration that you won't do business until then. If you permit early birds to buy, they'll be back for your next sale at the same early, sleep-spoiling hour.

16. If you don't like haggling, put up a sign indicating that all prices are firm. Some people will insist on trying to get you to lower your prices, no matter how low they are. If you think you're asking a reasonable price, stick to it. A fair price will find a customer. You can always ask the haggler to make a bid and give you his phone number. If no one else offers more, call the haggler after the sale. Don't be surprised if this person tries to haggle when you call, or even when he or she shows up to pick up the item. Don't be afraid to just say, "I'm sorry, I've decided not to sell." Letting someone browbeat you can put you off yard sales for good.

17. To avoid having to answer, "How much is this?" over and over, use price stickers. Tags can fall off or be switched by the unscrupulous.

18. When you're selling items from other households along with your own stuff, be sure to label their merchandise as belonging to their households. Ask your yard sale cohosts if they want to haggle, and if so, direct hagglers to them (have them do the same for you). Only they know what price they'll be happy taking. If they believe you foolishly accepted too low a price, they'll be less likely to join in your next sale. Imagine how you might feel if your neighbor sold a silver teapot you expected to sell for $50 for $.50.

19. If the yard sale is in your home or your garage, be sure to indicate which items aren't for sale.

You can do this by putting sheets over non-sale items, by running a tape to fence them off, or by locking doors. Take extra care when staging a sale with your neighbors, if you're using their home. Selling Uncle Joe's urn might make a humorous sitcom episode, but it can be remarkably unfunny in reality when you're playing a starring role.

20. If you have a lot of unsold merchandise as the end of your sale nears, reduce prices by 25 or 50 percent. It's better to get less money and be rid of your clutter.

21. Avoid placing merchandise where customers might trip over it.

22. Don't let customers move heavy purchases if you think they can't safely do so.

23. Don't take personal checks, except from personal friends.

24. Have a supply of singles and coins to make change. A cash

Yard Sale Managers

Professional yard sale managers will put together a sale for you for a percentage of the proceeds. They can give you an estimate of what your clutter will fetch. Some may be willing to price your items for a fee, so that you can sell them on your own.

Be wary of sales managers who offer to buy items from you. Some shady characters call themselves yard sales managers and offer free estimates just to get first shot at buying your stuff. More than one clutter clearer has been offered a lowball price for a valuable antique by such predators.

box can be easily stolen, so use a fanny pack turned round or an apron with pockets.

25. Buyers will be reluctant to buy more than they can carry, so have lots of boxes and bags on hand.

26. It's rather shocking, but some people will steal your clutter. If you see a thief, ask him or her to leave. If the person won't depart, don't risk a confrontation—just call the police. Someone nutty enough to steal an old tennis racket may be nutty enough to bend it over your head if challenged. You should also be careful about admitting customers into your home, where they might appropriate your checkbook, credit card, or other valuables. Common ploys include asking for the use of your phone, a visit to your bathroom, or a drink of water. Politely say no, and point them toward the nearest pay phone, gas station rest room, or garden hose.

27. Arrange for a charity to pick up unsold items at the end of the sale.

FLEA MARKETS

Consider selling your accumulated clutter at a flea market. The market organizer rents spaces and advertises the event, sparing individual dealers these expenses. Since the sale isn't at your house, you don't risk having a thief entering your home. Don't take this route if you have just a few inexpensive items to sell. You may not make back the fee you pay.

ESTATE BUYERS

When a person dies, the executors will often sell the household goods as a block to an estate buyer. If you have a good-size load of clutter, call a buyer and ask him or her to make an offer. The bid may seem surprisingly low. Professional buyers must get merchandise at a low price in order to resell at a profit. You may want to remove from your collection of clutter any items that you suspect have particular value, and explore more lucrative ways of selling them.

CONSIGNMENT SHOPS

Consignment stores will take clothing in good shape and sell it for you in return for a percentage

of the sale price. There are consignment stores that specialize in men's, women's, and children's clothing. Children's consignment stores may also sell related items, such as strollers and toys.

AUCTIONS

If you have a large quantity of clutter to dispose of, an auction can be a quick way to sell it. Since auctioneers earn a percentage of the take, they're motivated to get you as high a price as possible. Some auctioneers combine lots from sellers to hold large sales that attract more bidders. There's a risk here for the clutter-prone. Auctioneers are expert at exciting the audience's acquisitive impulses, and it's all too easy to come home with more clutter than you brought.

ONLINE AUCTIONS

There are several online auction sites, the best-known being eBay. Everything from baseball cards to used cars can be sold through this site.

To sell your clutter on eBay, you first must register and provide a credit card number. Next, you send in a description of your item with a computer image of it, and choose a category for it to be listed under. You typically set an opening bid for your item, and are charged a modest "insertion fee." If you sell the item, you'll also be charged a "final value fee" based on a percentage of the price you received.

Online auctions are great places to sell items you think may have value as collectibles. Collectors frequent such sites and may bid your item up to a fair value. You can generate collector attention by posting your intention to sell your item on a Web site devoted to collectors of that type of item. Taking your collectible to a dealer instead of an online auction might

Getting an Estimate for Uncle Sam

To produce an estimate for Uncle Sam for your donated object, you can consult guidebooks and price lists for the type of object you're donating. Check Web sites for collectors. They may be able to suggest guidebooks or experts. Keep a paper trail detailing how you arrived at your estimate.

Be careful to consult only authentic experts. A reputable expert should be able to provide proof of expertise through certification or membership in professional associations. He or she should also be able to provide references. Be cautious of experts who buy and trade the objects for which they provide estimates. They may attempt to persuade you to sell your object to them at a low price. Also be cautious of experts who try to please you with too high an estimate. An estimate may not be accepted by the IRS if it exceeds what other experts give for similar items.

If you want to claim over $5,000 for a donation, you need to fill out a special IRS form and provide a professional appraisal. The IRS may track the sale of the item to verify its worth.

not earn you as much, because the direct connection to the collector is missing, and dealers need to buy cheap to stay in business.

If you don't have a computer or access to the Internet, or if you aren't computer savvy, you can use eBay with the help of a "trading assistant" who does the dealing for you in return for a percentage of the sale price. Visit the eBay site for information on finding an assistant.

SPECIFIC CLUTTER DISPERSING TIPS

There isn't one strategy that will lead you to a good home for all of your clutter. It may take a

little planning and research to find a happy disposition for the things you've bravely decided to part with.

APPLIANCES

The American Council for the Blind accepts used household appliances. Contact the group at www.geappliances.com/geac/donations/.

AUTOMOBILES

Cars can be donated to charity, giving you a substantial tax deduction. Charities may use them in their work, repair and make them available to the needy, or sell them and put the proceeds to charitable use. The IRS warns taxpayers to be wary of scam artists, who falsely suggest they are tax-exempt charities. These crooks are just looking for free cars to resell. You could wind up paying more taxes *plus* a penalty if your deduction isn't allowed.

To determine if an organization is tax-exempt, check the IRS Web site www.irs.gov, call the IRS information number (800) 829-1040, or go to your local IRS office. IRS Publication 78 lists tax-exempt

Sharing Your Wheels

Car sharing can be an attractive alternative—especially for city dwellers—to owning an automobile, eliminating a large piece of clutter from your life. Subscribers to San Francisco's City CarShare pay a deposit and a monthly subscription fee for access to a car 24 hours a day, 7 days a week (www.citycarshare.org). They pay an additional fee based upon mileage and hours used, but this is less than the cost of an ordinary rental car, not to mention the cost of owning a vehicle. An electronic key opens the car and tracks usage. Similar services are offered by Zipcar (www.zipcar.com) and Flexcar (www.flexcar.com). One unexpected group that has found these services attractive is college students. They often have difficulty paying for a reliable vehicle or finding parking. Car sharing helps them avoid these problems.

organizations. An example of an IRS-recognized, nonprofit organization that accepts car donations is the American Lung Association Vehicle Donation Center (www.donateyourcar.com).

BICYCLES

Have a bike you're not using? Pedals for Progress (www.p4p.org) gathers used bicycles and spare parts, then ships them to developing countries where they can be an important means of transportation. The organization requests a small monetary contribution to help cover handling costs and provides you with a receipt for the donation for tax purposes.

COINS

Travelers often return home with a pocket full of foreign coins. Running them down to a bank that's willing to exchange them for a handful of U.S. currency can be a bother. Instead, you can donate the coins to UNICEF's Change for Good program. It takes foreign coins of any kind and funnels the money to international programs for needy children. The charity can be reached through Travelex America, Change for Good/UNICEF, JFK Airport, Terminal 4 IAT, Jamaica, NY 11430. Travelex America, which provides financial services for travelers, has offices in airports around the world where you can drop off your spare kopeks before you leave the airport.

COLLEGE TEXTBOOKS

Old textbooks can occupy a lot of bookshelf space. You can sell them through www.textbook-buyer.com. Publishers frequently replace texts, however, and older

editions (even just a semester old) may bring very little.

7 COMPUTER CONSIDERATIONS

Unlike Cher, computers age quickly. The snappy bit-juggler of today becomes a tabletop anachronism in just a few years, unable to handle newer versions of the programs you require. There are buyers for old computers—check the Yellow Pages under "Computers—Dealers." Most will want to inspect your machine before offering a price, and that price will be way, way below what you paid.

While your old computer may be too limited for your needs, it might be welcomed by others.

1. Computers for Schools (www.pcsforschools.org) can help you find a school in need of used computers. Share the Technology (www.sharetechnology.org) also matches computer donations to schools, nonprofit groups, and people with disabilities. The Children's Dream Foundation (www.thecdf.org) accepts computers

for children with cancer. Boys' and girls' after-school programs also accept computers to equip their clubhouses.

2. A neighbor's kid might appreciate your old machine. Get the word out that you have one to give away.

3. Senior centers may be looking for computers.

4. Local social welfare agencies run job-training programs that require computers. Homeless shelters may need them to help people to surf the Internet to find jobs and to prepare résumés. The National Cristina Foundation (www.cristina.org) transfers thousands of donated computers to charities. Check www.techsoup.org, a Web site helping nonprofits deal with technology, for other charities that may be interested in your old computer.

5. By law you're required to leave the licensed operating system on a donated computer. Don't allow personal data to remain, however. Deleting files isn't enough to destroy this data, because a computer-knowledgeable person can reconstruct deleted files. To completely clean out your data, you need a disk drive utility program that writes over free space after you delete files.

Include all the accessories needed to use your computer, such as the keyboard, mouse, and printer. Include the original disks that came with your computer, with proof of license. Keep a list of what you've donated, so that you can demonstrate the fair market value of the donation.

6. If your computer is obsolete or no longer functional, disposing of it is more of a problem. The Environmental Protection Agency identifies cadmium, lead, mercury, and various flame retardants as toxic chemicals that are commonly found in PCs. The agency estimates that half of all the heavy metals found in landfills are from discarded electronic products.

Your local sanitation department, the Computer Recycling Center (www.crc.org), PCDisposal.com (www.pcdisposal.com), or the Electronic Industries Alliance

4 Ways to Lose a House

Perhaps the greatest decluttering task is ridding oneself of a house while keeping the house's lot. This isn't as uncommon as you might think. In certain highly desirable neighborhoods, a building lot can be worth more than the house that occupies it. The traditional solution for an unwanted house is to hire a demolition company. There are less wasteful alternatives, such as the following:

1. You can donate your home to the local fire department. It may ignite the building in a controlled manner, then run drills to practice firefighting. The department may then use city crews to clear away the rubble left behind, saving you the cost of a demolition crew.

2. You can donate the building to charity that will arrange for it to be moved to a new location for use as low-income housing.

3. There are community organizations that recycle building materials. Usually, they just accept renovation or construction leftovers, but some groups will recycle whole houses. Recycle North, in Burlington, Vermont, does this. It has developed techniques that allow a crew to strip down a home in about the time it would take a demolition crew to knock it down. The siding, plywood sheathing, windows, and other parts are resold or donated to home-building programs such as Habitat for Humanity.

4. Older homes often have architectural fixtures—fireplace mantles, columns, decorative windows, oak doors—which can be sold to architectural salvage firms.

(www.eiae.org) can help you find a recycler who will dispose of a computer safely. Your city's Chamber of Commerce may be able to identify retail stores that recycle electronics.

7. Computer manufacturers also offer recycling options. Dell Computer (www.dellrecycling.com) accepts trade-ins of old computers. It also maintains a Web site where you can auction off your old machine, and offers a recycling option for machines that are useless. Gateway (www.gateway.com) offers rebates for old computers when you buy one of its new machines. For a modest fee, Hewlett-Packard (www.hp.com/recycle) and IBM (www.ibm.com/ibm/environment/ products/ptb_us.shtml) accept old computer equipment for recycling.

FURS

You may own a fur that has been languishing in the back of your closet for too many winters. Consider donating it to the homeless—a fur coat can save a life during a frigid winter. Or give your fur back to the animals. The Black Beauty Ranch (www.blackbeautyranch.org), a sanctuary for unwanted, abused, and exotic animals, accepts furs to help warm and comfort orphaned or injured animals. The ranch is also seeking many other items used in the care of animals. Your local Humane Society or animal shelter may have similar needs.

HOTEL TOILETRIES

When decluttering, you may find you have a collection of unused hotel toiletries, including little soaps, shampoos, and skin cream. Check with a women's shelter to see if these supplies would be welcomed.

PROM DRESSES

The Cinderella Project in Atlanta, Georgia, accepts donations of used prom dresses. It passes these on to young girls who can't afford formal wear for school dances. Check www.youthcommunication-vox.org/301pg13.htm for details. A state-by-state list of similar programs is available at www.glassslipperproject.org.

Unsuspected Treasures

While you may be sagacious enough to recognize the worth of an antique rolltop desk or a mint-condition Barbie doll when you see it in the attic, there are a lot of other objects that may have unsuspected value. Here's a short list of treasures that might escape your notice.

- Vintage clothing, including bowling or Hawaiian shirts
- 1950s and 1960s Baby Boomer toys
- Real jewelry that's mixed with costume pieces
- Bicycles with balloon tires from 1930 to 1960
- Vintage fountain pens
- Antique marbles
- Golf clubs
- Merchandising materials for such products as Coca-Cola
- Fishing lures and tackle
- Military souvenirs
- Blue jeans
- Cigarette lighters

SEVENTEEN

Decluttering Saboteurs, Enablers, and Allies

"There's nothing quite as irksome as someone else's mess."

—**Sue Grafton**

The plan to get ride of clutter is complicated by the very nature of clutter. Clutter isn't always under our sole control. When you live with someone, his or her clutter problem becomes your clutter problem. If your spouse eats a tub of ice cream, the body fat it produces won't wind up on your hips; but if your spouse buys a set of the complete works of Stephen King, those countless horror books will haunt your bookshelves. And there are competing and compounding forces involved. Your bookshelves might manage to hold King's works, but not if you insist on acquiring a complete collection of Agatha Christie's mysteries, too.

Choosing between the two mountains of books can be contentious, leading to subjective arguments over whose stuff is more valuable. Keeping both collections is a kind of mutual enabling that can produce overwhelming clutter. Dumping both will cut away a nice chunk of clutter, but at the expense of making both parties unhappy. Clearly, to produce a satisfactory result, you have to find a way to work together.

The keys to reducing clutter with another person are amiability and agreement on goals. Like Don Quixote and Sancho Panza, Batman and Robin, and the Lone Ranger and Tonto, you need a friend who will go along with you when you see windmills become giants, who will join you throwing Bat-arangs at the Joker, and who, when the claim jumpers come a-shooting, will stand by you and match your fire, bullet for silver bullet.

8 WAYS TO MAKE YOUR PARTNER YOUR ALLY

1. Enlist your partner in your decluttering. Find out what he

or she would like to improve, then incorporate these wishes into your plans. You may be surprised to learn that your partner is more eager than you are to see your household clutter gone.

2. Be considerate when evaluating your companion's possessions. Don't presume that just because you think something is worthless, it is. You may not share your spouse's admiration for doo-wop music and therefore be eager to dispose of the half-ton collection of old LPs lining your living room shelves. But those records could be all that keeps your spouse, after a

day of being bullied by a beetle-browed boss, from crawling under the bed with a fifth of Jack Daniels. It's better to put up with some clutter and keep your companion happy than to insist upon draconian purges.

3. Be explicit about which possessions you value. You can't expect your companion to know what's important to you if you don't speak up.

4. As you declutter, you'll discover items that one of you wants to keep, but the other wants to throw out. If you can't resolve this, set the disputed item aside. Eventually you'll have a heap of such items. Agree to each get rid of one of your items from the pile. After you've both made your choices, repeat until you can no longer bear continuing.

5. Be equitable. Don't expect your companion to accept your collection of road signs if you won't permit her collection of spoons. Remember, you're sharing your home.

6. Have you ever gotten into an argument while doing a dirty, stressful job? Wasn't fun, was it? Arguing makes hard work harder. To avoid arguments, be courteous even when you want to be otherwise. It's easy to get angry when confronting a mountain of clutter created by your companion's bad behavior, but arguing won't move you toward your goal of a clutter-free home. Be persuasive rather than accusatory. Also be prepared to admit when you're wrong. Your behavior is unlikely to be perfect, either.

7. Team projects benefit from a little cheerleading. Your high school football team didn't require the help of the cheerleaders to win—the girls' snappy routines didn't score any touchdowns—but the cheerleaders helped the team rev up the energy they needed to do their best. The cheerleaders made winning more likely. Try to be a cheerleader for your declutter team. You don't have to jump around waving pom-poms and chanting aggressive slogans, but be sure to acknowledge every task that's done correctly and make a fuss over excellent work. Don't you

perform better when your good efforts are recognized?

8. Never dispose of your ally's stuff without asking. Living together requires consideration, compromise, and consultation.

DEALING WITH AN UNCOOPERATIVE COMPANION

"I can't take it anymore, Felix, I'm cracking up. Everything you do irritates me. And when you're not here, the things I know you're gonna do when you come in irritate me. You leave me little notes on my pillow. Told you 158 times I can't stand little notes on my pillow. 'We're all out of cornflakes. F.U.' Took me three hours to figure out F.U. was Felix Unger!"

—The Odd Couple

Conflict makes good theater. That's why Neil Simon's classic play of mismatched roomies, *The Odd Couple*, was a hit on Broadway and became a classic film with Jack Lemmon as the obsessively neat Felix Unger and Walter Matthau as the slob's slob Oscar Madison. Felix and Oscar struggle to resolve their polar-opposite lifestyles, while Felix contemplates suicide and Oscar contemplates murder. On the screen, this is great comedy, but if your home situation resembles theirs, you know that such great differences can strain relationships.

9 WAYS TO RESOLVING CLUTTER DISAGREEMENTS

Not all "odd couples" are at odds. Proverbially, opposites attract. Most of us know a couple in which one partner is gregarious and the other is reclusive, or a pair in which one is plump and the other thin, or a couple in which one wakes up before the crack of dawn while the other lives like Dracula, chipper as an undead cricket long past midnight. How do such dissimilar people get along? If we look closely, we see that these

Nagging Isn't Pretty

Pop psychologists suggest that nagging can be ameliorated by rewording. Instead of complaining, "You never pick up your socks!," they say you should be less confrontational and less universal in your criticism, while incorporating your feelings into your request. You might say, "When you leave your socks on the floor, you make me feel unimportant to you, and this makes me feel anxious." is more polite and might work for a time. Unless your spouse is unusually unperceptive, though, both the blunt and the subtle statement will eventually convey exactly the same information: "Pick up those socks!" and if you repeat the request over and over, it will be perceived as nagging, no matter how you prettily word it.

It may not be worth the effort of hiding nagging in prettier language or supplications for sympathy. Instead, be clear and polite: "Please pick up your socks." Don't endlessly repeat yourself. If your companion still doesn't comply, you can leave the socks on the floor, pick them up yourself, throw them out, or pack up your own socks and move out.

couples usually work hard to overcome the problems that come with their differences. Here are several ideas about dealing with differing attitudes toward clutter.

1. Establish boundaries so each partner has his or her own territory somewhere in the home. In *The Odd Couple*, Felix takes over Oscar's apartment, scrubbing and cleaning and reordering a home that hasn't seen such attention in years. Oscar feels put upon, so

he and Felix agree that Oscar's bedroom is under his sole control. If Oscar wants to store leftover pizza under his pillow, he can. It's his territory. If you and your companion differ in the level of clutter you can tolerate, you too can divide up your living space, permitting each of you a portion under your control.

2. Be prepared to compromise. If you want a trimmed-down, clutterless home and your companion doesn't think this is important, try to meet somewhere in the middle. If your spouse believes, for example, that it's necessary to have ten white shirts in order to play the role of a crisp, efficient executive, and you think five white shirts (and more frequent trips to the laundry) would suffice, adjust your standards to accommodate your companion. Maybe seven shirts would do.

3. Mitigate your impositions on each other. Perhaps your companion doesn't want your shoes in the hallway, but you find it convenient to keep them there. A shoe bench may be the answer, organizing your clodhoppers so that they're less offensive to your companion.

4. Tell your companion what you believe is important, and how you hope to achieve your goals. The two of you may not reach an agreement, but you can't expect good behavior if you don't ask for it. One of the most irritating arguments is the "you-should-know" gambit. Telepathy has not been perfected. If you want your companion to act upon what's going on inside your head, you must express yourself.

5. While you must communicate your point of view, don't nag. A tidy environment is a worthy goal, but it doesn't justify using unpleasant means to achieve it. Indeed, nagging may produce the opposite effect, if the recipient of it rebels.

6. Don't make threats. If you tell clutterers to dump their clutter or you'll dump it for them, you'll be surprised at how often they'll just squint their eyes like Clint Eastwood and refuse. If you follow through on your threat, you can very

well produce tribulation far worse than living with the disputed clutter.

7. Don't be lazy. Mark Twain once quoted his mother as saying, "Never learn to do anything: If you don't learn, you'll always find someone else who'll do it for you." It's an amusing observation, but it expresses a philosophy that won't be appreciated by the person who winds up hauling your load. In love songs, the enamored claims to be willing to climb the highest mountain and swim the deepest seas. If you quail at clearing the supper table, you can hardly expect your beloved to be impressed by your devotion.

8. One of the most widely shared conceptions of how the world should be ordered is fairness. Divide decluttering chores between you and your partner. If there's a task you both loathe, alternate who does it.

9. When you're done cutting clutter, don't hog the resulting free space. Would you be happy if you'd helpfully tossed out some of your prized possessions, and your reward was to have someone else's clutter put in their place?

THE GOOD NEWS

If you can work together to cut the clutter in your home, your efforts will be compounded—the results better and the rewards sweeter—by being shared. Not only will you have a neater home, but your teamwork can also help build a better relationship so you can take on other problems and overcome them.

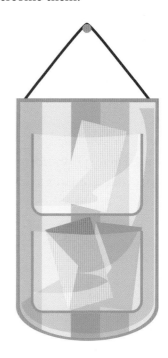

EIGHTEEN

Keeping It All in Perspective

"Success is the ability to go from failure to failure without losing your enthusiasm."

—Winston Churchill

As with any attempt at self-improvement, you'll have ups and downs in your struggle with clutter. There will be days when clutter flees your home like dew disappearing with the budding dawn of an August morn. But there will also be days when clutter arrogantly shoves its way into your home, rudely plops itself into your favorite chair, and bangs its heavy feet down on your coffee table. At times like these, mentally review some of the ideas we've presented in this book.

18 IDEAS FOR DECLUTTERING

1. Simplify. If you aren't sure you need an item, you probably don't. Get rid of it.

2. Don't let the prospect of utility in the future cause you to stack up useless junk today. If you can't think of an immediate purpose for any basket, margarine tub, or other seemingly useful item that comes your way, dump it. If you feel you must stockpile a particular kind of item, set a limit on how many you'll save.

3. If you haven't used something in years, recycle it or throw it out. It'll probably be more years before you notice its absence, and you can buy a new one then and save yourself years of storage costs.

4. If it's broken, get it fixed or throw it out.

5. If it's in good shape, don't let this oblige you to keep it. Keep only items that you'll use.

6. Store like with like.

7. When sorting, try to handle objects only once. If you can't, try to advance the object toward its permanent location.

8. Don't store items in "temporary" spots. Temporary becomes permanent.

9. Keep your stored items in good order. If you can't find something, you can't use it and may be forced to buy another. This doubles the space needed to satisfy the object's purpose.

10. Store stuff near where you'll use it.

11. Label boxes with detailed descriptions of what's inside and when it was put there.

12. Have a place for everything and keep everything in its place. Allocating a specific space to a particular object will make it more likely for you to store that object there, where it'll be easier to find when needed.

13. You'll be tempted to store items where they easily fit. This may allow you to store more stuff in a small space, but it'll make finding items more difficult. It's better to waste a little space and be able to find the item when it's needed.

14. Make your own plans for storing your stuff. Someone else's plan may not fit yours. Conversely, if you can't think of a way to organize a group of items, experiment with someone else's organization. If you don't know how to store your shoes, for example, go to a shoe store for ideas.

15. Don't limit yourself by following standard conceptions of how to organize your home. You might not find it useful to store blankets in the blanket chest at the foot of your bed. Maybe your household files would be more comfortable there.

16. Assign chores to your children. Match your expectations to their capabilities, reward good-faith efforts, give gentle guidance, and penalize slacking off. As your children grow older, expand their chores to include tasks that they'll have to handle as adults.

17. Work with your spouse to reduce clutter—without nagging or resentment, but with understanding and a sense of fair play.

18. Keep your perspective. If your decluttering efforts take over your life, you'll be like a dieter who goes too far and becomes anorexic. Remember that you're removing clutter from your life in order to become happier and more productive. If decluttering makes you unhappy and leaves no time for other pursuits, you're doing something wrong.

A PARTING SHOT

If you want a neat, tidy home, you have to spend the effort to neaten and tidy it. Wishing alone

will never make anything real, but you shouldn't forget that working requires a steady supply of wishing to motivate yourself. If you don't have a dream of what you're working for, then your work will seem like drudgery, and you'll fail—if not in your work, then in your satisfaction with it. We have to work and dream together. So imagine success! Imagine enjoying it. Then go and make it real. Start by finding a spot on your bookshelf and putting this book away where it belongs.

Acknowledgments

The authors want to thank the many colleagues, friends, and family members who helped in the creation of this work, generously sharing their stories and tips. Prominent among these are our editors Ellen Phillips and Karen Bolesta; Megan Buckley, Janet Rosen, Lori Perkins, Susan de Russy, Diane and Glen Sherman; Claire Curry, Peter Skinner, Lee Berg, and Judy Labenshohn. Sheree Bykofsky would also like to extend her greatest gratitude to Ed Morrow for his mind-boggling professionalism, humor, and talent and to Rita Rosenkranz for her inspiring friendship and brilliance. Rita would like to thank Sheree for lassoing an idea and shepherding it to the bookshelves, and Ed, whose expertise and commitment helped bring the idea to life. In turn, Ed would like to thank Sheree and Rita for their great creative skill and expert guidance.

The authors also wish to acknowledge the many sources used in writing this work. The sources are referenced in the work, but if any errors or omissions have been made, please accept our deepest apologies.

Index